EX LIBRIS

Medieval People

MICHAEL PRESTWICH

Medieval People

Vivid Lives in a Distant Landscape
From Charlemagne to Piero della Francesca

with 179 illustrations, 171 in colour

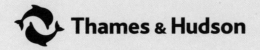
Thames & Hudson

For my grandchildren,
Ben, Joshua, Hannah, James, Oliver and Alexander.

Frontispiece: Dante Alighieri, in a painting by Domenico di Michelino of 1465. The poet expounds his Divine Comedy, one of the greatest works of medieval literature. Behind him, there is an image of purgatory. Hell is to the left, and Paradise to the right.

First published in the United Kingdom in 2014
by Thames & Hudson Ltd, 181A High Holborn, London WC1V 7QX

Medieval People © 2014 Thames & Hudson Ltd, London

Designed by Karolina Prymaka

British Library Cataloguing-in-Publication Data
A catalogue record for this book is available from the British Library

ISBN 978-0-500-25203-1

Printed and bound in China by C & C Offset Printing Co. Ltd

To find out about all our publications, please visit **www.thamesandhudson.com**.
There you can subscribe to our e-newsletter, browse or download our current catalogue, and buy any titles that are in print.

Contents

5.

An Age of Transition 232

1400–1500

The Medieval World

The term 'medieval' has many different implications. It can suggest a romantic world of knights and ladies, of courtly love and heroic deeds of arms. It is often thought of as referring to an age of faith, one of religious certainties. It is also used as a term of abuse, with implications of ignorance and brutality. This is not surprising, for the medieval period was many things. It was an age of change as much as of continuity, as empires rose and fell, and old concepts were challenged by new ideas.

When did the Middle Ages begin? There can be no definitive answer to this question. For some commentators, it was with the decline of the Roman Empire, while for others that was the start not of the medieval period, but of the Dark Ages. It could, then, be argued that the Middle Ages did not begin until the eleventh century, or even later. For Petrarch, writing in the fourteenth century, a dark age was ushered in by the fall of Rome which continued until his own day. This book commences in the eighth century with the reign of Charlemagne; his establishment of a new empire in western Europe in 800 marked a fundamental moment of change.

There is less argument about the close of the Middle Ages, although one suggestion is that it occurred 'at any point between the thirteenth and the twentieth centuries, according to taste'. There is broad agreement, however, that it can be placed around 1500. The fall of Constantinople to the Turks in 1453, the invention of printing in the mid-fifteenth century, the discovery of the New World in 1492, and the French invasion of Italy in 1494–95, have all been seen as crucial, as has the papal condemnation of Luther in 1520.

Many of the popular characterizations of the Middle Ages have little validity. Much that is often thought of as 'medieval' was nothing of the sort. People in the Middle Ages did not believe that the earth was flat. Torture was far less common than in subsequent centuries. While there was of course much superstition in the Middle Ages, accusations of witchcraft were rare; it was the early modern period that saw large-scale witch-hunts. Medieval warfare involved hard hand-to-hand fighting, but the Thirty Years War in the seventeenth century saw much more brutality than the Hundred Years War of the fourteenth and fifteenth centuries. Medieval scholars may have considered alchemy a valid science, but so did Isaac Newton. Nor was the Middle Ages lacking in innovations. The list of technological advances includes mechanical clocks, guns, printing, blast furnaces, spectacles, stirrups and

The 'Psalter' world map, created in England in about 1265, has East at the top and Jerusalem at the centre.

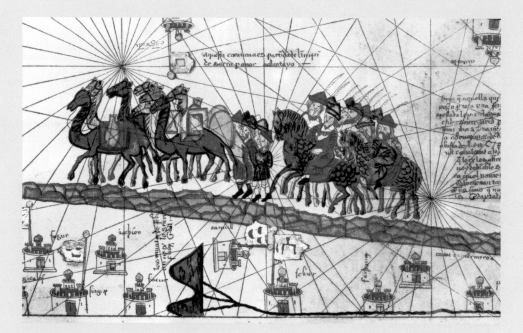

Detail from the Catalan Atlas of 1375, showing Marco Polo, with his father and his uncle, travelling on the Silk Road through Asia to the Far East.

the compass. While it is easy to dispel at least some of the myths about the period, there are no obvious overarching generalizations to replace them. My hope, however, is that this book will provide an indication of the richness and complexity of the centuries from 800 to 1500.

The focus of this book is largely on Europe and the Mediterranean world, but it extends into Asia with the Mongol conquests under Chinggis Khan in the thirteenth century, which opened up routes to the Far East, as Marco Polo's journeys show. In intellectual terms, it is not possible to understand the Middle Ages without appreciating the immense importance of the work of such Muslim scholars as the Persian Ibn Sīnā, with his achievements in medicine and philosophy. It was through the world of Arab scholarship that much Classical learning was transmitted to western Europe.

Many of those in this book, notably emperors, popes and kings, have been selected for their undoubted importance. In Ibn Sīnā and Thomas Aquinas there are great philosophers. Distinguished soldiers discussed included El Cid and John Hawkwood. Among the writers of history, Matthew Paris and Jean Froissart were particularly notable. I have included others, such as the Venetian nuns of the convent of Sant'Angelo, because their careers illustrate particular facets of the age, though they themselves may have had relatively little influence on the course of events. Some individuals close to the bottom of the social spectrum, such as the French peasant leader Guillaume Cale, also feature. Many careers spanned different fields. Benedetto Zaccaria was both merchant and admiral. The artist Piero della Francesca was a mathematician of distinction. Richard of Wallingford was an abbot, a clockmaker and a leper. With scholars, authors and artists my aim is not to provide detailed analysis of their ideas and works, but to describe their lives and the challenges they faced.

The quality of the sources about particular individuals has been important in making my choice. There would have been no point in examining the career of a solitary hermit living by the banks of the river Wear, Godric of Finchale, had his life not been written about at considerable length. Autobiographies were uncommon in the Middle Ages, but Guibert de Nogent wrote an intriguing account of an appalling childhood, while Pedro IV of Aragon and Charles IV of Bohemia were responsible for autobiographical chronicles. The Arab nobleman Usāma ibn Munqidh also wrote a fascinating memoir.

The medieval world may have been male dominated, but not to such an extent that women could not make their mark. They could be important in many ways: this book shows them as queens, in Eleanor of Aquitaine's case of both France and England; as authors, with the remarkable history written by Anna Komnene; and as military commanders, with Matilda of Tuscany and Joan of Arc. They could also be spiritual leaders. One notable visionary was Hildegard of Bingen, whose interests extended from music to herbal medicine. In many ways, the women in this book are more remarkable than the men, given the difficulties they faced in making their voices heard.

The French heroine Joan of Arc leading an unsuccessful attack on Paris in September 1429, from a late fifteenth-century manuscript.

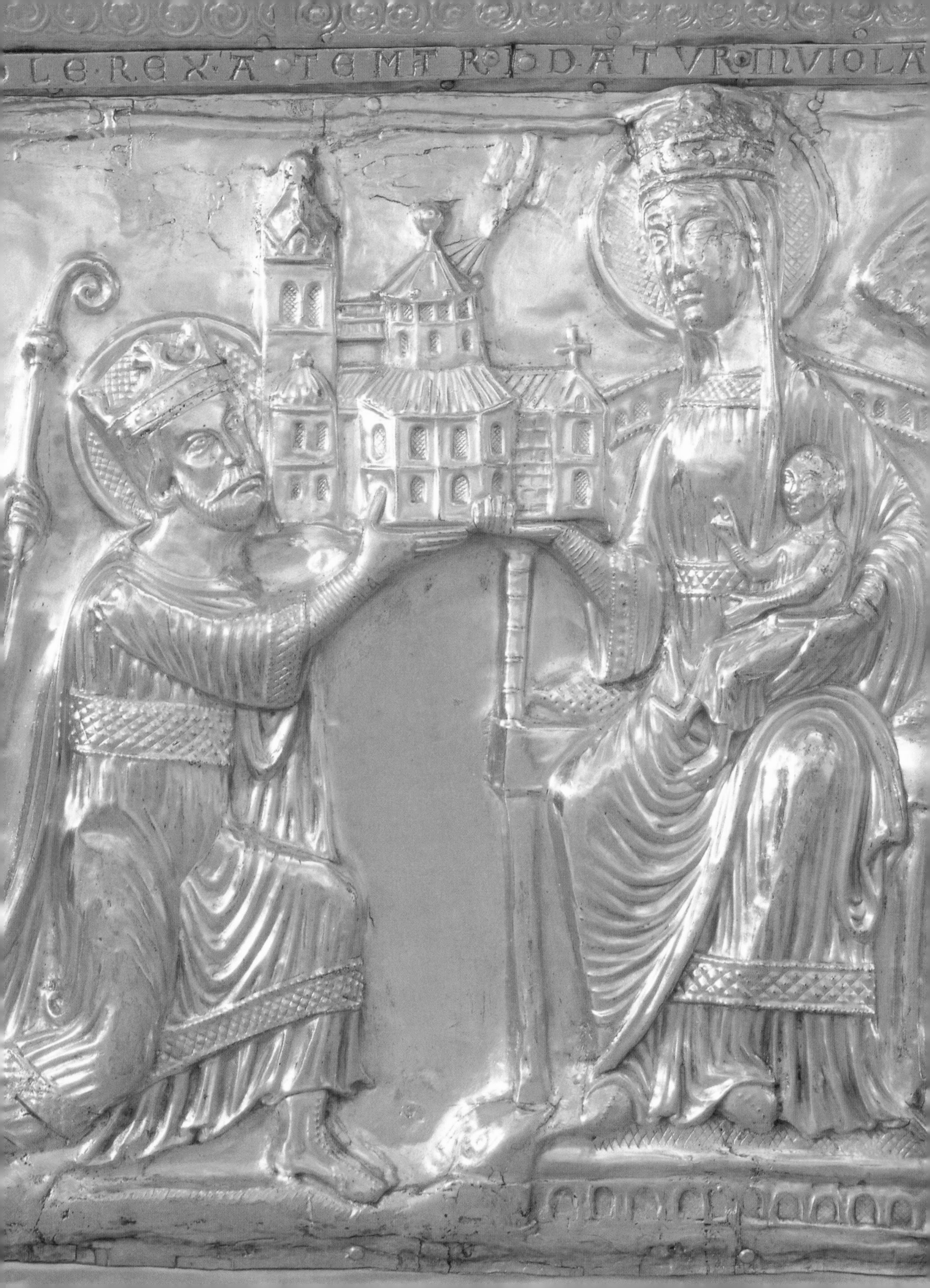
LE·REX·A TEMT R D·ATVR INVIOLA

1.

An Age of Empires

800–1100

Of all the Germanic peoples who settled in what was once the Roman Empire, the most successful were the Franks. In the fourth century, they were settled in the Rhineland region; by the early sixth century, their king, Clovis, had established his rule over much of the old Roman province of Gaul. When the Frankish ruler Charlemagne was crowned emperor in 800, his empire stretched from the North Sea to the Pyrenees, and eastwards to the Adriatic. His was a new dynasty, which had replaced the previous Merovingian kings in 751 when his father, Pepin, was crowned. Although the Carolingians were new to the royal title, they were not new to power, having been influential since the early eighth century. Charles Martel, from whom the dynasty takes its name, had held the key position of mayor of the palace under the Merovingians, and defeated a Muslim army invading from Spain at the battle of Tours in 732.

Charlemagne's empire, however, was not a structure that could be kept together, nor did he intend it as such. It had thrived as it expanded, but it began to fall apart once that expansion ceased. When Charlemagne's son, Louis the Pious, died in 840, the empire was divided between the latter's three sons. By the end of the ninth century, Carolingian rule had largely collapsed, due to dynastic divisions on the one hand, and external pressures from the Vikings, Magyars and Arabs on the other.

Viking expansion transformed much of Europe in this period. Under the Vikings, trade, piracy, conquest and colonization combined in an extraordinarily productive mix. Viking traders in the east used the great Russian waterways to travel as far as the Black Sea, and the principality of Kiev was of Viking origin. In the west, in the ninth century, coastal raids were followed by deeper incursions, with longships sailing up the Seine to Paris and beyond. New Viking states were established, such as the duchy of Normandy, the product of an agreement between the Carolingian ruler of France, Charles III, and a Viking leader. King Olav I of Norway, who died in 1000, was a representative of this changing world: he was both a traditional Viking raider and a convert to Christianity.

The career of the Norman Emma, queen to the English king Æthelred and to the Danish king Cnut, illuminates the connections that existed between England, Scandinavia

A gold panel from the thirteenth-century shrine at Aachen, showing the emperor Charlemagne dedicating the church to the Virgin Mary.

and Normandy. In 1066, the Normans achieved an astonishing triumph when Duke William defeated the English king Harold at Hastings. Even more remarkable was their success in the Mediterranean. They had begun to infiltrate southern Italy in the first quarter of the eleventh century; by 1061, they had started the conquest of Sicily from the Arabs, a process they completed by 1091.

In 911, the same year as the foundation of the duchy of Normandy, the last Carolingian ruler in Germany, Louis the Child, died. A new dynasty, known as the Ottonian, or Liudolfing, was established in 919 by Henry the Fowler, duke of Saxony. In the year 1000, the young emperor Otto III emphasized his links to the Carolingian past when he had Charlemagne's body exhumed. The Ottonians, however, were in a position to assume leadership only of the eastern part of the former Carolingian empire. The central part of that empire, which included Italy and Burgundy, lacked any unity, and these lands were soon subdivided into a complex patchwork.

In the west, after the death of its last Carolingian ruler, Hugh Capet took the French throne in 987. His Capetian dynasty would last, with direct descent from father to son, until 1328. In France, as Carolingian authority and institutions collapsed, power was increasingly concentrated in duchies, counties and smaller lordships. Castles, providing administrative and military bases for nobles, were built by rulers such as Fulk Nerra of Anjou, instead of communal defences such as town walls. The lordship exercised from such castles was based on force rather than on legitimate traditional authority. Yet to see this as evidence of a general crisis or even revolution is to wear blinkers that limit vision largely to France. In northern Italy, it was cities rather than local nobles that were beginning to take over as older power structures declined.

The cultural achievements of the Carolingian and Ottonian worlds were notable. While the imperial courts were important, monasteries such as Corvey and Reichenau formed the intellectual and artistic powerhouses of western Europe. Magnificently illustrated manuscripts demonstrate the wealth and confidence of these institutions. The deep Classical learning to be found in them is displayed by the plays and other writings of a canoness from the abbey at Gandersheim, Hrotsvit. The true intellectual powerhouses of this period, however, lay not in the west, but in the Muslim world. Just as much as Christian Europe, Islam was heir to the learning of the ancient world. Scholars such as Ibn Sīnā, known in the West as Avicenna, advanced knowledge across a broad front from medicine to philosophy.

Spain provided an interface between western Christianity and Islam; the porous frontier in the peninsula saw Islamic learning transmitted to the Christian world. By the late eleventh century, however, in the age of the warlord El Cid, attitudes were beginning to change. Differences were sharpened by an increasingly zealous Islamic ideology and a newly aggressive Christianity. El Cid himself, however, was prepared to serve both Muslims and Christians.

The Church in the west went through regular cycles of reform and decline. Papal reform began in 1046, when the German emperor Henry III deposed three rival popes. Reformers questioned the right of emperors and kings to appoint bishops and to invest

Carolingian art echoed that of ancient Rome. This manuscript illustration shows Charlemagne's grandson Charles the Bald being presented with a book.

them with spiritual authority. Clerical marriage and the buying and selling of positions in the Church were attacked. The papacy became increasingly radicalized, notably under Gregory VII, who was elected pope in 1073. However, the papacy's spiritual weapons, such as excommunication, were not sufficient in face of the hostility of the emperor Henry IV. Material assistance was needed, and Gregory's alliance with Matilda, countess of Tuscany provided him with invaluable support, in what has become known as the Investiture Dispute. A compromise was not reached until 1122 in the Concordat of Worms.

In 1095, the papacy demonstrated its leadership of the Christian west when Pope Urban II preached the crusade. There was immense enthusiasm for a holy war which promised the remission of penance, the acquisition of lands in the east and the recovery of Jerusalem. The arrival of the crusaders in Constantinople presented the Byzantine emperor Alexios Komnenos with considerable problems, as the history written by his daughter, Anna, records. The Byzantines had first to deal with an unruly rabble led by Peter the Hermit, and then to manage the ambitions of the nobles in the main expedition. Given the inadequate planning of the crusade, and the fact that the army took the difficult overland route to Constantinople and onward across Asia Minor, it is astonishing that the crusaders should have captured Antioch, let alone gone on to take Jerusalem itself. In the aftermath of this triumph, new crusader states were established, headed by the kingdom of Jerusalem. It was to prove much harder to defend them than it had been to found them.

Charlemagne

FIRST MEDIEVAL EMPEROR IN WESTERN EUROPE

742–814

harles the Great, or Charlemagne as he has become known, suffered from insomnia. He kept a wax writing tablet under his pillow, so that when he woke he could try to write, though forming the letters was beyond him. This was an exceptional failing in an extraordinary man, who became king of the Franks jointly with his brother, Carloman, in 768, sole ruler in 771 and emperor in 800.

Charlemagne's contemporary biographer, Einhard, described him in detail. He was tall and well built. His head was large, his hair fair, his eyes piercing. His neck was rather short, and his nose on the long side. His voice was shrill. Normally, he wore Frankish dress, much as his people did. He particularly liked roasts, and in his final years was angry with his doctors when they urged him to eat his meat boiled. Another writer, Notker, considered that 'the emperor struck terror into everyone'. In old age, Charlemagne could be impatient. He wrote to one official regarding bridge tolls: 'We have given you orders before, out of our own mouth, and you have not understood us.' He had a questioning mind. In an interrogation of his bishops and abbots he asked: 'Who is that Satan or enemy whose works and pomp we renounced at baptism? This is to be seen into, lest any of our people should follow him in his wrongdoings.'

Charlemagne was a great Christian warlord. His most formidable opponents were the Saxons, a Germanic people similar in many ways to the Franks, but unlike them in being pagan and having no kings. A series of campaigns developed from raids into full-scale conquest, which was not finally achieved until 803. The war was brutal; in 782, a reported 4,500 prisoners were massacred by the Franks. Saxons were pushed into rivers in mass forced baptisms. Charlemagne's armies also fought in Aquitaine, Italy, Brittany, northern Spain and Hungary. Failure was rare. In 778, his forces suffered a famous defeat at the hands of the Basques at the pass of Roncesvalles, later commemorated in the *Song of Roland*, but this did not halt Frankish expansion.

The key to Charlemagne's military success was not so much brilliant generalship as superb organization. His armies were recruited by means of sophisticated systems of military obligation. Attention was given to horse-breeding. Care was taken over logistics and provisioning, with legislation requiring 'flour, wine, sides of bacon and other food in abundance, hand querns, adzes, axes, augurs, slings and men who can use them properly'.

Instructions were even given for the construction of waterproof carts, which could be floated across rivers.

Government of Charlemagne's vast dominions, which extended across much of western Europe, was no simple matter. Regular assemblies enabled him to keep a finger on the pulse of his empire. Much was done by word of mouth at these gatherings; even at its largest, there were no more than a dozen clerks in Charlemagne's writing office, issuing administrative and legislative instructions known as capitularies in growing profusion as the reign proceeded. Special commissioners, called *missi*, were sent round regularly to check up on the conduct of the counts, who were responsible for government at a local level.

The royal estates were the backbone of Carolingian rule as Charlemagne journeyed around his lands, moving from one palace complex to another. Detailed instructions commanded, for example, that no one should press grapes for wine with their feet, and required that in each royal estate 'they shall always keep fattened geese and chickens sufficient for our use if needed, or for sending to us'. Sample estate surveys were made and issued as models of the documents that royal officials should produce.

In his later years, the aging emperor was no longer capable of constant travel around his lands. He settled on Aachen as the central hub of his empire, and turned to Italy and the Roman past for inspiration for his new palace. The church of San Vitale in Ravenna was the model for the magnificent palatine chapel, where fine polished marbles gave an extraordinary opulence. The palace complex at Aachen incorporated baths fed by hot springs. Charlemagne greatly enjoyed swimming, a highly unusual accomplishment for a medieval ruler. According to Einhard, it was because of the baths that he chose Aachen.

The powerful Christian element to Charlemagne's rule strongly reflected his own personal piety. Counts and their officials were to deal with crimes 'so that with God's indulgence all these evils may be removed from among our Christian people'. In 802, the *missi* were to enquire 'concerning adultery and other unlawful acts, whether committed in bishoprics and monasteries and convents or among laymen'. Charlemagne was much concerned to improve the standard of the lower clergy; one capitulary

A bronze statuette probably representing Charlemagne. He bears an orb in one hand, and would have had a sword in the other.

even included a clause forbidding priests, monks and clerks from drinking in taverns. He was keen that priests should use proper language, and not express themselves in uncouth ways.

Charlemagne possessed considerable intellectual curiosity if not necessarily much aptitude; his inability to write increased his appreciation of the written word. He developed his court as a centre of learning, and encouraged the establishment of schools in cathedrals and monasteries. Though he complained on one occasion that he did not have men around him of the quality of the early Christian fathers Jerome and Augustine, the scholars he recruited from the 780s were exceptional. There was Alcuin from Northumberland, Theodulf from Spain and Paul the Deacon from Italy. Scholars worked on many topics, from biblical commentaries to histories. The task of copying Classical texts was of crucial importance in preserving the heritage of the past. To help with this, a style of writing, now

An amulet made for Charlemagne, containing a relic of the Cross.

known as Carolingian minuscule (the basis of modern lowercase typefaces), was improved under Alcuin's influence. In illustrating books, artists combined late-Roman and Byzantine elements with Germanic and Celtic traditions. It was, however, words not pictures that Charlemagne regarded as being of fundamental importance. As he put it in one decree: 'Often some desire to pray to God properly, but they pray badly because of incorrect books.'

On Christmas day, 800, Charlemagne, king of the Franks, was crowned emperor by Pope Leo III in Rome. This elevation was surely deserved, in terms of his achievements and the scale of his conquests. In fact, that was not why the coronation took place. The pope faced serious unrest in Rome, and turned to Charlemagne for support. He crowned an apparently reluctant Charlemagne because he needed a protector. No pope had crowned an emperor before, and Charlemagne is unlikely to have welcomed such a precedent. With hindsight, the coronation was a moment of immense significance. There were now two empires, the Byzantine in the east, based on Constantinople and directly descended from the Roman Empire, and a new, upstart empire in the west.

Charlemagne's lavish palatine chapel at Aachen, built to a central plan, was modelled on the church of San Vitale in Ravenna.

Hrotsvit of Gandersheim

AUTHOR AND DRAMATIST

c. 935–c. 1000

Conquered and converted under Charlemagne (see pp. 16–19), Saxony became the powerhouse of empire in the tenth century. Henry the Fowler laid the foundations; his son, Otto I, expanded his authority in Germany, and, following the Carolingian example, invaded Italy and gained the imperial throne in 962. The astonishing political success of this Ottonian dynasty was accompanied by an intellectual revival centred on the court and on the great monasteries which thrived under imperial patronage.

One of those religious houses was Gandersheim, founded in the mid-ninth century by Liudolf, duke of Saxony. The sisters at Gandersheim were secular canonesses, not nuns, and so were not bound by full monastic vows. It was an aristocratic establishment, whose abbesses were normally members of the imperial family. Gandersheim was no refuge from the secular world. Otto II's empress, Theophanu, was a frequent visitor, and her daughter, Sophia, was educated there.

Hrotsvit, whose name means 'Strong Voice', was probably born in the 930s, and may well have lived until about 1000. She probably entered the house at Gandersheim at a young age. Her teachers there were Rikkardis, whom she described as extremely learned and kindhearted, and the abbess, Gerberga, who was a niece of Otto I. Her education was remarkable, for she read widely in the works of the early Christian fathers, particularly Prudentius, as well as Classical authors such as Horace, Ovid, Vergil and Terence.

Both inspired and shocked by her reading of Terence, Hrotsvit decided to write plays herself. This was highly unusual for any author, male or female; these were probably the first to be written in western Europe since Classical times. In one, *Pafnutius*, a beautiful prostitute called Thais was persuaded to renounce her wicked ways. Her penance was to be shut up in a small cell, with a tiny window for the supply of food and drink, but with no door, nor, to Thais's considerable concern, any sanitary facilities. After five years in her cell going over her sins, she died,

A Byzantine intaglio in a setting of gold and pearls shows the connection between the imperial worlds of Germany and Constantinople. Otto II's empress, Theophanu, was from Byzantium.

The young emperor Otto III, enthroned with members of his court around him, shown in the Reichenau Gospels, a magnificent example of Ottonian culture.

and her soul went to heaven. There was a didactic purpose to the play beyond its obvious moral message, for in it Pafnutius explained some difficult musical technicalities. Similarly, in another play, *Sapientia*, Hrotsvit provided a lesson in mathematics, in which, for example, she explained what an evenly uneven number is.

Hrotsvit excused the rustic simplicity and uncultured style of her writings. This, however, was no more than a conventional remark. In fact, she had impressive mastery of rhetorical devices, and composed verse in fluent hexameters. At Gerberga's request, she wrote a history of the emperor Otto I in Latin verse. In the preface, she emphasized the difficulty of her task: it was like wandering through an unknown forest, in which all the paths were covered by deep snow. She explained that, when she reached the point of time in the present where there were no longer any written sources to rely on, she laid down her pen. Her feminine nature,

The abbey at Gandersheim. The church with its Romanesque west front dates from about 1100; in Hrotsvit's day the building was much simpler.

she indicated, meant that she could not describe any more of Otto's military campaigning, nor did she wish to explain the deposition and replacement of the pope. The value of her history, however, is that it contains much more about royal women than do the works of male chroniclers.

Hrotsvit is one of the outstanding individuals in the cultural renaissance that took place in Germany in the later tenth century. As with the Carolingian empire, the court was central to it, with women such as Gerberga and the empress Theophanu playing an important role in patronage. The great monasteries, above all those at Corvey and Reichenau, were also crucial. It was there that manuscripts were copied, and some of the finest of all medieval illustrated books produced. German, Frankish, Italian and Byzantine influences came together in a court art which glorified the Ottonian dynasty.

King Olav I of Norway

HEROIC VIKING RULER

c. 960—1000

The achievements of the Vikings were astonishing. From their Scandinavian homes, they travelled east through the Baltic, down the great Russian rivers and reached the Black Sea. To the west, they sailed to the British Isles and France. They settled in Iceland, set up a colony in Greenland, and voyaged to America. They established kingdoms, principalities and duchies. Some of these, such as the kingdom of York, were short-lived. Others, such as the principality of Kiev and the duchy of Normandy, became part of the fabric of medieval Europe.

A thirteenth-century Icelandic work, the *Heimskringla*, gives a dramatic account of the Norwegian king Olav I. He was born while his mother lay in hiding from her husband's killers; and as a boy he was sold into slavery for a cloak. Freed, he went to Novgorod, where he served its ruler, Vladimir. He began a typical Viking career of raiding, and married a

Olav I drowned when he attempted to escape his enemies by diving into the sea at the naval battle of Svold in 1000.

A modern reproduction of a Viking ship, the Sea Stallion. Such ships could be rowed or sailed, and made Viking trade and expansion possible.

princess of the Wendish Baltic people. However, an encounter with a hermit in the Scilly Isles resulted in his conversion to Christianity, and he ceased his attacks. After his first wife died, he married a sister of the Viking king of Dublin. He then joined a rebellion in Norway against Earl Håkon, who controlled most of the country. Success came swiftly, and in 995 Olav was elected king. A third marriage proved disastrous; his bride pulled a knife on him during their wedding night, but he woke in time to prevent her killing him. He developed the town of Nidaros (now Trondheim) as his capital, establishing a merchant settlement there. Olav's reign, though, was short. In 1000, he was defeated by a combined Swedish, Danish and Wendish force in a naval battle at Svold. He dived into the sea to escape his foes, and drowned.

According to the *Heimskringla*, Olav was a truly heroic figure. He scaled the massive cliff of Hornelen (not climbed again until 1897), and then carried one of his followers back down it. He was able to juggle three daggers simultaneously, and could run across the oars of his longship as it was being rowed. He was ambidextrous, able to throw two spears at once. A merry, cheerful man, he was also violent, happily torturing his enemies.

Such accretions of legend in the *Heimskringla* make for good reading, but less good history. The evidence of the *Anglo-Saxon Chronicle* is rather more reliable. It suggests that Olav took part in the raid on southeast England in 991 which culminated in the battle of Maldon. The bravery of the defeated Anglo-Saxons is commemorated in a notable poem. In 994, Olav joined forces with the Danish king Svein Forkbeard to attack London and ravage the south coast. Olav probably converted to Christianity while in England, with King

Æthelred acting as his godfather and paying him a substantial tribute. When Olav returned to Norway and overthrew Earl Håkon, he brought a brutal Christianity with him. The account in *Heimskringla* has the ring of truth here. 'The king then went to the north part of Viken and invited every man to accept Christianity; and those who opposed him he punished severely, killing some, mutilating others, and driving some into banishment.' Lasting conversion proved to be a far more gradual process, achieved more by missionaries than by sword-wielding kings – but with his aggressive brand of Christianity, his alliances with powerful families in Norway, and his development of the trading town at Nidaros, Olav personified an important phase in the development of Norwegian kingship. His career as a Viking raider looked back to the past; his reign as king looked to the future.

Ships were essential to the Vikings' success. Olav had a particularly splendid ship built, the *Long Serpent*. It had thirty-four benches for its rowers, and the carved prow and stern were both gilded. Such a vessel was clinker-built, with a single mast and sail, and a side steering oar. The construction with overlapping planks gave flexibility, and an ability to ride through rough seas. A shallow draft meant that the Vikings could go far up river in the lands they raided. There were several different types of ship, all built on the same basic principles. The *knar*, for example, was a trader, broader in the beam than a longship, with half-decks at bow and stern. Vessels such as the famous Oseberg ship were almost certainly confined to coastal waters, others could venture into the wild seas of the Atlantic.

The Vikings were not successful in every endeavour. According to the saga of Olav's life, Eric the Red spent one winter with him. Eric was responsible for the earliest Viking settlements in Greenland, but these always remained small, and were abandoned in the later Middle Ages. Eric's son, Leif Ericson, discovered Vinland on his voyages, and there seems little doubt that this was America. A Norse settlement has been identified at L'Anse aux Meadows in Newfoundland, and there may well have been others. Little came of this, however, and there was no permanent colonization of the New World. The opportunities in Europe were surely far more attractive than the undeveloped lands of America.

The start of the saga of the life of Olav I, in the fourteenth-century Icelandic manuscript known as the Flateyjarbók.

Fulk Nerra

CASTLE-BUILDING COUNT OF ANJOU

972—1040

By the late tenth century, power in France had largely devolved into the hands of regional and local lords. One of the most formidable of these was Fulk Nerra, count of Anjou from 987 to 1040. Adept at playing neighbouring rulers off against each other, and making use of the Capetian kings of France as occasional allies, he employed a mixture of military power, bad temper and piety to great effect.

Fulk was notorious. The monks of Saint-Florent complained 'of his overwhelming ferocity'. His anger was understandable when, in 999, his first wife, Elizabeth of Vendôme, took a lover and seized the castle at Angers. Fulk besieged the place, and captured his wife when she fell from the walls. He had her burned, and then put the town to the flames. After he went on pilgrimage, however, his 'ferocity was replaced by a certain sweetness for a time'. That ferocity, however, was too valuable a political weapon to be abandoned for long.

It may seem surprising that a violent and bad-tempered man such as Fulk should have gone on four pilgrimages to the Holy Land, but his piety was a consequence of his behaviour. He explained that he had shed much blood, and was terrified by the fear of Gehenna (the destination of the wicked). By one account, on his final pilgrimage, in the year before he died, he was dragged naked to the Holy Sepulchre, where he cried out, 'O Lord receive wretched Fulk, your oathbreaker, your fugitive. O lord Jesus Christ look after my repentant soul.' Not everyone was convinced by Fulk's religious zeal. When he built a new monastery at Beaulieu-lès-Loches, the archbishop of Tours refused to consecrate the church as Fulk was a man 'who has seized more than a few of the estates and serfs of the mother church of my bishopric'.

Fulk's military strategy, which belies his hot-headed reputation, was careful. The warfare he engaged in was dominated by sieges, punctuated by raids and ambushes; he fought only two battles in his whole career. His use of castles was the key to his success. Castles were new in the tenth century; they were a clear reaction to the chaotic conditions of the time. Fulk constructed a complex network of castles to defend and consolidate his territories, and as bases from which he could exercise his lordship. Many of his castles were earthwork constructions, with a mound or motte topped with wooden defences, but his castle at Langeais, built in 994, is famed as the first stone keep, ancestor of the great towers that dominated the castles of the twelfth century. In reality, Langeais was hardly at the cutting edge of castle

A sixteenth-century woodcut depicting Fulk Nerra, showing him in Classical guise. Some contemporary sources used the terminology of ancient Rome when describing his rule.

design. Although it proved strong enough to withstand two sieges, what Fulk built was little more than a hall, with windows that looked back in their design to the Gallo-Roman past. It was not long before more formidable stone towers began to dominate the landscape. At Montboyau, in about 1016, Fulk built what was described as a *donjon*. The great keep at Loches, a complex three-storeyed structure, almost certainly dates back to his day. It was a major advance on Langeais, and made a forcible statement about its builder's power and

Castles were key to Fulk Nerra's power. That at Langeais is generally regarded as the earliest stone keep, and took the form of a two-storeyed hall. It was powerful enough to withstand two sieges.

prestige. Fulk was establishing a new kind of military and political authority.

Much of the vocabulary of the chroniclers at this time echoed the phrases of ancient Rome. Counts might be 'consuls', kings might be 'emperors'. Entries to towns were described as if they were the Classical ceremony of the formal arrival at a city, the *adventus*. This creates problems for historians. Was the use of Roman terminology a genuine reflection of the ways in which rulers around the turn of the millennium behaved, or was it a forced literary artifice that had little relationship to reality? In fact, it is more convincing to see Fulk as a ruler working out new ways of establishing his political authority than as a neo-Roman reintroducing Classical ceremonies to reinforce his lordship.

After Fulk's death, the intense rivalry between Anjou and the other great regional power, Normandy, continued. In an attempt to defuse it, Fulk's descendant, Geoffrey, count of Anjou, married Matilda, daughter of King Henry I of England. Their son, Henry II, came to the English throne in 1154, and with his accession the Angevin cause triumphed. The descent of the English crown thus went straight back to Fulk Nerra, from whom, perhaps, Henry II inherited his evil temper. It is no surprise that the Angevin family was popularly supposed to have been descended from the Devil, a story which Henry II's heir, Richard I, was happy to see propagated.

Ibn Sīnā
(Avicenna)

PERSIAN SCHOLAR AND POLYMATH

980–1037

The intellectual powerhouses of western Europe were the monasteries, schools and, in time, universities controlled by the Church. The courts of its emperors, kings and noblemen had only a small part to play. It was very different in the Islamic east, where the patronage and power of rulers was an essential support to learning. This was an astonishing world of great cultural achievements. It was a far more urbanized society than western Europe, with huge and splendid cities such as Sāmarrā, the Islamic capital for much of the ninth century, and Baghdad. Scholars were greatly valued; talent was well rewarded. An immense amount of work was done to translate Greek philosophical and scientific works into Arabic, providing the foundation for new advances. There was tolerance, and encouragement of new ideas. By the late tenth century, however, the Islamic world had begun to fragment, as dynasties failed, and local rulers gained increasing independence from the Abbasid caliphate in Baghdad.

Avicenna, or more properly Ibn Sīnā, was a Persian scholar, born in 980 near Bukhārā in modern Uzbekistan. His father had a keen interest in learning, and provided his precociously talented son with a tutor. By the age of ten, the boy had mastered the Qur'ān. He studied law, and had a tutor in philosophy. He had an extraordinarily retentive mind, and claimed later that as a teenager he knew as much as he would in adulthood. The young and good-looking Ibn Sīnā quickly acquired a considerable reputation. When the ruler of Bukhārā fell ill, his doctors consulted Ibn Sīnā, even though he was only eighteen. His advice worked, the prince recovered and Ibn Sīnā was given access to the palace library, a huge treasure

Ibn Sīnā's work was widely circulated in the Middle Ages. This illustration is from a fifteenth-century Hebrew version of his Canon of Medicine.

trove of learning. Political chaos forced him to leave Bukhārā, and he spent some years moving from court to court, both working as an official and practising medicine. In about 1025, he settled in Isfahan, in modern Iran, where he served the local ruler, 'Alā' al-Dawla, a considerable patron of learning. On Friday nights, scholars assembled in his court to discuss a wide range of intellectual issues. Ibn Sīnā was in no doubt that in these debates he showed himself to be supreme in all disciplines.

Geoffrey Chaucer (see pp. 225–28), writing four centuries after Ibn Sīnā's lifetime, numbered the Persian with the great doctors of Classical antiquity, Hippocrates and Galen, as one of the main sources of medical knowledge. 'Medicine', wrote Ibn Sīnā, 'is not a difficult science, and in a short space of time, of course I excelled in it.' He wrote much on the subject, most of it in Arabic rather than his native Persian. Particularly notable was his *Canon of Medicine*, which summarized the medical knowledge of his day, and continued to be used until the seventeenth century. The basis of his work was the concept, taken from Hippocrates and Galen, of the four humours – blood, yellow bile, black bile and phlegm – and the need to balance them. If a disease was characterized by heat, such as a fever, then cold was required to treat it. Ibn Sīnā's book was notable for the clear logic of the way in which he classified his subject into its component parts. Pain was categorized into fifteen

A page from a seventeenth-century Persian manuscript of Ibn Sīnā's Canon of Medicine.

different types. Some sections of the *Canon* were based on Ibn Sīnā's practical experience as a doctor; the use of wine to clean wounds, the value of certain herbs and the drinking of mineral waters were among the points that reflected practice rather than theory. The overriding emphasis, however, was on traditional authority and theoretical reasoning, rather than practical observation.

Medicinal herbs being collected. The great figures of medicine and philosophy are shown in the margins of this fifteenth-century illustration, with Ibn Sīnā at the top right.

The same desire to categorize, organize and classify knowledge, clear from his medical treatises, infused Ibn Sīnā's many philosophical writings, although initially he had found philosophy far harder than medicine. He developed complex arguments to reconcile the existence of God with a rational philosophy. In a famous argument, he put the case for the soul being quite separate from the body, suggesting that a man deprived of all sensory inputs would still be aware of his existence. He wrote of the soul that:

> As the guardian of higher things preserving the thought of the Primal Realities, it has no
> interest in food or drink and no need for kissing or coupling. Rather its task is to await
> the unveiling of realities and focus its perfect intuition and unsullied consciousness on the
> apprehension of the subtlest of principles, and read with the inner eye of insight the tablet
> of God's mysteries.

His great work was the *Shifā'*, which covered logic, the natural sciences, arithmetic, geometry, astronomy and music, in a coherent and systematic way. The book played an important part in the reintroduction of Aristotelian ideas to the west, and was fundamental to much of the scholastic philosophy of medieval Europe.

Ibn Sīnā's working method was to find the most difficult passage in any book; from assessing it, he could then decide whether the whole was worth reading. He would do his academic work for a couple of hours in the morning, prior to performing his official duties. His output was astonishing; one of his treatises is said to have occupied some 6,000 folios, and to have taken a mere six months to write. In all, he produced about 450 works. He had an arrogant, if well-justified, conviction in his own undoubted abilities. Ibn Sīnā may sound an austere figure, devoted to scholarship and remaining unmarried. However, he enjoyed wine, and if he started to fall asleep while working in the evenings, a glass would revive him. Nor did he abstain from the pleasures of the flesh – the student who wrote his biography noted, 'He was vigorous in all his faculties, the sexual faculty being the most vigorous and dominant.' Indeed, the scale of his indulgence was such that it was thought to have led to his death in 1037, though self-medication with inappropriate remedies is a more likely explanation.

Emma of Normandy

QUEEN TO TWO KINGS, MOTHER TO TWO MORE

c. 980–1052

A fleet of Viking longships, with ferocious figureheads and beating oars threatening slaughter, normally terrified those who saw it. In contrast, a book commissioned and inspired by Emma of Normandy, the *Encomium Emmae*, joyfully describes a Danish invasion fleet decorated with carved and gilded lions, birds and dragons, and with gold, silver and bright colours flashing in the light. Emma gloried in the Viking world, and wanted her menfolk to be noble, strong and skilful in arms.

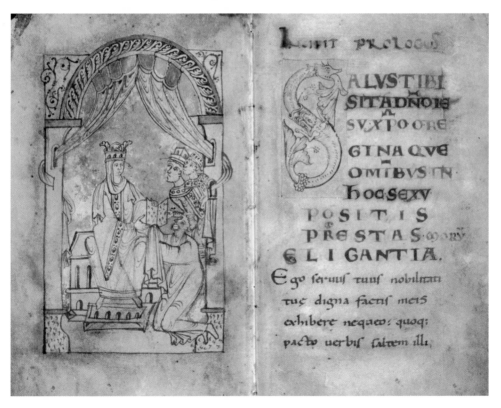

Emma of Normandy receiving a copy of the Encomium Emmae *from its author, from an eleventh-century manuscript.*

Emma, here given the Anglo-Saxon name Ælfgifu, and her husband Cnut, presenting a cross on the altar at the New Minster, Winchester.

Emma was a daughter of the Norman duke Richard I, and great-granddaughter of the Viking Rollo, who founded the duchy of Normandy. In a bid to forge an alliance in place of war, she was sent to England in 1002 to marry King Æthelred II, known to history as the Unready, following an unsuccessful attempt to invade Normandy. It was Æthelred's second marriage, and he had at least half a dozen children by his first queen. Emma provided him with two more sons, Edward and Alfred, and a daughter, Godgifu. It was no doubt to Emma's considerable annoyance that Athelstan, Æthelred's eldest son by his first marriage, remained heir to the throne until his death in 1014.

Æthelred died in 1016, and after the defeat and subsequent death of his eldest surviving son, Edmund Ironside, he was succeeded by the Danish king Cnut. According to the *Encomium*, once Cnut was enthroned, thoughts turned to finding him an appropriate queen. The fact that he was already married to an English lady, Ælfgifu of Northampton, was not seen as an obstacle. The search eventually came up with Emma. She met all the requirements, for she was of noble lineage, was exceptionally beautiful and was regarded as notable for her sound judgment. The marriage of Cnut and Emma was a success. 'It is hard to believe how much joy in each other arose in them both,' was one

well-informed verdict. Any husband was surely an improvement on Æthelred, and it is hardly surprising that a Norman woman, proud of her Viking descent, welcomed marriage to a vigorous and successful Danish king. Their genuine partnership produced a son, Harthacnut, and a daughter, Gunnhilda.

Cnut is one of only two kings of England to be known as 'the Great' (the other, of course, being Alfred), although in Cnut's case it is only in Scandinavia that he is so termed. England provided Cnut with resources on a scale that no other Scandinavian ruler could match. Emma wished him to be remembered as a friend of the Church, a protector of widows and orphans, a maintainer of justice and a bringer of peace. The reality, as Cnut dealt with his enemies and established his rule both in Scandinavia and England, was more complex. In 1025, he fought the Swedes; three years later, he invaded Norway. The appointment of his first queen, Ælfgifu, to rule in Norway on behalf of her son Svein was to prove mistaken; in the mid-1030s she was driven out, while Svein was killed in battle.

When Cnut died in 1035, Emma was faced with the problem of how to secure the succession, and for whom. Her preference was naturally for Harthacnut, but his absence in Norway until 1040 meant that Ælfgifu's son Harold Harefoot gained power. When Alfred, her elder son by Æthelred returned from Normandy to join his mother in 1036, he was soon captured by the powerful earl Godwin, who had him blinded and sent to the monastery at Ely, where he died of his injuries. Emma had failed, and in 1037 she 'was driven out without any mercy to face the raging winter', and took refuge in Flanders. In 1040, however, Harold Harefoot died. Harthacnut succeeded him, and Emma returned to England. Her son Edward followed, and according to the *Encomium's* happy ending, Harthacnut, overcome by love for his half-brother, invited him to share the kingdom with him.

Emma's vision of a happy family, with herself and her two sons ruling England, was soon shattered, for Harthacnut died suddenly in 1042. In the following year, King Edward suddenly turned on her, 'because she had formerly been very hard to the king, her son, in that she did less for him than he wished both before he became king and afterwards as well', and accused her of treason. One account suggested that she was plotting a Norwegian invasion. A later story had it that Emma had taken Ælfwine, bishop of Winchester, as her lover, but that she was exculpated when she submitted to a trial by ordeal, and walked over nine red hot ploughshares. Thanks to the intervention of St Swithun, she did this with no harm to her feet. This is not to be credited, but the tale helps to show something of Emma's reputation. The weak and inconsistent Edward, who was to be known as the Confessor, soon regretted his action against his mother, and Emma duly recovered her possessions. However, Edward married in 1045, and with a new queen in England, Emma was in no position to continue to play a large part in public affairs. She died in 1052, and was buried at Winchester, close to Cnut and her son Harthacnut.

The queens of the earlier Middle Ages have been described as 'peaceweavers'. Emma, however, was a spinner, not a weaver. The *Encomium*, written at Emma's direction, was a fine example of spin and distortion. Her marriage to Æthelred was written out of the story, as was the inconvenient fact that, when she married him, Cnut already had a wife. Instead, doubt was cast on Harold Harefoot's parentage with the implausible claim that he was the child of a maidservant, placed deceitfully in the bed of Cnut's concubine. The killing of Alfred was portrayed in extreme terms as martyrdom.

England's connection with Normandy began with Emma. At the time of her first marriage, the Normans must have hoped that a new Anglo-Norman dynasty would be founded. In the event, despite all Emma's struggles on behalf of her children, that was not to be. Instead, it was through conquest in 1066 that the Normans established themselves in England.

Odo of Bayeux

BISHOP WHO COMMISSIONED THE BAYEUX TAPESTRY

c. 1030—97

The Bayeux Tapestry never ceases to amaze. The vigour with which the Norman knights are shown charging the Anglo-Saxon forces, drawn up with their shields closely interlocked, jumps from the intricate stitching. Horses seem to neigh and stamp their hooves. The story flows from scene to scene in a tour de force of visual narrative. The Tapestry is unique, a remarkable survival which tells the extraordinary story of the Norman Conquest. In the dramatic battle scenes, the only Norman named, apart from Duke William himself, is Odo, bishop of Bayeux. He is shown equipped as a knight, though he carries a stout staff rather than a sword or lance; as a cleric, he was forbidden from shedding blood. In other parts of the Tapestry, Odo is given a leading role, advising the duke on building the invasion fleet, blessing the food and drink at a banquet, and sitting at the duke's right hand.

Odo, who was probably born in the early 1030s, was Duke William's half-brother. He was made bishop of Bayeux in 1049 or 1050, but his rise to real prominence came in the aftermath of the stunning Norman victory at Hastings in 1066. He was given the earldom of Kent, and exercised authority on behalf of William when the new king returned to Normandy in 1067. In 1075, he was one of the commanders of the royal forces that defeated a widespread rebellion, and in 1080 he led an army which dealt harshly with resistance in Northumbria. He was active in adjudicating some of the many disputes over land which resulted from the Conquest. Given the immense power that he wielded, it is not surprising that he acquired a reputation for harsh and oppressive behaviour.

Domesday Book shows that Odo was the largest landowner in England after the king himself, with estates in no less than twenty-two counties. This reveals the astonishing extent to which the landholding structure of England was transformed as a result of the Conquest. Odo received most of his lands in the first five years of Norman rule. The Conqueror's generosity to his half-brother enabled Odo to reward his own followers and supporters. Many were men of no great importance in Normandy for whom the Conquest offered splendid opportunities to gain wealth and status. A whole new aristocratic hierarchy was created in England, with Odo one of its chief authors. Surprisingly, he does not appear to have been a castle-builder on a grand scale. No doubt his tenants constructed simple motte-and-bailey fortifications, but unlike his contemporary, Bishop Gundulf of Rochester, whose name is

Bishop Odo at the battle of Hastings, shown on the Bayeux Tapestry, which he probably commissioned. As a cleric, he bore a staff rather than a sword, so as not to draw blood.

linked both to the castle at Rochester and to the Tower of London, there are no great castles associated with Odo.

Someone as powerful as Odo was bound to acquire enemies. In Kent, there was not enough room for Odo as earl and the archbishop of Canterbury, Lanfranc. Odo favoured the abbey of St Augustine's in Canterbury, which had a tradition of hostility to the cathedral. It seems very likely that Lanfranc was influential in persuading King William to arrest Odo late in 1082. The charges included his oppressive behaviour in England, but his plan to take a force of knights to Italy was the most serious matter. William was clearly alarmed at the scale of Odo's ambition; it was even claimed that he wanted to become pope. Odo was found guilty, and was imprisoned in Rouen until the king, on his deathbed, very reluctantly released him.

The situation after William's death in 1087 was difficult, for Normandy went to his eldest son, Robert Curthose, while his second son, William Rufus, received the kingdom of England. It was difficult for Odo to serve two masters. The choice, however, may not have been that arduous. Duke Robert was amiable, of no strength of mind, a man whom Odo could influence. William Rufus, in contrast, was no friend of the Church and was a man of questionable sexual habits and a furious temper. In 1088, therefore, Odo led a rebellion against Rufus, aiming to reunite England and Normandy under Robert. This failed disastrously. When Odo was besieged in Rochester, disease spread through his troops and he was forced to surrender, with the king's trumpets sounding out triumphantly.

Banished from England, his lands there lost, Odo saw out his career in Normandy, where he spent much of his energy building up his bishopric at Bayeux. In 1095, he attended

Bishop Odo blessing the food and drink at a feast held after the Norman landing in England. This scene in the Bayeux Tapestry was modelled on depictions of the Last Supper.

the Council of Clermont, where Pope Urban II (see pp. 46–48) preached the crusade. Most men in their sixties might have considered that they were too old to take up the cross, but not Odo. In the next year he set out on crusade, but on his way to the east early in 1097 he died in Sicily, at Palermo, by then in Norman hands.

It was typical of the ambitious and grandiose Odo that he should have commissioned the Bayeux Tapestry to commemorate the Norman Conquest of England and emphasize his own role in it. There have been countless theories put forward about the Tapestry's origins, but the most convincing is that it was made in England, in nine sections. The story of the Conquest is told from the Norman point of view, though it betrays some English sympathy by terming Harold *rex* (king). As well as Odo's prominence, and the fact that the Tapestry was preserved at Bayeux, there are other pointers to his involvement. The artist used some designs from manuscripts held by Odo's favourite abbey of St Augustine's; and among the few Normans named in the Tapestry are Vital, Wadard and Turold, all of them tenants of Odo.

Odo was a bishop for almost half a century. He was of the old school, resistant to the radical ideas of the reformers that were transforming the Church, and 'was more given to worldly affairs than to spiritual contemplation'. The verdict on him was, not surprisingly, mixed. Described as 'a slave to worldly trivialities', and the father of an illegitimate son, he nevertheless did much to benefit the church at Bayeux. He was a man of great ambition and considerable ability – a Norman through and through. He probably did not rate the Tapestry particularly highly among the many treasures that he presented to Bayeux cathedral, but that astonishingly vivid depiction of the Norman world is his lasting legacy.

Rodrigo Díaz
(El Cid)

HERO OF THE *RECONQUISTA*

c. 1043–99

Studying the past can be like peeling an onion. Each skin of prejudice and assumption laid by the past has to be removed in turn so as to reach the inner core of historical truth. Few individuals are concealed behind so many layers as Rodrigo Díaz, known as El Cid. His legend began to be constructed within fifty years of his death, and by the end of the twelfth century, his career was celebrated in a literary masterpiece, the great *Cantar di Mio Cid* (*The Poem of the Cid*). This work, which would become central to concepts of Spanish nationhood, presented a hero far removed from reality. Such later works are notable for the romantic gloss they put on events, but there is a very valuable early biography of him, probably written by an eyewitness of some of his campaigns.

In 711, a Muslim commander, Tariq, crossed the straits of Gibraltar. Within a decade most of the Spanish peninsula was in Muslim hands. Córdoba became the centre of a caliphate. By the eleventh century, however, Muslim Spain was hopelessly split, with the country divided between many regional powers, known as the *taifa* kingdoms. In the north, there were the Christian principalities of León, Castile, Aragon and Navarre and the county of Barcelona. The situation offered splendid opportunities for ambitious adventurers, the most remarkable of whom was Rodrigo Díaz.

Rodrigo was born to an aristocratic family in the 1040s, near Burgos in Castile. He took part in his first campaign in 1063, fighting with Sancho of Castile against the king of Aragon.

Charlton Heston in his most famous role, that of Rodrigo Díaz, El Cid.

As a knight, he fought on horseback. Spanish horses were particularly prized; the legend was that his favourite mount was called Babieca. Armed with sword and lance, protected by coat of mail and shield, Rodrigo was almost unbeatable. In a typical episode:

> Rodrigo the invincible warrior, placing all his trust in the Lord and his mercy, bravely and staunchly made a sortie with his well-armed followers on the enemy, shouting and terrifying them with threats. He rushed upon them, and began a huge battle with them.

When Sancho became king in 1065, Rodrigo, termed *campeador*, had command of his household knights. On Sancho's death, Rodrigo entered the service of the new king, Alfonso VI. Though he no longer held the command he had under Sancho, Rodrigo was clearly doing well, for the king arranged his marriage to an aristocratic lady, Jimena. In 1081, however, disaster struck, and Rodrigo was exiled, apparently the victim of jealousy. Once in exile, he was welcomed by the Muslim ruler of Zaragoza, al-Muqtadir, who 'exalted and raised him above his son, his realm, and all his lands, so that it seemed that he was the ruler of the kingdom'. Rodrigo served al-Muqtadir and his sons for the next five years. In one notable encounter, he captured the count of Barcelona. In another, he defeated a powerful Aragonese force.

Heroic exploits may have been part of Rodrigo's style of warfare, but so also was a brutality typical of the age. Count García Ordóñez was a rival at the Castilian court, and so 'because of the count's enmity and his infamy, Rodrigo burned his land, destroying and devastating it almost completely'. On another occasion, when he was attacking Alfonso VI's lands:

> He took a huge amount of booty, truly enough to weep over, and he impiously
> and irredeemably laid waste all the lands with fire and flame, savagely and mercilessly.
> He destroyed and devastated the land, emptying it of all treasure and wealth, which
> he kept for himself.

As a mercenary, Rodrigo cared more for profit than for principle. There is nothing in his biography to suggest that he was a man of anything more than conventional piety, and no indication that religious zeal played a part in his many campaigns. He was as happy to serve a Muslim as a Christian lord. He was not alone in this; his enemy García Ordóñez also took service with Muslim paymasters.

In 1086, the Almoravids, Berbers based in Morocco, invaded Spain and defeated Alfonso VI of Castile at Sagrajas. Rodrigo's military skills were much needed, and he was recalled. His relations with the king were difficult; when he was accused of treason, he again left Alfonso's service. Acting independently, he defeated the count of Barcelona. In 1093, he laid siege to Valencia, then under Muslim rule, and in the summer of the following year the city surrendered. He called himself 'prince', and ruled the city as his own, rather than as a vassal of Alfonso, until his death in 1099. A lasting principality of Valencia, however, was not to be. Rodrigo had no son to succeed him, and though his widow, Jimena, conducted a gallant defence of Valencia against the Almoravids, it was in vain. In April 1102, she left the city for Castile with her husband's corpse bumping along in the baggage train.

The Rodrigo of myth bore little relationship to the soldier of fortune of the late eleventh century. The *Cantar di Mio Cid* began the process of converting him into a Castilian hero of Christendom, loyal and chivalric, patriotic and honourable. His service in Muslim pay was omitted from the story; this was a man virtuous and brave, a hero whose deeds should be emulated. Rodrigo thus provided inspiration for the *Reconquista* (the war to drive the Moors out of Spain) in more modern periods, with a myth far removed from the reality of a man happy to make war on anyone, provided that there was a profit to be earned from it.

The courtyard of the eleventh-century Aljaferia place in Zaragoza. This was the residence of al-Muqtadir, whom El Cid served for five years in the 1080s.

Matilda of Tuscany

COUNTESS AND MILITARY LEADER

1046–1115

Early in 1077, the German king Henry IV appeared, barefoot and clad in a rough woollen robe, in the snow before the gates of the castle of Canossa, in northern Italy. He did this on three successive days, before he was finally admitted to appear before Pope Gregory VII and be released from excommunication. The central issue beween Gregory and Henry, in what became known as the Investiture Contest, was lay control of the Church, symbolized by the manner in which secular rulers invested bishops with spiritual authority. In the *Dictatus Papae* of 1075, Gregory set out an uncompromising programme, claiming among other things the rights to depose emperors and to absolve men of the fealty they owed to wicked rulers. Henry's appointment of an archbishop of Milan was a flashpoint which led to king and pope each declaring the other deposed, and to Henry's excommunication. At one level, the dispute was a question of principle, argued with bitter polemics; at another, it was a matter of practical power politics. To overcome his enemies, Gregory needed allies and money, as well as arguments.

Matilda of Tuscany, who owned the castle at Canossa, played a vital part in the great conflict between the papacy and Empire. She was born in 1046, daughter of Boniface, marquis of Tuscany. After he was murdered in 1052, and the death of her brother in 1055, she was left the heiress to vast swathes of land in northern Italy. Her mother Beatrice's second husband, Godfrey, duke of Lorraine, was a bitter opponent to the emperor Henry III. Matilda herself became the wife of Godfrey's son by a previous marriage, Godfrey the Hunchback. By 1071, Matilda had left Godfrey; but the marriage finally ended only in 1076, when an assassin thrust a spear up Godfrey's backside. After Beatrice died in the same year, Matilda was left in sole control both of the lands she had inherited and of those she had gained by marriage.

By the time of her inheritance in 1076, Matilda was already established as a close supporter of Gregory, who had become pope three years earlier. She was an essential ally for Gregory, for her lands formed a buffer between Rome and the Empire. She had attended papal councils and promised her possessions to the Church; he described her as his 'most beloved and loving daughter'. There were totally unwarranted suspicions about her relationship with the pope; the imperial bishops wrote to Gregory in 1076 of 'the stench of the gravest of scandals, rising from your intimacy and cohabitation with another's wife'.

The emperor Henry IV shown kneeling before Matilda of Tuscany and Abbot Hugh of Cluny. The abbot attempted to mediate in the dispute between Empire and papacy.

The events at Canossa, where Matilda helped to achieve reconciliation of a sort between pope and emperor by persuading Gregory VII to offer absolution to Henry IV, were a prelude to further negotiations, and then to war. The war began badly, when Henry's Lombard allies defeated Matilda's forces near Mantua in 1080. All Matilda could do was to maintain her defences, with a ring of fortresses around Canossa. At Sorbara, however, in 1084, her troops defeated Henry's Italian allies by means of a surprise cavalry charge. Gregory died in 1085,

having been driven out of Rome, but Matilda's fight continued. In 1088, at the instigation of Pope Urban II (see pp. 46–48), she married for a second time. Her new husband was Welf V, the son of the duke of Bavaria. He was a stout youth, some twenty-five years younger than his bride. Not surprisingly, the couple separated in the mid-1090s.

There was no question of Matilda handing over the command of her forces to her young husband. She was experienced, and had the respect of her men. In 1092, she had a crucial success over Henry IV, driving him from his siege of her castle at Canossa in an action fought in dense fog. Other victories followed. The collapse of Henry's ambitions in Italy, however, did not mark the end of Matilda's military activities; she turned her attention to cities that had supported the imperial cause, with successful campaigns against Ferrara, Parma, Prato and, at the end of her life, Mantua. She died in 1115, aged sixty-nine.

Matilda was no mere figurehead. She directed her military operations herself, from the recruitment of troops to the strategies that they followed. Later legend had it that as a girl she was trained to fight with lance and sword, but there is no evidence to support this. She was no Joan of Arc (see pp. 248–50), going into battle in person, leading her men from the front. Matilda was above all a strategist, fully conscious of the political implications of her decisions. She was fortunate in that Canossa and the other castles she held in the Appenines provided her with a reasonably secure base. Battle was risky, as Matilda was well aware; sieges and surprise attacks were far more the order of the day.

Matilda was much more than just a successful general. She knew several languages, and had a substantial library. She was personally pious, and convinced by the cause of Church reform. Learned men were attracted to her court and she offered patronage and support to a number of writers. She gave lavishly to the cathedral at Modena, but it is probably going too far to see her as the patron of the cathedral's architect, Lanfranc, or of its sculptor, Wiligelmo. She demonstrated an interest in the Classical past when she had Roman sarcophagi brought to Canossa for use in the family mausoleum that she created.

A remarkable woman, Matilda was strikingly determined and independent. In part this was the result of her two disastrous marriages, which left her little option other than to make her own way. Her view of her husbands is reflected in a lengthy biographical poem clearly written at her instruction, which simply airbrushes them out of the record. Matilda's position was very unusual. She was of high lineage, the representative of the house of Canossa in the absence of a male, and she expected allegiance accordingly. She had the ability to provide the military leadership that was needed, and which the reformed papacy urgently required. The papacy's spiritual weapons and fierce polemics needed to be backed up with her treasure, cold steel and determination.

Matilda of Tuscany, Hugh of Cluny and the emperor Henry IV, shown in the twelfth-century Vita Matildis, *a lengthy poem by Donizo.*

Pope Urban II

INITIATOR OF THE FIRST CRUSADE

c. 1035–98

In 1095, at Clermont in the Auvergne region of central France, Pope Urban II preached a sermon announcing a crusade to the Holy Land. The occasion marked the start of an astonishing movement, which saw western Europeans, from nobles to peasants, undertake a series of armed expeditions to the Holy Land in the name of their religion. The Crusades saw the foundation of a new kingdom of Jerusalem, and other states in the east, which lasted until the thirteenth century. Nor were crusades limited to the eastern Mediterranean; some were even launched against fellow Christians.

The background to Urban's decision to preach the crusade at Clermont was complex. The advance of the Seljuq Turks into Asia Minor, Syria and Palestine was one element, for this meant that pilgrimage to Jerusalem was no longer possible. The Byzantine Empire faced huge problems following the defeat of its forces by the Turks at Manzikert in 1071, and in 1095 the Byzantine emperor Alexios Komnenos sent emissaries to a papal council at Piacenza, asking for much-needed armed assistance. Importantly, Pope Gregory VII had already developed the concept of holy war. In 1080, he had offered absolution of sin and eternal salvation to those prepared to attack Byzantium and restore its deposed emperor.

There are a number of accounts of Urban's sermon at Clermont. While they differ in detail, the pope's overall message emerges clearly. He proposed a penitential armed expedition to recover Jerusalem and to liberate the Christians in the east. Those who joined could expect remission of all penance for their sins, receiving in effect a first-class ticket to heaven. According to one version, Urban suggested that the west was over-populated; the crusaders should therefore go to conquer new homes in the east. He also argued that it was better to fight to recover the Holy Land than engage in conflicts at home. The sermon was met with orchestrated chants of 'Deus le volt' ('God wills it'). In a brilliant move, the crusaders were given a badge of a cross to wear. This would both advertise their intention to others and make it difficult for them to renege on their vows. Urban did not intend to take part in person; command of the crusade went to a legate, Adhémar of Le Puy. The pope was on the road for fourteen months in southern France, ensuring that his novel message advocating the new concept of holy war was widely heard. Ceremonial processions backed up his message. The response was extraordinary. Many great men took the cross, while popular preachers, such as Peter the Hermit, encouraged the masses. The motivations of individuals to go on the crusade varied, of course, but the liberation of Jerusalem and the remission of penance were the most significant reasons.

Described by one chronicler as 'French by race, of high birth and great courtesy', Urban was a large man, pious, wise, modest and noted for his eloquence. He had been born in about 1035, as Odo of Châtillon, in a noble family in Champagne. He became archdeacon of Reims, before entering the great monastery at Cluny, where he rapidly became prior, second only to the abbot. Abbot Hugh recommended Odo to Pope Gregory VII, and in 1080 he was appointed cardinal bishop of Ostia. In 1084, Gregory nominated him as papal legate in Germany. This was no easy task given the opposition of the German ruler, Henry IV, to the papal reform movement. Odo backed the candidacy of Victor III to succeed Gregory VII in 1085; on Victor's death, he was elected pope himself in 1088, taking Urban II as his name. He encountered great difficulties in the early years of his pontificate, as he was in exile from Rome and faced considerable problems in gaining full recognition at a time when he was opposed by an anti-pope.

A fifteenth-century interpretation of Urban II proclaiming the First Crusade. In fact, Urban's sermon was delivered in the open air.

In this fourteenth-century illustration, Urban is shown on the left riding to Clermont, and on the right preaching the crusade there.

Urban was strongly committed to the reform agenda, which was renewed at a number of Church councils with decrees against married clergy, simony (the sale of Church positions) and lay investiture. At the Council of Clermont, which was attended by almost a hundred archbishops and bishops and ninety abbots, as well as preaching the crusade, the pope 'corrected many things which were done north of the Alps, and established many useful measures to amend practices'. These included prohibitions on the sale of Church positions, on the eating of meat by clergy during Lent, and on fixed prices for burying the dead. Excommunication was set as the penalty for assaulting or robbing members of the clergy.

Urban's character does not stand out from the chronicles and records, nor is there any contemporary life of him to provide personal details. For all his eloquence, he was not flamboyant. He had a solid grounding in canon law and theology, but did not write any scholarly treatises. Above all, unlike some of the reformers, he was a rational political realist. The weapons he chose to use were the ecclesiastical ones of excommunication and interdict, not war, with the exception, of course, of the crusade. Though he had displayed courage and determination, there was nothing in Urban's career before 1095 to suggest that he would take a radical new step. In preaching at Clermont as he did, to that great gathering in the open air, Urban demonstrated decisive leadership and set western Europe on a new course. The crusades he started would see great displays of valour, and some astonishing successes, but they would also have a disastrous impact on relations between Christendom and Islam.

Guibert de Nogent

AUTOBIOGRAPHER

c. 1060—1124

utobiographies were rare in the Middle Ages. Of the few that exist, Guibert de Nogent's *De Vita Sua*, written in about 1115, is exceptional in giving a full account of the author's childhood. In fact, the story begins before he was born. Guibert's parents belonged to a knightly family near Beauvais, in northern France. They had great problems in conceiving; their marriage was unconsummated for some seven years, until an old woman resolved the problem. Nor was his birth in about 1060 easy: his mother's labour lasted almost a day, and he was born prematurely. His father died when he was a baby, and though he adored his mother, she was not as caring as might have been expected. She hired a tutor who was 'utterly unskilled in prose and verse composition' and who believed in beating Guibert as often as possible. On one occasion, Guibert's mother discovered the bruises on his arms and back, and suggested that he should give up learning, and become a knight. The offer was unwelcome; Guibert was determined on a career in the Church, and claimed to love his tutor. When he was twelve, his mother withdrew from the world, setting up house close to a monastery, with an elderly nun as companion. At the same time, his tutor left to become a monk. Guibert was 'left deserted by mother, guide and master'.

Guibert's account of his appalling childhood has proved a great temptation to historians, anxious to apply psychological theories to it. One argues that 'it raises the question of whether his relationship to his mother and his fears together fit the Freudian model of a castration complex'. The tutor's role also raises questions, with its unattractive combination of violence and affection. There is also the issue of the effect on the twelve-year-old Guibert of being deserted by both his mother and his tutor. The safest conclusion to draw is simply that Guibert survived these various traumas in remarkably good shape.

Unsurprisingly, Guibert went wild for a brief time in his teens; but he soon entered on the monastic life that had always been his ambition. Though 'the carnal life began to stir my itching heart with fleshly longings', the worst he did was to write some obscene poems. He studied hard, particularly theology, and wrote a treatise on virginity. He was fortunate to be inspired by a notable visitor to his abbey, the great Italian scholar Anselm of Bec, who was to become archbishop of Canterbury. In 1104, Guibert became abbot of the little house of Nogent-sous-Coucy. There, he wrote prolifically. He produced a history of the First Crusade that was largely a reworking of the *Gesta Francorum* (*The Deeds of the Franks*), which

In this picture from one of his works depicting Christ in majesty, Guibert de Nogent is at the bottom left, wearing a blue robe, presenting a book.

was probably written by a soldier who, unlike Guibert, had taken part in the expedition. Among Guibert's works on religious questions was a treatise on relics, in which he displayed unusual scepticism. How could a church in Constantinople and one in Angers both claim to possess John the Baptist's head? What was saintly about St Pyro, when all that Guibert could discover about him was that he fell down a well when drunk? How could a church possess one of Christ's teeth, when he had been resurrected? There was no question, though, of Guibert attacking the worship of what he regarded as genuine relics. They were proper objects for contemplation.

Guibert's scepticism was, however, limited. His was a strange world, full of unlikely tales of devils. The Devil in person had paralysed his mother one night, after she had learned that her husband had been captured in war. Fortunately, a good spirit came and routed the Devil in a violent struggle which woke the servants. In the case of a sick man, 'swarms of devils rushed upon him from all quarters, tearing him and dragging him prostrate over the floor and striving with mad violence to pluck from him his holy habit'. In another story, the Devil strangled a monk who had broken the rules of his house. Unfortunately, the monk had been in the latrine when the abbot came to see him earlier, so he had been unable to confess his sins before he died. Guibert's Devil was also capable of appearing in disguise. He came to one man in the guise of St James and persuaded him first to castrate himself and then to cut his own throat.

When it came to writing about the local lords of his day, Guibert dipped his pen in vitriol. Thomas of Marle, lord of Coucy, was a particular target: 'No one can tell how many expired in his dungeons and chains by starvation, disease and torture.' Guibert vividly described how Thomas would hang his opponents up by the testicles. He also charged him with burning prisoners alive in a church. Guibert's hostility towards Thomas was not surprising, for Thomas had supported the people of Laon after they formed a commune and murdered their bishop.

Among the other villains who people his pages was John, count of Soissons, whom Guibert hated as 'a Judaizer and a heretic'. Although the count attended church at Christmas and Easter, displaying due humility, when a cleric explained the Easter story to him, he burst out laughing: 'What a fable, what windy talk!' He said that he only attended the church so that he could ogle the beautiful women. According to Guibert, the count, who made 'no exception of nun and sister in his abuse of women', lusted after a wrinkled old woman, who lived in a Jew's house. To his evident delight, the count came to a bad end, for he fell mortally ill after sleeping with the old woman, became violent and delirious, and died.

Guibert's depiction of a rapacious, violent nobility has proved exceptionally powerful, and needs balancing. One example of a virtuous lord was Simon de Crépy, count of the Vexin, Valois and Amiens. He defended his lands against the ravages of royal troops, and was noted for his piety, his almsgiving and the protection that he gave to the poor. He went on pilgrimage to the Holy Land, and ended his life not as a count, but as a hermit. The history of early twelfth-century France is thus more complicated than the traditional story of the struggles of the crown to extend its power and provide peace and protection from the depredations of oppressive lords. Guibert's autobiography nevertheless draws a vivid portrait of life in this period. Much more remarkable, though, is the insight it provides into the mind of a monk – one less distorted by a disastrous childhood than might be expected, and both sceptical and credulous in an intriguing and complex mix.

The execution of a supporter of Thomas of Marle, the most wicked of the lords described by Guibert de Nogent.

Anna Komnene

DISCONTENTED BYZANTINE PRINCESS AND AUTHOR

1083–1153

Anna Komnene could not deny that she was fortunate to have an emperor, Alexios Komnenos, and an empress, Irene, as parents when she was born in 1083; but she complained miserably that luck had not favoured her after that. She was exceptionally well educated in the Classics and in science, and possessed significant medical expertise. Her husband was the handsome, clever and well-connected Nikephoros Bryennios, with whom she had four children. She had hopes that he would gain the imperial throne in place of the rightful heir, her bitterly resented younger brother, John. When, in 1118, her plans were dashed, she was made to retire to a monastery. Here, in 1137, following her husband's death, Anna decided to take on the task of writing the life of Alexios Komnenos, which the empress had originally commissioned from Nikephoros, whose text had not even reached the emperor's accession.

The Byzantine Empire faced exceptionally difficult challenges during Alexios's reign. Complex court politics saw plots and rebellions frequently threaten his authority. External enemies menaced the empire on all sides. In the west, the Byzantines were finally ousted from southern Italy by the Normans in 1071. A decade later, the Norman leader Robert Guiscard defeated Alexios at Durazzo in modern Albania. In the east, the Seljuq Turks took most of Asia Minor following their great victory at the battle of Manzikert in 1071. Alexios hoped for western assistance against the Turks. What he got was the First Crusade. The initial arrival of a disorganized host largely formed of untrained but enthusiastic peasants under the popular preacher Peter the Hermit was particularly unwelcome. When the army of the aristocratic crusaders appeared outside Constantinople in 1097, the presence of a substantial Norman element suggested that they would be as much a threat to the Byzantine Empire as the Turks.

Anna, as a princess close to the throne, was in a superb position to observe such events, and she claimed to provide an accurate account of them in her book, known as the *Alexiad*. 'I am naturally averse to story-telling and the fabrication of history', she wrote. She also said she possessed 'a natural abhorrence of slander'. A particularly interesting aspect of her work was the view she took of the Normans and the crusaders. Anna considered the westerners

A twelfth-century illustration of the Church of the Holy Apostles at Constantinople.

thoroughly reckless, but also bold and courageous. They were, she considered, unreliable, uncontrollable, greedy and perfidious. She also found them verbose and sometimes ill-mannered. Their aim of reaching Jerusalem was, she thought, a smokescreen for a plan to dethrone Alexios and to capture Constantinople. Although she admired the bravery shown when western knights charged, their 'absolute refusal to cultivate a disciplined art of war' meant that once their initial onslaught was over and they had been dismounted they were easy prey.

One Norman in particular received Anna's attention. The chief villain in her book was Robert Guiscard's son, Bohemond, 'the supreme mischief maker'. Despite her frequent condemnations of Bohemond, Anna had a certain admiration for the Norman. She described him as exceptionally tall and perfectly proportioned, though with a slight stoop. His eyes were pale blue, his nostrils broad, his hair light brown and he was clean shaven. She felt that there was both charm and a savage quality about him; clearly, he was a hunk. Bohemond, of course, did what Anna feared, for rather than continuing with the crusade to Jerusalem, he seized Antioch, which had been a Byzantine possession.

Anna's book is remarkable for its insights into the warfare of the period. It demonstrates a considerable, and surprising, interest in technical matters. The battering ram used in Bohemond's siege of Durazzo in 1108 is described in great detail, as is the mine, which the besiegers constructed with a roof propped up with wooden posts, only for it to be nullified by the defenders' counter-mine. The Normans' wooden siege-tower, mounted on rollers and possessing many storeys and drawbridges, was particularly remarkable. All this has led to the suggestion that the descriptions of warfare were the work, not of Anna, but of her husband. This is unlikely. By her own account, Anna was in a good position to write about war, for she

In her life of Alexios Komnenos, his daughter Anna showed a keen interest in military matters. Here, Byzantine troops are shown in action in an illustration from the chronicle of John Skylitzes.

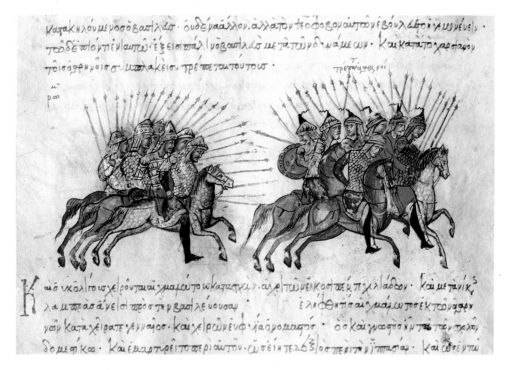

Byzantine heavily armed cavalry were highly effective, though Anna Komnene was particularly impressed by Norman knights. Another scene from John Skylitzes's chronicle.

had accompanied her father on some expeditions, and used a range of both written and oral testimony from veterans.

Anna, as has often been pointed out, was the first truly notable female historian. While her book is not in any sense a feminist tract, she gives full attention to the prominent role in government and administration played by her grandmother, Anna Dalassene. In contrast, Anna's mother, Irene, described as exceptionally beautiful, was a modest woman who rarely spoke. Anna surely felt disappointed that she never had such political influence as her grandmother, nor, with her slightly hooked nose and round face, such beauty as her mother. She displayed her maternal instincts when she expressed pity for Turks whose babies were boiled alive by Byzantine soldiers, and disapproval of those crusaders who, she claimed, roasted infants.

Anna's work has its problems. Personal prejudice did much to provide the book with its heroes, and its villains. There is little understanding of the world beyond the Byzantine Empire; for Anna, it was inhabited by barbarians whom she found hard to distinguish. The chronology of events is often far from clear. Yet, even though the character sketches may be somewhat overblown, they are far superior to the usual stereotypes. The life of Alexios is one of the most remarkable works of history written in the Middle Ages, for it has a rare vivid quality and a striking depth of detail.

2.

An Age of Confidence

1100–1200

The twelfth century was a period of growing wealth and achievement. There were powerful empires under the German ruler Frederick Barbarossa and the English king Henry II. Intellectual ferment saw old certainties questioned. Great churches were built in a style which challenged past conventions. Monasticism thrived. Yet this has also been seen as an age of crisis, when violent and aggressive nobles were barely tamed by advances in government and the application of justice.

In Germany, internal conflict was brought to an end with the accession of Frederick Barbarossa as king in 1152, though the rivalry between the two great families of Welf and Hohenstaufen continued to threaten stability. In England, the succession of King Stephen in 1135 was followed by bitter civil war, eventually ended when Henry II came to the throne in 1154. Through his marriage to the heiress Eleanor of Aquitaine, former queen of the French king Louis VII, Henry gained Gascony and other lands in southwestern France; as a result, he ruled a huge swathe of territory, from Normandy, through Anjou, and as far south as the Pyrenees. For much of the century, the French monarchy controlled a very limited area centred round Paris, but with the accession of Philip Augustus in 1180 a major expansion of royal authority began. In 1204, he conquered Normandy from the English. In southern Italy and Sicily, a new Norman monarchy saw different cultures combined in a sophisticated mix, notably under King Roger II.

There were many conflicts between Church and state. The Concordat of Worms of 1122 did not end disputes between papacy and Empire. In 1155 the German ruler Frederick Barbarossa, on his first expedition to Italy, was crowned as emperor by the pope. However, he soon faced the hostility of the papacy, and of the increasingly powerful north Italian towns. In England, Henry II quarrelled with his archbishop of Canterbury, Thomas Becket, over a number of issues, particularly his right to try clerics who committed criminal offences. The dispute reached a dramatic climax with Becket's murder in 1170, but after that cooperation between Church and state replaced conflict. By the end of the period, the papacy under

Henry II's knights, led by Reginald fitzUrse (who has a bear on his shield), shown murdering Thomas Becket in his cathedral at Canterbury in 1170, from an English psalter of about 1220.

Muslim forces attack the crusaders during the siege of Acre in the Third Crusade, as depicted in a fourteenth-century illustration.

Innocent III was in a position to exercise its influence, both spiritual and political, to an unprecedented degree.

In the Holy Land, as a result of the success of the First Crusade in 1099, a new kingdom of Jerusalem was created, as well as a principality of Antioch and counties of Edessa and Tripoli. There was some accommodation between Arabs and western Europeans; Usāma ibn Munqidh's memoirs show how some crusaders were ready to adopt eastern habits. This, however, was not sufficient to make Christian rule acceptable. These Latin states could not have survived without further crusades. Edessa was lost in 1144, leading to the Second Crusade; but the real crisis came in 1187 with Saladin's triumph in the battle of Hattin, a disaster which resulted in the preaching of the Third Crusade. The elderly emperor Frederick Barbarossa took the cross, but died in Asia Minor on his march to the Holy Land. The crusade was then headed by the kings of England and France; despite Saladin's efforts, it ensured the continued survival of the Latin states in an attenuated form for another hundred years.

Individuals responded to religious imperatives in very different ways. After a successful career as a merchant, Godric of Finchale chose the solitary life of a hermit. In Germany, Hildegard of Bingen found many ways to express her individuality and exceptional creativity within a monastic framework; she was one of the most remarkable women of the age. Héloïse, lover and victim of Peter Abelard, and reluctant nun, was another. She had great intellectual gifts, but it was her business skills that made her convent successful. She proved to be an excellent manager.

Learning and scholarship advanced in what has been termed 'the Twelfth-Century Renaissance'. How far the term is justified is arguable; if 'renaissance' is taken to imply a rebirth of Classical culture, it is applicable only to a limited extent. The new idioms in architecture owed nothing to the Classical past. Under the guidance of Suger, abbot and statesman, the church of Saint-Denis, just outside Paris, was rebuilt in the new Gothic style, with slender pillars and pointed arches. While monasteries were still important, the major intellectual advances were made in cathedral schools, such as Chartres and Orléans, and in what would become the university of Paris. Peter Abelard's application of a logical dialectic argument to theological issues was characteristic of the age. In Bologna, Gratian was applying similar techniques to the study and analysis of Roman law. Some lay rulers were patrons of learning and culture. At the court of Roger II, king of Sicily and southern Italy, Arab scholars such as the geographer al-Idrisi might rub shoulders with western Europeans and Greeks. Literature was not confined to Classical themes. The century saw the development of stories around the mythical King Arthur, derived from the highly imaginative and astonishingly successful history of Britain written by Geoffrey of Monmouth. In France, in the later twelfth century, Chrétien de Troyes wrote a series of popular Arthurian romances, which took the tales to a new level. He was active at the court of Marie, countess of Champagne, Eleanor of Aquitaine's daughter. In many ways, therefore, the cultural advances of this period are better regarded as a new start, rather than a rebirth or renaissance.

Abbot Suger

SKILLED POLITICAL OPERATOR

1081–1151

The French king Louis VII once claimed that in comparison with the wealth and military power of other European rulers he possessed nothing save bread, wine and joy. The remark is delightful, but disingenuous, for Louis had inherited a crown whose power and prestige had recently been transformed. One of the authors of that transformation was Suger, abbot of Saint-Denis.

Born in 1081, Suger joined the abbey of Saint-Denis when he was only ten. Appointed provost of the Norman possessions of Saint-Denis at Berneval in 1108, he was soon moved to Toury in the Beauce region of northern France. There he faced the hostility of a rampaging noble, Hugh of le Puiset, whose notoriety owes much to Suger's writings. Such turbulent barons were a real threat to the growing power of the crown; for them, ownership of a strong castle provided independence and placed them above the law. So the scholarly and physically unimpressive Suger found himself thrown into a world of castle-building and sieges. He nevertheless quickly developed keen military skills. In one siege, he had carts filled with dry wood and inflammable grease so as to set fire to a gatehouse. The *Life of King Louis* that he wrote is filled with vivid and enthusiastic descriptions of warfare.

Though he failed in the difficult task of tying Hugh of le Puiset down to the agreements he had negotiated with him on behalf of King Louis VI, Suger was a man of undoubted diplomatic acumen. In 1118, Louis employed him to meet Pope Gelasius II, when the pontiff came to southern France, and in 1121 he sent him to the south of Italy to hold discussions with the new pope, Calixtus II. On his return, Suger discovered that he had been elected abbot of Saint-Denis. The king's irritation that this had happened without his being consulted was soon assuaged.

Suger was no ordinary abbot; he saw himself as primate of France. A forged charter, purporting to have been issued by Charlemagne (see pp. 16–19), set out his ideal that the kings of France, and all the churchmen in the kingdom, should be subordinate to the abbot of Saint-Denis. Suger, high in the king's council, navigated political crises skilfully; even the difficulties created by Louis VI's hostility to the new reformist ideas in the Church did not threaten his position. He survived when his patron, the powerful chancellor and steward, Stephen de Garlande, rebelled and was stripped of office in the late 1120s. In fact, Suger may well have helped to engineer Garlande's fall. Even the death of Louis VI in 1137, and the change of personnel at court under his successor, Louis VII, did not see Suger lose power and influence. When Louis VII departed on crusade in 1147, Suger became one of the co-regents of the kingdom. A plot by Ralph of Vermandois, another co-regent, was dealt with by Suger, possibly with the aid of a cunningly forged letter. The abbot was a supreme political operator, who did much to improve the position of the French monarchy.

As abbot of Saint-Denis, Suger was concerned to reform the way that the abbey was run. He revised the liturgy, among other things adding prayers for his own soul. He was as much concerned with running the abbey as an efficient business as with its spiritual role. Lost estates were regained, and in many cases defended by newly built castles. New financial procedures were introduced. Discipline was strict, but there was none of the emphasis that the new Cistercian order placed on manual work, nor were the monks encouraged to adopt an ascetic way of life.

Suger was responsible for a major building programme at Saint-Denis. The main monastic buildings, such as the refectory and the dormitory, were rebuilt. The abbey church saw major changes; a new west front with two towers was built, and crenelated as if it were a castle. It had three portals, and featured a splendid array of sculptures as well as an innovative circular rose window. This was followed at the east end by a new choir, with magnificent stained-glass windows. Chapels radiated off an ambulatory, which had slender pillars, pointed arches and a ribbed vault. Suger wanted to join his works up with a new nave, but this project failed to get off the ground. He was a demanding and interfering patron. He described how he went in person to a wood to assist his workmen in selecting roof timbers, although it is likely that it was the expert master masons rather than their somewhat conservative employer who were responsible for the ingenious solutions to the many problems they faced.

Abbot Suger, shown in a stained-glass window in his church of Saint-Denis.

Suger's writings suggest that he took more interest in, and pleasure from, the furnishings of the church than from its innovative architecture. He employed workmen from Lorraine for two years on a great golden cross, standing on a pedestal featuring the four evangelists, and decorated with fine gemstones that had originally been in the English royal treasury. As for the altar, 'We had it all encased, putting up golden panels on either side and adding a fourth, even more precious one; so that the whole altar would appear golden all the way round.' Stained-glass windows of the highest craftsmanship told the story of Moses. Suger had no truck with arguments suggesting that all that was needed for the sacrament was a pure and holy intention; while that was important, so too for him were the gold, silver and precious stones that were surely appropriate for the vessels holding Christ's body and blood.

In this stained-glass window from Saint-Denis, Suger is shown crouching before a scene of the Annunciation.

Some have interpreted the building programme at Saint-Denis as the physical expression of complex theological ideas derived from the work of the fifth-century writer known as the Pseudo-Dionysius. This is implausible: Suger's writings do not include any theological works, nor does anything he wrote about Saint-Denis support this theory. No doubt he was aware of contemporary theological debates about the nature and significance of light, but surely what he appreciated above all was the colour that suffused the church from its magnificent windows: Saint-Denis was one of the leading buildings in an astonishing architectural transformation, from the Romanesque with its massive pillars and rounded arches, to the new Gothic architecture, with its slender columns rising to pointed vaults.

Suger was remarkably successful, combining his role as a statesman with energetic rule as the abbot of Saint-Denis. He was adept at all he turned his hand to, from politics and pastoral care to building up his own reputation. He was not above making use of (and perhaps even making) forgeries to support the claims of his abbey, and it is impossible to believe that his success in the politics of the Capetian court did not involve some questionable dealing. Yet even if he was sometimes guilty of exaggerating his own achievements, his political importance is undoubted, while the work he supervised at Saint-Denis marked a milestone in European architecture.

The abbey church of Saint-Denis. The east end, with its ambulatory and pointed Gothic arches, is a masterpiece of design.

Geoffrey of Monmouth

POPULAR PSEUDO-HISTORIAN

c. 1100—c. 1155

Bad history is more popular than good history. It is more exciting, more romantic, and it is untrammelled by any requirements to be accurate. Geoffrey of Monmouth knew just how to write bad history. His fame rests upon his *History of the Kings of Britain*, which he wrote in the 1130s. A couple of hundred manuscripts of the *History* still survive: this was clearly a best-seller.

Little is known of Geoffrey's career. His name suggests that he came from Monmouth in Wales; he may have had Breton links, for the lord of Monmouth was of Breton descent. By 1129, he was living in Oxford, where he had the title of master, which suggests that he taught in the schools that would later be recognized as a university. He realized the importance of having powerful protectors. During the difficult days of the civil war in King Stephen's reign, he dedicated one version of his *History* to Robert, earl of Gloucester, the half-brother of Henry I's daughter; Matilda, and another to Waleran of Meulan, a powerful magnate on the opposite side. He also greatly praised Alexander, bishop of Lincoln, and sent him a copy of what he claimed to be Merlin's prophecies. This careful cultivation of the important led to his appointment as bishop of St Asaph in 1152. He died some three years later, probably without ever visiting his see.

Geoffrey claimed that his *History of the Kings of Britain* was based on an old book in Welsh which the archdeacon of Oxford had obtained in Brittany and lent to him. This was surely mendacious, an attempt to give apparent authenticity to his inventive history. He did have some sources which he used, or rather misused, such as Gildas, who had written in the sixth century, and the late Roman, Orosius, and he probably also relied on Welsh tradition. Above all, he employed a splendidly rich imagination to blend fact and fantasy in a beguiling and skilful manner.

The *History* begins with the story of Brutus, who led the survivors of the siege of Troy to settle in Britain, which up until that time had been uninhabited, apart from by a few giants. The story runs on through King Lear and a number of other British kings to the Romans, and then to the arrival of Hengist and Horsa and the Saxons, and King Arthur.

An illustration from a fifteenth-century copy of Geoffrey of Monmouth's work, showing the arrival of Brutus in England, with the slaying of the giants who lived there, and the construction of a city.

The Arthurian story occupies many pages. When Geoffrey wrote, there were already stories of Arthur current on the continent, and even a complex carving at Modena in Italy showing the king and his knights. It was, however, Geoffrey who wove into a glittering fabric the story of the king, the magician Merlin, the adulterous queen Guinevere, Kay the seneschal, Bedevere the cup-bearer and Gawain.

It is conceivable that there was a historical figure, a late Roman cavalry commander perhaps, on whom the Arthurian myth was ultimately based. There was no such possible origin for King Lear, though. Here, Geoffrey surely had no sources save his imagination. In Godfrey's story, in contrast to the Shakespearean version, Cordelia survives her father's death, only to commit suicide five years later, the victim of hostility to the idea that a queen might rule in her own right.

Geoffrey's version of history is fascinating, for it provides a remarkable insight into the mentality of his day. His account is what people wanted their history to be. It is a thoroughly secular vision of the past, a history of kings, not bishops. Stories such as that of the martyrdom of St Alban are few, and are dealt with briskly. The version Geoffrey provided of the tale of St Ursula and the 11,000 Cornish virgins makes nothing of their sanctity, and little of their martyrdom. There is much detail about military matters; the descriptions of how troops were drawn up for battle are far more detailed and specific than any to be found in the chronicles of his day. Interestingly, however, there is virtually nothing about castles, which dominated warfare in Geoffrey's time. It is unlikely this shows that Geoffrey was aware that castles were a Norman innovation; it is more likely that he derived his ideas about warfare from reading Classical works in which castles did not feature. Geoffrey's ideals of kingship also had less to do with the realities of his own day than might be expected. There was, for example, no contemporary parallel for Geoffrey's King Belinus, whom he particularly praised as a road-builder whose code of justice ensured the safety of travellers.

The veracity of Geoffrey's work was soon doubted; the chronicler, William of Newburgh, wrote a savage criticism, describing Geoffrey as a shameless *fabulator*, or story

An early fourteenth-century illustration of King Arthur's knights in battle.

teller. However, such sceptics were few and far between; the stories in the book were too enjoyable to dismiss, the history too persuasive. As a result of Geoffrey's work, Arthurian tales became ever more popular. The great French late twelfth-century poet, Chrétien de Troyes, owed a great debt to Geoffrey and did much to develop the genre further, with a new emphasis on Arthur's knights, such as Lancelot and Percival, and on the Holy Grail. Yet more elements were added later, to be fully developed by Thomas Malory in the fifteenth century – but the basis remained Geoffrey's astonishing work.

The Arthurian story developed so skilfully by Geoffrey became part of the myth of English nationhood. King Edward I sought to identify himself with Arthur, and excavated what he thought were the graves of Arthur and Guinevere at Glastonbury. When a letter was sent in Edward's name to the pope to justify the king's claims over Scotland, the clerk added to the account a summary of

Merlin, reading to King Uther from a scroll. Geoffrey of Monmouth's history did much to popularize Arthurian tales.

Geoffrey's story of Brutus and his defeat of the giants, as well as emphasizing Arthur's subjection of the Scots. Yet there was a problem, in that Brutus and Arthur were part of a British, rather than an English, story. Geoffrey's depiction of the Anglo-Saxons as treacherous was troubling for the English, and his was not the only version of the past that was believed. There were alternative stories, such as that of Engle, an early king of the Angles after whom England was allegedly named. Alternatively, the name of the country might have derived from Hengist's supposed daughter, Ynge. Nevertheless, Arthur could not be written out of history. Geoffrey of Monmouth's fictional farrago was too deeply embedded, the myth too potent. His book may be bad history, but it is great literature.

Godric of Finchale

LONG-LIVED MERCHANT AND HERMIT

c. 1070–1170

Trade offered splendid opportunities for an ambitious entrepreneur. One such was Godric of Finchale, who came from a poor Norfolk family. Disdaining a farming life, he began his career buying and selling in local markets. He then spread his wings, trading internationally, between England, the Low Countries, Denmark and Scotland. He followed well established routes, pioneered by the Vikings in the North Sea world. A short, strong, well-built man, Godric became a ship's captain. He was careful to spread his risks, for he had a half-share in one ship, and took a quarter of the profits from another; this was a sophisticated trading world. The life written about Godric by his contemporary, Reginald of Durham, says nothing about the commodities he traded, save that he took care to take precious goods to places where they were scarce. Woollen cloth was probably the most important export, while he would have imported Baltic products such as timber and pitch to England and the Low Countries. It is also very likely that he engaged in piracy, though understandably his biographer, was silent on this subject, wishing to stress Godric's saintliness.

Like so many, Godric was inspired by the crusading message. He did not join the First Crusade and take the hard overland journey to the east, but sailed to Palestine after the capture of Jerusalem. He was in the east when the king of Jerusalem, Baldwin I, was defeated by Egyptian forces at Ramla in 1102. It was Godric who rescued him, taking him by sea from Arsuf to safety in Jaffa. During his voyage home, Godric made the pilgrimage to Santiago de Compostela. He went on further pilgrimages in the following years, notably to Rome. According to Reginald of Durham, a visit to the Farne Islands was important in inspiring Godric's faith; this was where St Cuthbert had lived a life of solitude among the seabirds and seals. This emphasis was not surprising from the pen of a monk at Durham, where St Cuthbert was buried.

Godric's piety gradually overcame his entrepreneurial zeal. In about 1108, he went on pilgrimage once again to Jerusalem. After washing his feet in the Jordan, he never wore shoes again. It was probably in 1112 that he settled in Finchale, by the river Wear, to live as a hermit. In time, Finchale became a pleasant retreat for the Durham monks; it is now a favoured beauty spot. For Godric, however, it was wild, unpleasant, remote, full of snakes and ideal for self-mortification. Two of the snakes became Godric's particular pets, until he finally ordered them to leave. Godric did not go as far as some of the holy men of the day, who weighed themselves down with pieces of armour, but he used to wear a mail hauberk directly on his bare, ulcerating flesh as a form of penance. He was, to use the contemporary phrase, a true 'athlete of Christ'. Foraging provided much of his food, though he also grew some crops in a small garden. He mixed his flour with ashes to make his bread unpleasant. In winter, he might spend all night in the freezing water of the Wear, even when this involved breaking the ice to get in. According to his biographer, he was often assailed by devils, but his prayers would drive them away.

Godric was far from unique in leading a spiritual life in solitude; there were many who did this. Like other hermits and recluses, Godric was not completely isolated from society. He acted among other things as a banker; an attempt was made to rob his cell, because people had deposited money with him for safety. Tales that Godric could foretell the future no doubt added to his popularity, as did his reputation for healing. Miracle stories show that people often came to Godric, the local holy man, to seek his advice. He successfully counselled a couple who had had three miscarriages, and dealt with a wife-beater. A man about to undergo trial by battle went to see Godric the day before the fight; in this case, the hermit's prayers did not work, for he was killed despite being innocent of the charges against him. Godric was not wholly isolated from his family: his sister, Burcwen, followed his example and lived a hermit's life in a cell close by. Nor was he cut off in his religious profession, for from about 1150 he established a close relationship with the monastery at Durham, and accepted the authority of its prior.

Hermits were often assailed by temptation. This illustration from a fourteenth-century manuscript shows a hermit by his hut, unmoved by the attentions of a devil.

A priory was built close to the river Wear at Finchale, near Durham, at the site of Godric's hermitage.

Godric was not a learned man, but he could speak French and understand Latin. He had a musical gift; his hymns are the first in Middle English to survive with both words and music. He was important to the monks of Durham; their association with him enhanced the reputation of the house. His life was remarkable in many ways, providing a unique glimpse into the very different worlds of an entrepreneur and a recluse. There were other merchants, and other hermits, but none combined the two roles as he did, nor had their careers recorded in such detail. Nor were there many who lived as long, for Godric survived until he was about a hundred.

Héloïse

VICTIM OF A TRAGIC LOVE AFFAIR

c. 1100—64

Paris in the early twelfth century was an intellectual hothouse. There was no university in the formal sense, but the reputation of the scholars who taught in the various schools in the city was formidable. One of the most celebrated was Peter Abelard, notable both for his clear-minded application of logic to difficult questions of philosophy and theology and for the love songs he composed and performed. He was a rock-star of the age, adored by women, on whom he spent most of his earnings.

In 1116, Fulbert, a canon of Notre-Dame in Paris, agreed that in return for board and lodging Abelard should tutor his niece, Héloïse, who was about sixteen. She was attractive and highly intelligent; he was at least twice her age. Tutoring soon led to seduction, and sexual experimentation. As he wrote: 'Our desires left no stage of lovemaking untried, and if love would devise something new, we welcomed it.' Letters attributed to them show that the two wrote to each other frequently, in an extravagant and affected language of adoration. Héloïse addressed Abelard: 'You are most cherished and loved in my heart, so suitable for my love, always the perfect answer to my prayers.' His reply was 'to one more glistening than silver, more splendid than any jewel, finer than all unguents in smell and taste'. The outcome of the affair was a baby son, called Astralabe, and a furious uncle. The baby was sent off to be looked after by Abelard's sister. Abelard married Héloïse, but in secret, so that his academic career would not be ruined. When the news finally broke, he despatched Héloïse to a nunnery at Argenteuil. Fulbert was incensed,

A seduction scene, from a fourteenth-century manuscript.

thinking that Abelard had found a convenient way of getting rid of Héloïse, and sent his servants to castrate him. Following this assault, Abelard abandoned Héloïse, leading her to think that he had been motivated by lust, not love. She complained that it was not any sense of vocation that had led her to a convent, but her obedience to him.

In 1129, Abbot Suger of Saint-Denis (see pp. 60–63), relying as he often did on forged documents, had Héloïse and her fellow nuns removed from Argenteuil. He considered them too frivolous and immoral. Their patron, the royal chancellor and steward, Stephen de Garlande, had lost power, and that gave Suger his opportunity. Héloïse was then invited by Abelard to become abbess of Le Paraclete, an oratory near Nogent-sur-Seine, which he had set up some seven years earlier, and then left after spending about five years there. Abelard, meanwhile, wrote a vivid account of his relationship with Héloïse and the disasters that had followed, which he sent to a friend. Someone passed it to Héloïse, who was understandably furious. She condemned Abelard for not writing to her, nor speaking to her when he visited Le Paraclete. He was, she felt, making an unacceptable demand that she obey him. It was then that the two began a famous correspondence, consisting of three letters from Héloïse and four from Abelard.

There has been much scholarly argument about these letters, but they appear genuine, rather than all being written by one person, or a later forgery. As a girl, Héloïse had been celebrated for her learning. The letters she wrote at Le Paraclete display a remarkable skill in the use of language, and an impressive knowledge of Classical as well as biblical sources. They are also highly personal in tone. Memories of her affair haunted her. 'During the solemnities of the mass, when prayers should be pure, obscene phantasms of those pleasures captivate my soul, so that I give my time to their foulness rather than to my prayers.'

Héloïse sought advice from Abelard on the rules that the community at Le Paraclete should follow. He envisaged a double monastery, one for men and one for women, with a single male abbot for both. His lengthy instructions advised that an abbess should not live in greater comfort than her nuns. If wine was to be drunk, it should be watered. The nuns should not enjoy bread hot from the oven, but should wait until it was stale. Their underclothes should be clean, and worn when they slept, which they should do alone. There is nothing to suggest that Héloïse accepted all this advice; it seems likely that she resented this level of detail from Abelard. He also provided hymns and sermons for the nuns, and answered difficult theological questions from Héloïse; she did not thank him for this either. In one letter, he explained that:

> It frequently occurs that the flesh of black women is on the one hand unattractive in
> appearance, and on the other soft to touch. Therefore the pleasure they provide is better
> and more appropriately enjoyed in private rather than in public.

The abbess Héloïse giving instruction in the art of love. A fifteenth-century illustration from a treatise attributed to Héloïse, though it was not in fact written by her.

Dieu et mon droit

Que ceulx qui ce liure veul
lent entendre doiuent sa
uoir que quant maistre pi
erre abaielart eut longue
ment regne et vse de ses arts sa consien
ce le reprist Il fonda vne abbaye pres

Héloïse's reaction to this is not recorded, but can easily be imagined. Abelard's letters contain no indication that he regarded Héloïse as an intellectual equal, and he was arrogantly happy to advise that an abbess should be diligent and devout in accepting advice from scholars.

Héloïse wrote far more than her three letters to Abelard. She gained fame as a writer 'by composing, by versifying, by joining new words, making known words new'. Her output, regrettably, is largely lost or unidentified, apart from some poems which may be her work. A dramatization of the Song of Songs attributed to Abelard is perhaps more likely to have been Héloïse's work, and it is very likely that she wrote some of the anonymous poems and songs of the period. What is known of her work provides no more than a glimpse of a remarkable mind. Had she been given to mystical visions, such as those claimed by her contemporary, Hildegard of Bingen, no doubt her writings would have possessed greater authority, and therefore popularity.

Despite her own formidable scholarship, Héloïse did not attempt to make Le Paraclete an intellectual centre. She was, however, highly successful as its abbess, building up the community and establishing six daughter houses. Abelard's explanation for her success was typically petty; he suggested that because women were frail, they received donations out of sympathy at their poverty. In fact, Héloïse was an excellent manager and fund-raiser, clear-headed and practical. She maintained good relations with St Bernard and the Cistercians, despite Bernard's action in putting Abelard on trial for heresy.

Héloïse outlived Abelard by twenty-two years. When she died in 1164, she was buried beside him. The story of Héloïse and Abelard has become famous as a tragic love story. The reality is more complicated, for it is a story not just of love, but of obsession and betrayal. Héloïse was a woman of great intellect and complex character, who never achieved all that she might have done. Thrust into a monastic life for which she had no vocation, deprived of the opportunity to nurture her son, Astralabe, it is astonishing that she did not display greater bitterness in her writings or a similar degree of self-pity to that shown by Abelard.

Al-Idrisi

CARTOGRAPHER

1099–1165

During the 1100s, the island of Sicily was a cultural melting pot. It had been part of the Byzantine Empire until it was taken by the Arabs in the tenth century. The Normans had begun to infiltrate southern Italy as early as 1018, and in 1061 they embarked upon the conquest of Sicily, which they completed with the capture of Palermo in 1091. Under Roger II, the descendant of a minor Norman noble, Tancred of Hauteville, the island became a kingdom in 1130.

The tall and corpulent Roger drew not only on his Norman heritage but on the Byzantine and Arab past. He adopted Byzantine regalia, but his magnificent cloak bore

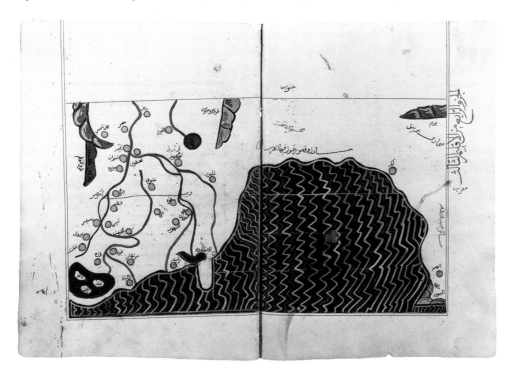

One of the sectional maps from al-Idrisi's treatise.

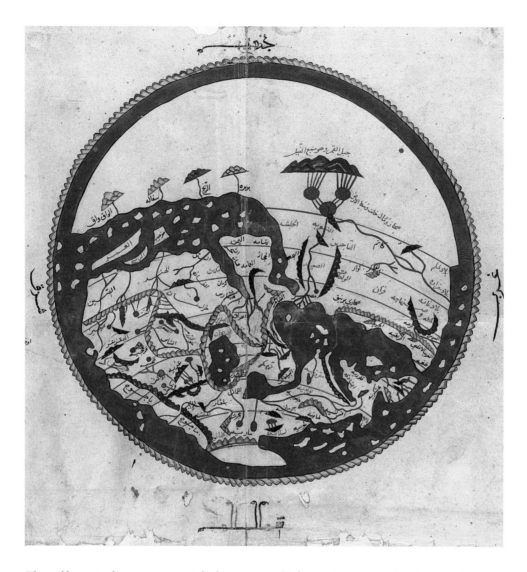

The world map found in some versions of al-Idrisi's treatise. This does not show the same climatic zones as in his work, and probably pre-dates it.

an Arabic inscription. He was a man of immense scientific curiosity. 'His knowledge of mathematics and literature was immense; his profound study of the sciences led him to extraordinary discoveries.' It was thus not surprising that he turned to a Muslim scholar, al-Sharif al-Idrisi, for geographical expertise. Arab merchants had far more extensive links, and wider knowledge of the world, than any European traders. There was a much stronger tradition of map-making in the Arab world than in Christian Europe: the ninth-century caliph al-Māʾmūn, who wished to measure the distance of the surface of the earth, had employed scholars to make a large world map.

Al-Idrisi was born in Ceuta, in North Africa. A member of a noble family, he travelled from an early age, first in North Africa and Spain, where he studied in Córdoba, and then further afield, possibly even as far as England. In 1138, Roger commissioned him to produce a map of the entire known world, and to accompany it with a textual commentary. The work, which took fifteen years, was supervised by the king himself. Many written authorities, all but two Islamic, were consulted, and experts interviewed. All too often they failed to produce clear answers, so travellers were sent out, and interrogated. Only when they agreed was a conclusion accepted. Eventually, a map was prepared, and engraved on a huge silver disk, said to be six feet across.

A book, *al-Kitab al-Rujari*, or *The Book of Roger*, was needed to explain the map. In it, the world was divided into seven climatic zones, from south to north, following the Classical geographer Ptolemy. One of al-Idrisi's innovations was to divide each zone into ten sections, each of which was then described. Distances were given, towns were described and details of the local economy set out.

The quantity and quality of information available to al-Idrisi varied considerably, and shows how far the known world extended. There was, for example, an astonishingly detailed description of the way divers collected pearls in Bahrain. Several pages were devoted to Damascus, with its magnificent mosque, silk industry and fruit and grain production. The price of dates in Basra was noted. Sicily, naturally, was carefully delineated, with Palermo's splendid buildings, both ancient and modern, and its delightful streams of running water, receiving the highest praise. Al-Idrisi even recorded the factories producing a widely exported form of spaghetti.

For distant England, al-Idrisi probably used information provided by a sailor familiar with the coast, for many of the distances between coastal towns that he provides are accurate, in contrast to what he knew of inland districts. A section of his description reads:

> From Southampton to the town of Shoreham is sixty miles. The latter lies on the edge
> of the sea and is a fine and cultivated city containing buildings and flourishing activity.
> From there along the coast to the town of Hastings is fifty miles. This is a town of large
> extent and many inhabitants, flourishing and handsome, having markets, workpeople and
> rich merchants. From there along the coast eastwards to the town of Dover is sixty miles.

Al-Idrisi included information, not necessarily first or even second hand, about central Asia, China, India and Ceylon. His approach was essentially rational. Save for some inhabitants of Norwegian forests who had no necks, he did not populate distant parts of the world with strange beings, as many later medieval authors would do.

The world map that al-Idrisi produced to accompany *The Book of Roger* is, however, problematic. Some later manuscripts of the treatise contain a small circular map of the world. In this, south is at the top, following normal Islamic practice. The map extends from Spain in the west to the eastern coastline of China, and shows mountains, seas and rivers, with much emphasis given to the twin sources of the Nile. Parts of the world are reasonably recognizable, such as Spain, the Arabian peninsula and the Mediterranean. Others, such as the British Isles and Scandinavia, are not. The difficulty is that a thirteenth-century manuscript of the eleventh-century *Book of Curiosities* contains a version of the same map. This strongly suggests that al-Idrisi was not its author, and that it pre-dated his work. His text shows that his world map was different, for it showed the seven climatic zones, with the seas, rivers, deserts and cultivated lands. Towns were carefully placed in respect of their latitude and longitude, and of the distances between them. This was not a symbolic representation after the manner of the world map in the manuscripts.

It is possible to put all the sectional maps in al-Idrisi's book together to form a single whole, but this makes a rectangular map, whereas the great map commissioned by Roger II was engraved on to a silver disk. This does not mean that al-Idrisi considered that the earth was flat; he took the view that the world was spherical. Half of the sphere was covered with water; half was habitable, though not the southern parts, where the heat of the sun was too great. This was the conventional view. The author of the Norwegian *King's Mirror*, writing in the thirteenth century, explained both that the world was round, like an apple, and how this meant the days were so short in northern winters and the heat of the sun so great in Mediterranean climes.

Al-Idrisi continued his work in Sicily for a time after Roger II's death in 1154, but he eventually returned to his North African homeland, where he died in 1165. His work was widely used in the Arab world, for example by the great fourteenth-century historian Ibn Khaldūn. In Christian Europe, however, al-Idrisi had no influence. With no Latin translation of *The Book of Roger*, he remained unread, and unequalled. The great silver disk engraved with his world map was probably lost in the course of the Sicilian rebellion of 1161.

The western European tradition of map-making was very different from al-Idrisi's attempt to represent realistically the world he knew. This pattern for world maps had been established by Isidore of Seville in the seventh century. Known as T-O maps, they resemble a capital T set within a circle. East is at the top, with Europe bottom left and Africa bottom right. The splendid Hereford World Map, or *Mappa Mundi*, of about 1300, takes this form. This is a symbolic representation of the world, bearing little relation to reality. The map depicts various monstrous races in the margins of the world, such as the Sciapods, who possess a single giant foot on which they hop when not using it as a sunshade. Other men have a huge lip to protect themselves from the sun. The Blemmyes have their faces in the middle of their chests. Intriguing and delightful as these are, what the Hereford World Map emphasizes above all is that the Christian world centred on Jerusalem. It represents theology and superstition, not geographical knowledge, in stark contrast to the pioneering work of al-Idrisi.

Hildegard of Bingen

NOTABLE NUN

1098–1179

Although the medieval Church was male dominated, many female saints and martyrs were worshipped. In particular, the cult of the Virgin – identified as she was as the Queen of Heaven – developed apace in the twelfth and thirteenth centuries. Holiness, consequently, was not an exclusively male preserve; and while it was convenient in many cases for families to send some daughters off to adopt the religious life, this also provided career opportunities for some exceptionally able women. Hildegard of Bingen was one such individual: a visionary theologian, botanist, composer, creator of a secret language and correspondent of popes and emperors.

Hildegard was the tenth child of a well-to-do family. She began to have visions from an early age, and perhaps as a result was sent in 1106 to a monastery at Disibodenberg, not far from the Rhineland town of Bingen, to be raised under the care of an anchoress called Jutta. The small community Jutta led eventually became a convent, linked to the neighbouring Benedictine house. Hildegard claimed to have acquired no more than a basic education from Jutta. But in 1136, after Jutta's death, she became abbess, and in about 1150, so as to escape Benedictine supervision, she moved the convent some forty miles to a new site,

A depiction of one of Hildegard von Bingen's visions. She is shown in the small panel, dictating her work. Flames from her head show her inspiration.

at Rupertsberg. The sisters were all from wealthy, well-connected families, for Hildegard would not accept those of low birth. She did not take a severe view of how monastic discipline should be applied; she was, for example, ready to allow her nuns to wear underwear. This she considered useful as a means of reducing lustful feelings.

When she was forty-two, Hildegard claimed that she had a vision in which 'a light of extreme brilliance flowed through my brain'. This, she explained, gave her an instant understanding of the scriptures. She was commanded in the vision to write down and communicate all that she knew. However, Hildegard did not do this in a straightforward way. As Guibert of Gembloux, one of her secretaries, explained, 'Many turn away from, and abhor, the books of Hildegard, because they are written in an obscure and unaccustomed style, not understanding that this is the characteristic of a true prophetess.' She wrote three mystical theological works, of which the first, *Scivias*, is the most celebrated. Part of it was shown to Pope Eugenius III, at the Synod of Trier in 1147–48, who approved it. In her text, Hildegard explained Christian doctrine in terms of visions:

> Then I saw a great round tower, of white stone, standing all complete. It had three windows
> at the top, from which such brightness shone that the roof of the tower, built like a cone,
> could be seen clearly in the light.

One explanation of Hildegard's visions is that she was a migraine sufferer. It was perhaps from personal experience that she wrote that if a migraine spread right across the head, it was quite unbearable, and almost impossible to cure. Yet no number of migraines could possibly explain the quantity and complexity of Hildegard's visions.

Music was intensely important to Hildegard, who saw it as an expression of her theological ideas. Her ability to use musical notation was, she believed, a God-given gift. The words that went with her music did not fit any normal poetic structure; they were almost prose. Hildegard's melodies are characterized by an extraordinary range, difficult for many singers to achieve.

Hildegard also wrote a work on natural sciences, much of it devoted to plants, and a medical treatise. Her physiological ideas were conventional, based on the four elements of earth, air, fire and water, which were linked to the humours of black bile, blood, yellow bile and phlegm. Any imbalance of the humours would cause illness. Hildegard did, however, view health in practical as well as theoretical terms, and was much more interested in, and informed about, sex than might be expected from a nun. She followed the normal medieval view, which gave women a positive role in procreation, writing:

> When a woman is making love with a man, a sense of heat in her brain, which brings with
> it sensual delight, communicates the sense of that delight during the act, and summons
> forth the emission of the man's seed.

Elsewhere, she explained female sexual enjoyment in more detail:

One of Hildegard's visions from her Scivias, *showing a mysterious huge egg-shaped object that appeared to her, possibly representing her interpretation of the universe.*

When the breeze of pleasure proceeds from the marrow of a woman it falls into her womb, which is near the navel, and moves the woman's blood to pleasure; and because it spreads out around the womb, and is therefore more mild, because of her moisture where she burns with pleasure, or from fear of shame, she is able to restrain herself from excessive pleasure more than a man.

The fire of pleasure, as she put it, burned more strongly in a man than a woman. But men, as she also pointed out, were not so potent after the age of fifty, and not up to it at all after eighty; for women, desire normally ceased at fifty. Alongside such questionable observations,

Hildegard had some strange ideas. She suggested that people conceived in damp and cloudy weather were likely to have bad breath. Ointment made from a mixture of fat from a dead sparrowhawk and herbs, and applied to the genitals, was an implausible remedy for excessive sexual urges. On the other hand, she sensibly advocated regular tooth cleaning.

Among all her activities, one of the most surprising is that Hildegard invented a new alphabet, of twenty-three letters, and a secret language of about a thousand words. It is not clear what it was for, though it probably related both to Hildegard's music and her scientific interests, with many of the words relating to the natural world. A wasp in this language was an *amzia*, a gnat an *arschia*.

Hildegard had a very considerable reputation and corresponded widely. Her fame was such that in 1148 Odo of Soissons, an academic in Paris, wrote to ask for her advice on the nature of the Trinity. She once sent a letter to Eleanor of Aquitaine (see pp. 94–97), telling her to keep calm. Quite exceptionally for a woman in the twelfth century, she preached, not just within the confining walls of her convent, but on four tours of Germany, in which she called for reform of the Church. Yet her legacy was limited. Her works did not receive wide circulation; there are only two main manuscripts. There was no large-scale miracle cult associated with her. Her fame has, however, burgeoned in modern times. She has been portrayed, with little justification, as a feminist, and as anticipating New Age thinking. Her use of herbs is viewed as a form of alternative medicine. Her popularity is such that, in 2012, the pope declared her to be the thirty-fifth Doctor of the Church. Hildegard, however, should be seen in the context of the twelfth century, not the twenty-first.

Thomas Becket

MARTYRED ARCHBISHOP AND SAINT

1120–70

Thomas Becket's mother was a Muslim princess who followed his father, Gilbert, to England after he escaped from captivity on the crusades. She was recognized by Gilbert's servant as she walked the streets of London in search of her lover. That, at least, was the legend, and like much that has been said about Thomas, there is no truth to it. In reality, Thomas Becket's parents were reasonably well-off Londoners of Norman origin.

Thomas began his career in the household of Theobald, archbishop of Canterbury. He was undoubtedly clever; his exceptional abilities even extended, according to one commentator, to an acute sense of smell. However, his education did not extend to formal training in the higher academic disciplines, notably those of canon law and theology. In 1155, he entered royal service as chancellor, an astonishing appointment for a man with no experience of government. Seven years later, King Henry II engineered Thomas's election as archbishop of Canterbury. Relations between king and archbishop, however, soon broke down, with Thomas's refusal to accept the guidelines of the 1164 Constitutions of Clarendon, which attempted to define the relationship between Church and state. Thomas was put on trial at

An early fourteenth-century illustration of the implausible story of how Thomas Becket's mother was recognized on the streets of London.

Northampton and fled abroad. Although he eventually succeeded in reaching a settlement with the king, which ended his exile in 1170, it was all too evident that there was no real agreement between them. Henry addressed his knights: 'What miserable drones and traitors have I nourished in my household, who let their lord be treated with such shameful contempt by a low-born clerk!' Thomas's savage murder in Canterbury cathedral swiftly followed.

'Humble at heart, yet proud in appearance, humble with the poor, but overbearing with the great, a lamb within and a leopard without', Thomas was very different things to different people. It was hard to understand how it was that the extravagant and worldly chancellor became the committed and unworldly defender of the rights and privileges of the Church. Did he undergo a Damascene conversion, or was he chameleon-like in his capacity to take on the colours of whatever role he was playing?

There is little doubting Thomas's ambition, as he rose from merchant's son to be one of the chief men in the kingdom. As he climbed upwards at each stage of his career Thomas had little difficulty in casting aside any baggage from the past, abandoning friendships as he went. He did not, however, forget his enemies. He and Roger of Pont l'Evêque had been rivals in Archbishop Theobald's household, and it was galling to Thomas when Roger became archbishop of York in 1154. His fury in 1170, when Roger crowned the heir to the throne, Henry II's son Henry, led almost inexorably to the final tragedy of his martyrdom.

Thomas believed in making a show. He was extravagant as chancellor, throwing himself with enthusiasm into the grandeur of the post. His house was said to glisten with gold and silver ornaments. When he went on an embassy to Paris, he had a magnificent following of 200, and took twenty-four changes of clothes for himself. As archbishop, his extravagance took a different turn. His household was splendid, and the food in his hall was opulent, but he ate modestly himself, and had the leftovers distributed to the poor. Where his predecessor, Archbishop Theobald, had been generous in giving alms, Thomas was twice as bountiful. Even in the dark days after Thomas fled from his trial at Northampton into exile, he remained grand in manner; an innkeeper and his serving girl had no difficulty in identifying him from his posture and the way that he ate.

Thomas's admirers saw one clear element of consistency in his career: he remained chaste throughout his life. He and the king may have enjoyed chasing game together, but Thomas did not share Henry's taste for pursuing women. He believed in mortifying the flesh; when in exile at Pontigny, he took to immersing himself for hours in a cold stream 'in an effort to purge himself of the stings of desire that still seemed to dwell in him'. It was only on his death that the hair shirt he had always worn was discovered, along with the vermin that infested it. Claims that Thomas led a secret life of chastity and self-mortification provided his supporters with a way to equate the grand and arrogant chancellor with the martyred archbishop.

Thomas Becket confronting King Henry II, in an illustration from an early fourteenth-century chronicle. A royal geneaology is below.

Thomas Becket's death at the hands of Henry II's knights. The top of his head was sliced off with a sword. After his murder, a great many lice crawled out of his clothes.

Thomas's achievements as chancellor, however, were limited. He successfully negotiated a treaty with France, and he distinguished himself in war, even defeating a French knight in single combat. He also gained considerable wealth; he held the Tower of London, the estate or castlery of Eye in Suffolk, and Berkhamstead castle. No doubt he contributed to the good government of the country following the difficult days of the civil war in King Stephen's reign, but his role in imposing taxes on the Church did nothing for his popularity. The significant reforms of Henry's reign, notably in the law, came after Thomas's years of royal service were over.

Equally, as archbishop, Thomas failed to provide the leadership that the Church needed. He did not have the support of most of the English bishops in his dispute with the king, nor did he even have the backing of the monks of his own cathedral. When he was first elected, he was justifiably concerned to restore all the lands and rights of his see, but his long exile in France meant that he was unable to defend it from the depredations of royal officials. He was not a man capable of effective compromise, as the final breakdown of his relationship with Henry II, which culminated with his brutal martydom, all too starkly show.

Had he not been martyred, Thomas would surely not have had a high reputation. However, in his death he achieved far more than he had in life. Although he was not inconsistent in all things, and was indeed a man of genuine piety, he was, above all, ambitious, arrogant and unbending. A key issue in his quarrel with the king had been whether clergy who committed crimes could be punished in royal courts. The matter involved difficult and technical questions of canon law, but Thomas's martyrdom effectively settled the matter. Within a few years, it was agreed that clerics could claim immunity from the jurisdiction of the king's courts, except in cases where they had infringed forest law or where they held secular land. A cult quickly developed at Canterbury around Thomas, who was canonized in 1173. Miracles soon abounded; the martyr's blood, suitably diluted, healed many. As befitted a man who once hunted with the king, he even proved to be good at curing sick falcons. Notably celebrated by Geoffrey Chaucer (see pp. 225–28), the journey to the murdered archbishop's shrine in Canterbury cathedral became the most important and popular pilgrimage in England for the remainder of the Middle Ages.

Usāma ibn Munqidh

ARAB WARRIOR AND AUTHOR

1095–1188

The crusades brought western Europeans into direct contact with a very different, and in very many ways superior, civilization. The establishment, at the end of the eleventh century, of the kingdom of Jerusalem and the other Latin states – the principalities of Antioch and Edessa and the county of Tripoli – saw westerners settle in Arab lands. They were faced with a much more urbanized society, with far more sophisticated trading networks, than anything they were used to. The militant ideology that had led them to conquer the Holy Land was far less appropriate for the task of settling their new territories. One of the most vivid accounts of the resulting clash of cultures comes from a Syrian nobleman, warrior and poet, Usāma ibn Munqidh.

Usāma was born in 1095, the year that the First Crusade was preached by Urban II (see pp. 46–48). He was brought up in northern Syria, the nephew of the ruler of Shayzar, from where he was exiled in 1138. He then served in the courts of Mosul, Cairo and

A Muslim assault on a crusader camp, from an early fourteenth-century French manuscript.

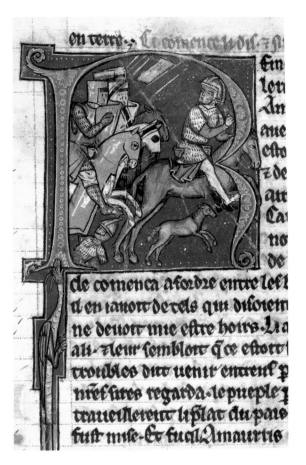

The sultan of Damascus shown fleeing from pursuing crusaders.
Usāma's book contains many accounts of encounters between
Muslims and westerners.

Damascus, where he became well acquainted with some of the great figures of the age, notably Nur ad-Dīn and the renowned Saladin (see pp. 98–101), both redoubtable opponents of the crusaders. Usāma, a prolific author whose more unusual works included a book about walking sticks, wrote his memoirs in his old age.

Usāma was intrigued by the cultural differences between the Franks (the term he used for the crusaders) and his own people. The crusaders were undoubtedly formidable warriors; their mounted and armoured knights in full charge were fearsome. Their religious ideology, particularly in the hands of the military orders of the Templars and the Hospitallers, gave them an additional edge. Although Usāma acknowledged their military skill, seeing them 'as animals possessing the virtues of courage and fighting, but nothing else', he claimed never to have been defeated by them. Usāma himself wore a double coat of mail, with a quilted jerkin, and fought with lance and sword, just as a crusader knight did. He explained that the Muslims had developed a compound lance, so as to increase the weapon's length. Their horses were excellent, and highly valued.

Muslim forces were quite as adept at siege warfare as the crusaders, with the use of stone-throwing engines for offence, and crossbows and arbalests prominent in defence. Like the crusaders, Muslims had a religious motivation for war. Usāma, who was conventionally devout, duly gave praise to Allah – 'mighty and majestic is he!' – for victories over the crusaders. Surprisingly, however, Usāma made nothing of the doctrine of holy war, *jihād*.

On the whole, Usāma held the Franks to be 'an accursed race, the members of which do not assimilate except with their own kin'. Crusaders newly arrived from the west were particularly objectionable. There were, however, examples where successful cultural assimilation did eventually take place. Usāma tells the story of how he once dined with an elderly knight. He was initially unwilling to eat, but his host explained that there should be no problem: 'Eat, be of good cheer! I never eat Frankish dishes, but I have Egyptian women cooks and never eat except their cooking.' On another occasion, he recounts how a crusader's maidservant was captured and sent to a Muslim lord. She became his mistress, and bore him a child. When the lord died, she escaped to a crusader settlement, where she married a shoemaker, while her son remained a Muslim, and lord of a castle. In a similar case, Usāma's father was so impressed by the conversion of a captive crusader to Islam that he provided him with a wife and all necessary expenses. After the couple had two children, the convert abandoned his wife, took his sons, aged five and six, and returned to the crusader lands. Another knight, who befriended Usāma, was about to leave the Holy Land when he told him that he wanted to send Usāma his son to educate him – but of course nothing came of it.

In order to show just how uncivilized (and hairy) the crusaders were, and how immodest their women, Usāma told the following tale. One of them, visiting a bath-house, noticed that the owner had shaved his pubic hair, and demanded the same treatment for himself. Pleased with the results, he had his servant fetch his wife, so that she could follow his example. 'So,' said the bath-house keeper, 'I shaved all that hair while her husband was sitting looking at me.'

Crusader methods of justice also astonished Usāma, who described a case determined by means of trial by battle, in which the defeated party was killed and his body then hanged. 'This case illustrates the kind of jurisprudence and legal decisions the Franks have – may Allah's curse be upon them.' He also saw a man tried by ordeal, in which the accused was dropped into a huge cask of water. Should he sink, he was innocent. In this case, he floated, and suffered blinding as punishment.

Usāma was particularly intrigued by the differences between Arab and European medicine. He was appalled by one crusader diagnosis: a woman was declared to have a devil in her, and was treated by cutting a cross in her head and rubbing salt into it. Not surprisingly, she died. Yet he also told how one western physician cured a man of infection by careful washing with vinegar, and how in another case an ointment of herbs, olive oil and vinegar proved effective.

It is dangerous to take all Usāma's anecdotes as factually accurate, but they provide a unique insight into the attitudes of an aristocratic Syrian towards the crusaders. Though he found some crusaders were becoming civilized, it was a vain hope that these invaders could be fully assimilated into the society of the Middle East.

Frederick Barbarossa

GERMAN EMPEROR

1122–90

Frederick Barbarossa lies in the Kyffhäuser hills, a saviour awaiting the call when his country is at its greatest need. So goes the unlikely legend about an emperor who has also been seen as typifying the aggressive side of the German national character, and as diverting German resources to his futile Italian ambitions. Such conceptions obscure, rather than illuminate, the reality of an ambitious and energetic man.

Frederick, duke of Swabia, was still a young man when elected German king in 1152 and crowned emperor in 1155. He was described by a chronicler according to the template established by Einhard for Charlemagne (see pp. 16–19). He was shorter than tall men, but taller than those of medium height. His barber kept his golden hair short; his beard was reddish in colour. He had sharp eyes, and good white teeth. His neck was plump, though not fat. He was strongly built, with broad shoulders, and his thighs, supported by stout calves, were sturdy. The physical description was not matched by any meaningful analysis of his character. He enjoyed hunting, showed due reverence to the clergy and was eloquent in speaking German.

Frederick's father was a Hohenstaufen, his mother a Welf, and it was hoped that when he came to the throne he could end the damaging feud between these great families. This was not so easily done. Henry the Lion, duke of Saxony, was a Welf; his claims on the duchy of Bavaria were disputed by Henry Jasomirgott of Austria. Frederick rapidly achieved a notable success in 1156, when he granted Austria, previously a march, to Jasomirgott to hold as an imperial duchy. The Lion received a reduced Bavaria, as well as keeping Saxony. Skilfully, Frederick had ensured that no one lost face disastrously.

The relationship between Frederick and Henry the Lion only broke down spectacularly some two decades later, in 1175, when the Lion refused to provide military service for a campaign in Italy. In 1180, the Lion was put on trial in his absence, and in the following year he submitted to the emperor and was exiled for three years. This was as much a triumph for the Lion's enemies in Germany, men such as Albert the Bear and Philip, archbishop of Cologne, as it was for Frederick. The fall of the Lion was followed by a reorganization of the German duchies, with the creation of the new duchy of Westphalia, and the grant of Bavaria to Otto of Wittelsbach. The political geography of Germany was transformed, though the bitterness between Welf and Hohenstaufen remained.

Italy had always been alluring for Frederick. The wealth of the cities of the north, if it could be taxed, promised resources that far exceeded anything that Germany could offer. Yet there was an acute danger that an alliance between a hostile papacy and resentful Lombard cities could prevent Frederick from achieving his goals. A further problem was the summer heat in Italy, and the malaria-carrying mosquitoes. The towns proved formidable foes. On Frederick's first Italian expedition, in 1154, Tortona, a small fortified place, held out for a couple of months, despite its walls being battered by siege engines and mined, and the water supply poisoned.

Relations with the pope began badly, when Frederick initially refused to hold Adrian IV's stirrup at their first meeting in 1155. Nevertheless, the imperial coronation went ahead, though Frederick had to send troops to secure St Peter's before the ceremony, for the citizens of Rome were in full rebellion. The death of Adrian IV in 1159 created a new and difficult situation. The imperialists among the cardinals elected Victor IV, the rival faction Alexander III.

The papacy obtained support from the cities of Lombardy. The Lombard League, headed by Milan and formed in 1167, was more powerful than any alliance the emperor could construct. In 1176 the forces of the League met Frederick in battle at Legnano. The emperor, his forces reinforced by mercenaries recruited from the Low Countries, was roundly defeated. Frederick himself was lost for three days after the defeat, eventually reaching Pavia. A truce followed, with a final peace negotiated in 1183, in which Frederick showed considerable statesmanship.

Frederick enjoyed and encouraged the world of chivalry, his sons even more so. The peak of German chivalric celebration came, in 1184, with the court held at Mainz. A splendid wooden palace was built, with a tented city all around. There was a great ceremony for the knighting of Frederick's sons, and much feasting and jousting. Reality struck when disastrous weather brought

A gilded bronze reliquary in the form of Frederick Barbarossa's head, presented by the emperor's godfather to the abbey at Cappenberg.

events to a sad and premature close. Lyric poetry also had its place at court. The Archpoet, a twelfth-century hippy, was connected with Frederick's chancellor, Rainald of Dassel. His best-known lines are:

> Meum est propositum in taberna mori
> ut sint vina proxima morientis ori.

Which could be translated as 'I'd like to kick the bucket in the pub, with a drink beside me as I die.' The Archpoet could be awkward; he refused Rainald's request that he should write an epic setting out Frederick's deeds in Italy.

Before he was elevated to the German throne, Frederick had taken part in the Second Crusade, with no great distinction. His position as emperor meant that he now saw himself as the secular leader of the Christian west, and he took the cross again in 1188, for the Third Crusade. 'A glorious old man, he inspired young men to follow his example and fight for Christ.' He led a substantial German contingent on the overland route to the east. There was a good deal of fighting with the Byzantines, 1,500 of whom were slaughtered in one town, as well as inappropriate liaisons with local women. As the army crossed Asia Minor, victuals were short, and they were harassed by the Turks. In the extreme heat of June 1190, Frederick decided to cool off by swimming across the river Göksu. He was swept away and drowned.

Frederick's crusading army collapsed in disarray. His empire, however, did not; he had left a capable son to succeed him, Henry VI. It was the demise of Henry in 1197, leaving a three-year-old son, that led to crisis in the Empire, as the Welfs sought to regain power, and Pope Innocent III (see pp. 105–9) attempted to take advantage of the situation. Perhaps Frederick's true legacy does not lie in the achievements of his reign or the events that followed his death, but in the hold that the legend of Barbarossa, asleep in the Kyffhäuser hills, has exerted over the German imagination.

Opposite *The emperor Frederick Barbarossa, in a portrait dating from 1188. He bears a crusader's cross on his tunic and his shield.*

Left *Frederick Barbarossa's death by drowning in Asia Minor, shown in a thirteenth-century chronicle.*

Eleanor of Aquitaine

QUEEN 'BY THE WRATH OF GOD'

1124—1204

The figure of Eleanor of Aquitaine is enveloped in myth and contradiction. There is the scandalous queen, who, when married to Louis VII of France, had an affair with her own uncle. There is the mother, fiercely protective of the interests of her sons against her second husband, Henry II of England. In addition there is the patron of literature, and of the troubadour culture of southern France, perhaps suggested by her tomb effigy in Fontevraud abbey, which shows her reading a book and ignoring the presence of Henry lying beside her.

Born in 1124, Eleanor was heiress to the great duchy of Aquitaine in the south of France. She was brought up surrounded by a sophisticated court in Poitou; her grandfather, Duke William IX, was a poet who supported the troubadours with their songs of love. How far Eleanor, as a girl of thirteen, herself helped to bring this culture to northern France when she married Louis VII in 1137 is questionable; but later, when she married Henry II of England, she sponsored the Provençal troubadour Bernard de Ventadour at the English court. There is, however, little to show that she helped to develop ideas about courtly love. A satirical handbook about love was written by Andreas Capellanus, a clerk at the French court towards the end of the twelfth century. In the book, Eleanor and her daughter by Louis VII, Marie, countess of Champagne, pronounced judgments at Poitiers in courts of love. In one ruling, a woman who abandoned her lover for another was told to return to the first man, a clear reference to Eleanor's leaving Louis VII for Henry II. There is no doubt that Marie was an important literary patron, notably of Chrétien de Troyes. However, mother and daughter had little contact after Eleanor's marriage to Louis was annulled when Marie was only seven; and the tale of the courts of love has no more credence than Andreas's advice that men should cure their shyness by raping peasant women. As for the book that Eleanor is shown reading on her tomb, it is far more likely to be a psalter than a romance.

The romantic vision of Eleanor, as a woman for whom love was all important, can easily shift into scandal. It was said that she felt that in Louis VII she had married a monk, rather than a king. Louis, however, was devoted to her, and in 1145 took the exceptional step of bringing her on crusade. At Antioch, Eleanor fell into close company with her uncle Raymond, ruler of the principality. When there were arguments over strategy, she sided with Raymond. Gossip soon abounded about her relationship with him. Eleanor threatened

Louis with divorce, but on the couple's return from the east the pope successfully reconciled them. Back in Paris, however, the rumours flared up once more. Eleanor was said to have had an affair with Geoffrey, count of Anjou, when he came to Paris with his son Henry; though it was to be Henry, nine years her junior, and the future king of England, that she would marry. Finally, in 1152, Eleanor's marriage to Louis VII was annulled, on the grounds that they were too closely related. The real reason for the breakdown was her failure to produce a male heir.

Within eight weeks, Eleanor had married Henry, who succeeded to the English throne in 1154. Politics, not love, was the motive: she brought with her the vast lands of Aquitaine and Poitou, while he could provide her dominions with protection. There were no more rumours of affairs on Eleanor's part. The boot was now on the other foot, with Henry's many illicit liaisons, notably that with Rosamund Clifford. The marriage was successful in one important respect: by 1168 Eleanor had borne Henry nine children. The family, though, was to prove utterly dysfunctional.

Eleanor's role in politics and government during the years of her marriage to Louis VII had been very limited, in contrast to the previous queen, Adelaide of Maurienne. Rarely away from Louis, Eleanor had little opportunity for independent action. As Henry II's

Queen Eleanor, in a French wall-painting of around 1200. It is thought that it may show her being led into captivity after the rebellion of 1173–74.

The wedding of Eleanor of Aquitaine to Louis VII of France is shown on the left of this fourteenth-century illustration. On the right, Louis and his troops embark on the Second Crusade.

queen, there were more openings for her. During the long periods that Henry spent in his continental dominions, she acted as regent in England. There is a determined tone in the few of her instructions that survive. Ordering the men of Abingdon to do their service to the abbot, she wrote, 'If you do not do this, the justice of the king and my own justice will cause it to be done.' In 1168, she returned to her homeland of Poitou, ruling there successfully, and with a degree of independence from her husband.

Crisis came in 1173, with the rebellion against Henry II of his heir, also named Henry. Eleanor supported her son, while his brothers Richard and Geoffrey joined in the rising. Matters went badly for the rebels; the young Henry was feckless and incompetent. Eleanor was captured, and duly placed in comfortable, if thoroughly unwelcome, captivity. Henry II's mistress Rosamund died in the mid-1170s; inevitably, later legend made Eleanor responsible, with horrendous tales of torture involving, among other things, the use of toads. Henry did not, however, divorce his wife; to have done so could have led to the loss of Aquitaine. Her custody became increasingly nominal in the later years of Henry's reign, but it was not until the king's death in 1189 that she was fully free.

With the accession of her son Richard I, Eleanor had a new political role to play: the controlling matriarch. Before Richard's coronation, she reversed some of Henry II's decisions, and was very active in England during Richard's absence on crusade. In one letter, she termed herself 'Eleanor, by the wrath of God, Queen of England'. She took a leading part in securing Richard's release after he had been captured by the duke of Austria while returning from the east; in 1194, she accompanied the archbishop of Canterbury to Germany to deliver the first instalment of her son's ransom. She also worked to ensure that her youngest son, John, did not usurp his brother's authority. On Richard's death in 1199, Eleanor interrupted her retirement at Fontevraud to do her best to ensure that her subjects in Poitou would be loyal to John and not support the rival candidate to the throne, his nephew Arthur of Brittany.

Eleanor did not conform to the normal role of a queen. In many ways, her interests were more those of a duchess of Aquitaine. Traditionally, it was expected that a queen should intercede with her husband, asking him to exercise mercy in appropriate cases. No doubt Eleanor did this on occasion, but there is nothing to show that this was a major preoccupation. A queen should be pious, and while Eleanor's care for Fontevraud abbey fitted in with this assumption, the scale of her patronage of the Church was not exceptional. Queens might also be expected to act as peacemakers, but Eleanor's status as former queen of Louis VII meant that she was hardly suitable to assist in Anglo-French negotiations. Her forceful support of her sons was more likely to end in war, as in 1173, than in peace.

It is hard to disagree with the chronicler Richard of Devizes, whose description of Eleanor was deliberately full of contradictions. She was 'a matchless woman, beautiful and chaste, powerful and modest, meek and eloquent'.

Eleanor of Aquitaine's tomb effigy at the French monastery of Fontevraud.

Saladin
(Ṣalāḥ ad-Dīn Yūsuf ibn Ayyūb)

MUSLIM LEADER AGAINST THE CRUSADERS

1137–93

The small child was stolen in the night. Distraught, her mother was advised to go through the enemy lines, and ask Saladin himself for help. She was brought before him, wailing and tearing at her clothes. Saladin wept on hearing the tale, and ordered a search of the camp. An hour later, the child was found, and returned to her crusader mother. It was acts like this which led to the view in the west that Saladin, although a heathen, was a chivalrous and noble man, and a worthy opponent.

Ṣalāḥ ad-Dīn Yūsuf ibn Ayyūb, known as Saladin, was a Kurd, born in Tikrit, in modern Iraq, in 1137. Little is known of his early years, which were mostly spent in Syria gaining a good Islamic education. He first came to prominence when he was appointed vizier in Egypt in 1169, and 'he gave up wine and the pleasures of the world, and devoted himself to serious business and to work'. When the Egyptian Fatimid dynasty came to an end in 1171, Saladin soon established his authority there as sultan. He then extended his power over Syria, completing his work when Aleppo surrendered to him in 1183. This unification of the Arab Middle East was his greatest achievement. In part, he owed his success to military skill, notably with the defeat of the forces of Aleppo and Mosul at the Horns of Hama in 1175. His diplomatic skill was also important, while his religious conviction gave him the drive to succeed.

Since their creation almost a century before, the crusader states had depended for their survival in large measure on the weakness of the Islamic powers. Saladin's success in unifying Egypt and Syria transformed the situation. At Hattin, in 1187, he defeated and captured Guy de Lusignan, king of Jerusalem, in an overwhelming triumph. 'God, having granted his aid to the Muslims, sent them victory.' Jerusalem itself then fell on the anniversary of the ascension of the Prophet, and the crusaders soon held little more than the towns of Tyre, Tripoli and Antioch. In the west, the news was shattering. It led to the preaching of the Third Crusade, in which Saladin faced his greatest foe, Richard I of England. 'God alone could protect the Muslims against his wiles; we never had among our enemies a man more crafty or bolder than he.'

The Third Crusade began in 1189 with the lengthy siege of Acre. In July 1191, the town finally fell to the crusaders. Richard I then marched south. Successful harrying of the crusader army was followed by disaster at Arsūf, when the heavily armed crusader cavalry proved too powerful for Saladin's forces. Saladin now found it increasingly difficult to

This early thirteenth-century silver vessel depicts a triumphant Saladin.

maintain morale. An attack on Richard's camp failed, as the crusaders 'displayed such hardihood in the face of death that our troops lost heart at their sturdy resistance'. Saladin made generous offers to his men, but they would not charge. The armoured western knights, backed up by crossbowmen, were all too formidable. The situation drifted into stalemate when Richard halted his advance on Jerusalem just a few miles short, and withdrew. Lengthy and frustrating negotiations took place; Saladin had no trust in Richard, but his hopes of driving a wedge between him and another crusade leader, Conrad of Montferrat, came to nothing when the latter was assassinated. Eventually, in September 1192, an agreement was reached which allowed western pilgrims access to Jerusalem. Saladin, who had suffered ill-health for some time, died in the following year.

As a commander, Saladin had an excellent sense of strategy. He was well aware of the importance of good intelligence. When Richard I was ill, he wanted nothing more than fresh pears and peaches. Saladin was only too ready to oblige, for his messengers could carry fruit one way and intelligence the other. He was also a master of the latest siege technology, and made good use of stone-throwing machines to batter defensive walls. Mining was also employed to good effect. Castle after castle fell to his troops. However, his greatest success in battle, at Hattin, was due at least as much to crusader failings as to his qualities as a general. The outnumbered enemy, exhausted, hungry and above all thirsty, were hardly a

The fortress of Qal'at el-Gindī, in the Sinai peninsula, constructed by Saladin in about 1170. Saladin was a master of the warfare of castles and sieges.

formidable foe. It was a different matter when he faced Richard I at Arsūīf. The biggest weakness in his forces was the navy. Despite efforts to improve and modernize his fleet, Saladin was unable to counter the sea power that Richard I and the crusaders had at their disposal, a fact that was crucial at Acre.

Although chivalry was not an Islamic concept, the values that Saladin espoused were not dissimilar to those held by western knights. He was generous and humane, and was a man who kept his word. He was viewed with some justification as tolerant of religions other than Islam. However, he did not invariably display these qualities. The treatment of prisoners by both Saladin and the crusaders failed to match chivalric ideals. After the battle of Hattin, Saladin had the captive Templar and Hospitaller knights put to death. At Acre, Richard I ordered the killing of a large number of Muslim prisoners, said to number 3,000. 'The Franks rushed upon them all at once, and slaughtered them in cold blood with sword and lance.' To his credit, Saladin did not take revenge in like manner. He 'acknowledged that it was an abominable act, but said that it was the king alone who had decreed and commanded it to be done'.

Saladin was personally indifferent to the possibilities of profiting from office, and so did little to prevent corruption by others, while his policy of giving full authority to his sons or to favoured individuals was dangerous. He consistently abolished those taxes which were against Islamic law, showing a creditable devotion to his religious principles, but also a lack of financial awareness; lack of money was a significant problem in his later years. He did, however, appreciate the importance of trade. He made treaties with Pisa, Genoa and Venice, so as to encourage their merchants to come to Egypt. The actions of the maverick crusader Raynald de Châtillon, who plundered caravans and engaged in piracy on the Red Sea, were completely unacceptable to Saladin, who personally executed Raynald after Hattin.

A pious Muslim, committed to *jihād*, or holy war, Saladin died before he could fulfil his promise to make the pilgrimage to Mecca. His Islamic heritage was important to him; he knew the genealogies not only of the Arab heroes of the past, but also of their horses. He was an upright man, who kept nothing for himself when the capture of Jerusalem meant that vast wealth was available from booty and ransoms. He was no great patron of learning, and took a matter-of-fact view of literature, objecting to a poetic reference to silvery leaves, on the understandable grounds that leaves are in fact green. Remarkably, he earned the full respect of his enemies. William of Tyre, the great historian of the crusader states, summed him up: 'He was a man wise in counsel, valiant in war, and generous beyond measure.'

Saladin's troops, as imagined by a western fourteenth-century artist.

William Marshal

TOURNAMENT CHAMPION AND STATESMAN

1147–1219

'Have I not the hammer and anvil with which to forge finer sons?' So said John FitzGilbert, the marshal, in 1152 when he learned that his son, who had been handed over to King Stephen as a hostage, was to be killed. However, after threatening to hurl the boy into Newbury castle from a siege engine, Stephen was charmed by him, and spared him. This boy was William Marshal, who would grow up to become a chivalric hero, earl of Pembroke, marshal of England, and saviour of the realm in the aftermath of King John's disastrous reign.

William's life is described in a lengthy narrative poem, the *Histoire de Guillaume le Maréchal*. Written soon after his death, this records many of the stories William must have told about his career. It was designed to show William as a chivalric hero, and this creates problems, for there may be some inventive exaggeration. Did he really, when in brief captivity, bind up his wounds with bandages smuggled in a loaf of bread by a female admirer? The tale is perhaps too good to be true.

William was a fourth son, so his prospects were slender. He had to make his own way in the world, and he did so with staggering success. Born in 1147, at thirteen he was sent to Normandy to be trained in the household of his relative, William de Tancarville. Here he acquired his famed prowess with lance and sword. He would also have learned about the knightly values of loyalty, liberality, courtliness and piety.

William spent many years on the tournament circuit, and proved to be one of the outstanding champions of the age, a superstar. Tournaments in the twelfth century were not the courtly jousting festivals of the later Middle Ages; they were battles in miniature. Fierce blows were exchanged: after one tournament William was found with a blacksmith hammering his helmet back into shape so that he could take it off. Prizes for the most gallant brought honour rather than fortune, as William discovered when he was awarded a two-and-a-half foot long pike (which was probably rotting by the time he received it). It was by taking horses, and capturing rival knights for ransom, that profits were to be gained.

So noted an exponent of chivalry was an obvious choice to act as a tutor to Henry II of England's son, the Young King. This would test William's loyalty, for the foolish and unreliable Young King rebelled in 1173–74. William supported him; a knight should not show disloyalty to his lord. In 1182, however, William left the Young King's service. He suffered exile for a time, but his reputation remained intact, and he returned to the Young King's service shortly before the latter's death in 1183. William remained in royal service when Richard I became king in 1189. On the death of his brother in 1194, William gained the family lands and the hereditary position of marshal. Over the next decade, the defence of Normandy against the French occupied much of his attention.

Richard I died in 1199. In the next reign, that of King John, the Marshal had his loyalty put to the test. The loss of Normandy in 1204 meant that he faced the prospect of losing his estates there. Although these were worth far less than his possessions in England, Wales and Ireland, the Marshal made a deal with the French king Philip Augustus, and performed homage to him for his lands in France. This meant that when John demanded that the Marshal accompany him on campaign in Poitou in 1205, he was met with a refusal. In the next year, the Marshal left John's court, for Wales and then Ireland, where he held Leinster. John may have been a disastrous king, but he had sharp political instincts, and realised the value of restoring the Marshal to the fold. Back in favour by 1212, the Marshal stood by John in the political disputes which led to Magna Carta. The principle of loyalty overrode any inevitable misgivings he had about John's rule.

For a poor knight on the make the chivalric virtue of liberality was not always easy to display. On one occasion, early in his career, William met a monk who was eloping with a young woman. When the monk showed his money, and explained that he intended to live off the interest it could earn, William seized it all from him. He did this, he explained, as usury was a sin. This may seem ungenerous, but William then showed his liberality by divid-

ing the money between his companions. On one occasion, when he did well in a tournament, he gave away his winnings. Later in his life, as a result of a good marriage to a wealthy heiress, William possessed the title of earl of Pembroke, broad acres and full money chests. He could more easily afford to be generous. He was not notably lavish with grants of land to his followers, but they were sufficiently rewarded with cash and with offices. One of William's concerns as death approached was to ensure that the members of his household were given the robes that were due to them.

Of all the chivalric virtues, courtliness is, in the Marshal's case, the hardest to assess. The *Histoire* is sadly uninformative about the

William Marshal's effigy, on his tomb in the Temple Church, London.

manners of the court, and the treatment of ladies, but its hero was evidently *molt corteise*, 'most courteous'. He was surely good company, cheerful and well-mannered. There is no suggestion that he was prone to swear by God's eyes, legs or teeth, as King Richard and his brother John did. However, the culture of courtly love could lead to misunderstandings, and, as the *Histoire* explains, there was gossip suggesting that William had an improper relationship with the Young King's queen. The tale is perhaps too similar in its theme to some of the romantic literature of the day, and William would surely never have been so disloyal.

William Marshal was a man of conventional piety. He founded three religious houses, one of them in consequence of a vow he made when he feared shipwreck as he crossed the Irish Sea. A chivalrous knight should go to the Holy Land and, after the death of the Young King, William went on pilgrimage to Jerusalem, where he spent two years. The final demonstration of his faith came on his deathbed when he became a knight of the order of the Temple.

The Marshal's greatest achievement came after John's death in 1216. He ensured the succession of the young boy, Henry III, in face of the very real danger that Louis, heir to the French throne, who was backed by many of those who had opposed John, would overthrow the English monarchy. The Marshal had the sense to realise that the royalists should adopt Magna Carta, and reissue it in revised form. He commanded the victorious royalist forces at the battle of Lincoln in 1217, but more importantly, as regent, he began the process of restoring good government. There was little in his earlier career to suggest that he would make a great statesman, but that is what he proved to be.

The great keep at Pembroke castle in Wales, built by William Marshal. Such circular towers were fashionable in England and France in the early thirteenth century.

Pope Innocent III

INFLUENTIAL PONTIFF WITH A SENSE OF HUMOUR

c. 1160—1216

When the church of Santa Maria in Trastevere was reconsecrated in 1215, the city of Rome was lit up with lamps, and purple banners streamed from the rooftops. This was one of the splendid ceremonies during the Fourth Lateran Council, held by Pope Innocent III in order to authorize a new crusade and to reform the Church. Major political questions, such as the succession to the Empire, were hotly debated. Seventy-one decrees dealing with Church reform were passed, without much discussion. Issues of confession, marriage, the payment of tithes, and excommunication were covered, and clerics were forbidden to take part in judgment by ordeal, or to be involved in sentences of death. Nor were they to attend theatrical performances, wear red or green clothes, or store household goods in church. The council was attended by representatives from across Europe and demonstrated how widely accepted Innocent's authority was.

The future pope, Lothar of Segni, was born in about 1160, and brought up in Rome. He studied in Paris, where he gained expertise in theology, and for a shorter time in Bologna, the great European centre of legal learning. His subsequent rise was rapid. In 1189, he became a cardinal deacon; soon he was a cardinal; and then, at the exceptionally young age of thirty-seven, in 1198 he was elected pope, taking the name of Innocent III. As pontiff, Innocent had a clear view of his authority. The relationship between papal power and that of lay rulers was in his view akin to that between the sun and the moon, the latter deriving its light from the former. He expected obedience from lay rulers, and claimed the 'power to root up, to break down, to destroy, and to overthrow, and to build and to plant'. The pope had a plenitude of power, at least in theory.

In practical terms, Innocent transformed the material basis of the papacy. He brought the city of Rome under a significant degree of control, and greatly extended papal authority over what would become known as the Papal States. The march of Ancona, the duchy of Spoleto and the county of Assisi all became papal territory. This was almost as much a family achievement as a papal one; Innocent owed a great deal to his brother, cousins and other relatives.

Hearing cases under canon law occupied much of Innocent's time. He sat in public three times a week to determine issues that could not be resolved by judges delegated to hear cases in the countries they arose. The pope was a skilled lawyer, adept at cutting through procedural nonsense, saying on one occasion: 'We don't want all these preliminaries; get to the point of the matter.' It was not always a matter of finding a compromise. In England, the chapter of Canterbury cathedral was in dispute with the archbishop over his building of a church in Lambeth. Innocent backed the chapter, and the Lambeth church was destroyed. Lesser men, too, might also receive his justice; he was clear that judgment should be delivered without regard to the status of individuals. One such case involved a crusader, who had been captured by Muslims and during a famine had, he claimed, been forced to kill and eat his daughter. He also killed his wife, but could not bear to eat her as well. Innocent's verdict was one of lifelong celibacy, and three years wandering barefoot, after which the case would be reconsidered.

Although Innocent claimed a plenitude of political power, there were limits to what he could do. Controlling monarchs was problematic. Use of the interdict and excommunication could have some impact, but the leverage at the pope's disposal was very limited. The French king Philip Augustus decided to divorce his Danish queen, Ingeborg, after just one night, ostensibly on the grounds that they were too closely related. He then married his mistress, Agnes of Meran. Innocent took a firm line, and imposed an interdict on the French kingdom, but he was never able to persuade the king to take Ingeborg back. In the disputed succession to the Empire, Innocent's role was influential, but his support was not enough to ensure success for the Welf candidate, Otto IV, against the Hohenstaufen, Philip of Swabia. Nor, after Philip's death, was he able to keep Otto to the promises he had made earlier. In the end, Innocent was unable to prevent the outcome he had feared: the Hohenstaufen emperor Frederick II (see pp. 129–32) ruling both Germany and the Regno of southern Italy and Sicily.

Innocent could preach crusades, but not control them. In the Fourth Crusade, firm papal instructions that the crusaders were to proceed directly to the Holy Land, and not attack Byzantine lands, were ignored. Innocent was, however, a realist and a pragmatic politician, and came to take the view that the ensuing sack of Constantinople and the establishment of a Latin empire of Byzantium were acts of divine judgment, a necessary precursor to the reconquest of the Holy Land. The Albigensian Crusade against the heretics in southern France saw Innocent again fail to control a movement he had authorized. He wanted conciliation and moderation; what he got was the horror of heaps of burning bodies.

There was, however, much that was appealing about Innocent. He did his best to reduce the grandeur of the papal court, replacing gold and silver vessels with wooden ones. In the summer, he camped at Subiaco, in the mountains not far from Rome. The noise of the cicadas, the shouts of the peasants, the moaning of the sick, the plagues of flies, were all intolerable. The only thing that made life bearable for his followers was the spiritual guidance the pope provided.

This fresco from the underground church of the monastery of Sacro Speco at Subiaco shows Innocent III wearing a cloth tiara and the white papal pallium, marked with crosses.

The dream of Innocent III, in which St Francis of Assisi held up the collapsing towers of the Lateran church.
This vision is said to have led to the pope giving approval to the Franciscan order.

Innocent III seated on a simple throne, from an early thirteenth-century English manuscript.

Innocent could be witty and occasionally sarcastic. When dealing with a complex case concerning Evesham abbey, he dismissed one lawyer's argument with the words: 'For sure, you and your masters must have drunk a lot of English ale when you learned that.' There was much amusement when the prolific author and would-be archbishop of St David's, Gerald of Wales, was accused of having stolen a horse in his homeland and ridden it to Rome. The key issue was whether the beast was a stallion or a gelding; inspection revealed that it was the latter. Innocent found this hilarious, and Gerald recovered his horse.

Despite his failure to control the crusaders in Constantinople and southern France, and the eventual ineffectiveness of his intervention in the Empire, Innocent undoubtedly enhanced the moral authority of the papacy. He redefined the nature of papal power, and provided it with a more secure base in the Papal States. The Fourth Lateran Council showed how triumphantly he had succeeded.

3.

An Age of Maturity

1200–1300

In the thirteenth century, the rise of the Mongols transformed Asia. These nomadic tribesmen, welded into a single people by Chinggis Khan, were astonishingly successful, creating an empire which stretched from China to eastern Europe. They were seen both as a threat – particularly with their invasions of the west, which began in 1237 with attacks in Russia – and as possible allies for the crusaders against the Mamluks who ruled Egypt. One effect of the Mongol conquests was to open up routes across Asia to China; a succession of European travellers, of whom the most famous was Marco Polo, took the new land-route east, some hoping to convert the heathen, others aiming to make profits from trade.

Crusading in the thirteenth century was far better organized, and far less effective, than in the past. In 1221 and 1250, well thought-out strategies for attacking Egypt foundered in the marshes of the Nile delta. In 1250, the French king Louis IX was captured as his army retreated in disarray towards the Egyptian coast. The survival of the Latin settlements in Palestine hung by a thread, which was finally severed in 1291, when the last crusader city, Acre, fell to well-armed and well-equipped Mamluk forces. This meant that the two military orders, the Templars and the Hospitallers, had lost their main raison d'être. Accusations, many of them bizarre, against the order of the Temple led to its destruction by Philip IV of France; the last master, Jacques de Molay, was burned at the stake in 1314.

Crusading, however, was not limited to the defence of the states in Palestine. Crusaders also fought in those Baltic lands where conversion to Christianity had not taken place. The advance was spearheaded by the German military order of the Teutonic Knights. As they pushed yet further east, into Christian territory, they were defeated in 1242 by Russian troops under Alexander Nevsky on the frozen Lake Peipus.

Since the twelfth century, the Church had felt increasingly threatened by the growth of heretical movements, particularly in northern Italy and southern France. Many of those considered to be heretics maintained a dualist position, holding that there was a good god responsible for the spiritual world, and an evil one controlling the material world. Yet how

This fourteenth-century fresco by Andrea da Bonaiuto in the church of Santa Maria Novella in Florence, shows St Thomas Aquinas enthroned between Biblical figures, as virtues fly above him.

The Sainte-Chapelle in Paris was built on King Louis IX's orders, in the most up-to-date Gothic style, to house his collection of sacred relics.

far the heretics in Italy, France and elsewhere were a coherent, well-organized body, with common doctrines and ideas, is open to question. Their opponents clearly held that they were, but it is hard to credit that the Church faced a conspiracy on the scale that was suggested. The murder of a papal legate in 1208 led to the declaration of the Albigensian Crusade against the Cathar heretics in southern France, which developed into a vicious war of conquest led by Simon de Montfort. The appalling brutality of the crusade has helped to give the Middle Ages a bad name. The new orders of friars, the Dominicans and Franciscans, particularly the former, were another weapon against heresy. With their dedication to preaching and to poverty, the friars were in some ways not dissimilar from the heretics they opposed.

The thirteenth century also saw renewed conflict between papacy and Empire. The emperor Frederick II's power was largely based in his lands in southern Italy and Sicily, where an up-to-date, bureaucratic government had the capacity to raise the funds needed for his campaigns against the Lombard towns. In Germany, there was little possibility of reviving strong centralized imperial authority, though there was still some potential for Frederick and his officials to play a judicial role. Known to contemporaries as 'the wonder of the world', Frederick was a man of wide interests, and his court reflected this, with its philosophers and scientists.

This period saw many architectural triumphs. Gothic forms reached new heights with buildings such as Louis IX's Sainte-Chapelle in Paris. Castle-building too was highly sophisticated. There were magnificent fortresses in the Holy Land; while in Italy, Frederick II's Castel del Monte was particularly remarkable, more for its aesthetic qualities than for military strength. The famous chain of castles built by King Edward I to hold down the Welsh display the architectural skills of masons recruited from Savoy, notably James of St George. A draughtsman, Villard de Honnecourt, recorded many of the period's new architectural details in an extraordinary portfolio.

In Italy, a commercial revolution was taking place, as merchants developed new forms of partnerships, new methods of spreading risk, and new ways of making profits in spite of clerical prohibitions of usury. In the north Italian cities of Lucca, Siena and Florence, firms of merchant bankers were able to raise large sums, both to finance trade across the Alps, reaching the cloth-producing cities of the Low Countries, and also to lend to the papacy, and the English and French monarchies. The approach of the Genoese was more individualistic, but no less successful, as the career of Benedetto Zaccaria shows. An exceptional businessman, he also had much-sought-after expertise in naval warfare.

Meanwhile, difficult philosophical and theological ideas aroused fierce argument, creating ferment in the universities of the thirteenth century. A key issue facing scholars was how to integrate Aristotelian concepts, and those of Islamic writers, with traditional Christian teaching. The Dominican friar Thomas Aquinas, with his voluminous writings, played a leading role in this process. It was dangerous work, given the possibility that it might be declared heretical, but Thomas was thorough and careful, and avoided any such fate.

Among the many chroniclers who described the events of the period, the English monk Matthew Paris stands out. Gossipy and well informed, his interests extended well beyond the England of Henry III on which his work was centred. He was also a fine draughtsman, and was exceptional in illustrating his own work.

Chinggis Khan
(Genghis Khan)

SUPREME NOMADIC CONQUEROR

c. 1160—1227

Rising from obscure origins in Mongolia, Chinggis Khan, often known as Genghis Khan, created the largest empire the world had ever seen. At his death in 1227, his authority extended from the shores of the Black Sea to those of the Pacific Ocean. The Mongols were the most formidable and the most destructive of all the nomadic peoples whose origins lay in the steppes of central Asia.

Chinggis Khan's original name was Temüjin. The story of his childhood is told in the *Secret History of the Mongols*, a work that entwines myth and reality. He was born in the 1160s. His father died, probably poisoned, when Temüjin was thirteen, and his mother was forced to leave the clan. Living in poverty, she fed the family on wild fruit and roots. Temüjin and his brother, Khasar, killed their half-brother in a squabble over a fish they caught, to his mother's understandable irritation. Captured for a time by a rival clan, Temüjin managed to escape. Eventually, his tribe recognized his ability and chose him as their khan in 1189. He then led them in a complicated history of triumphs, betrayals and double-dealing against other steppe peoples, such as the Naimans, the Merkids and the Tatars. If people resisted him, he 'struck the breath from their bodies with the whip of calamity and the sword of annihilation'. At a gathering in 1206, the union of all the Mongol peoples under the supreme rule of Temüjin was confirmed. It was then that he took the title of Chinggis Khan.

Mongol expansion under Chinggis Khan at first took the form of raids intended, above all, to win gold, precious cloths and women. In 1211, his horsemen defeated the formidable army of the Jin of northern China. Two years later, the Mongols advanced in three huge hosts which ravaged Jin territory before departing with astonishing loads of booty. In 1215, the Jin capital, Zhongdu (now Beijing), was besieged and captured. His ambitions were not confined to China. To the west of Mongol territory lay the empire of the Qara-Khitai, which collapsed swiftly before his onslaught. Beyond that was the Muslim Kwārazmian empire, which stretched from the Indus valley to the Persian Gulf. The Mongols invaded in 1219, and in the following year Samarkand and Bukhārā were among the cities taken and pillaged. At the latter, Chinggis Khan told the citizens: 'If you had not committed great sins,

A fourteenth-century Chinese portrait of Chinggis Khan, painted on silk. It is taken from a page in an album depicting several emperors.

Chinggis Khan fighting Chinese troops in a mountain pass,
as shown in a fourteenth-century Persian manuscript.

God would not have sent a punishment like me upon you.' His ablest general, Sübe'etei, continued the campaign by attacking the kingdom of Georgia, crossing the Caucasus and defeating a Russian army, before returning to Mongolia. In the last year of his life, Chinggis Khan once again turned his attention to China, and the Tangut people of the north. After he had their ruler suffocated, he stated: 'While we eat, let us talk of how we made them die and of how we destroyed them. Let us say: "That was the end, they are no more."'

The scale of the destruction the Mongols wrought was massive. At Nishapur, in Persia, orders went out that not even cats and dogs were to be left alive. Four hundred skilled craftsmen were taken prisoner and led away, while all the other inhabitants were killed, their skulls left piled up in gruesome heaps. One estimate is that in China the death toll reached a barely credible eighteen million. Not only was there horrific slaughter in cities both in the Middle East and in China, but the irrigation systems vital to agriculture were also destroyed. Scientific analysis suggests that the Mongol invasions led to such widespread abandonment of cultivation in China as to have had a noticeable effect on CO_2 emissions and hence the global climate.

Mongol armies were very large, with virtually all the male population expected to fight. They were well organized, divided into units of ten thousands, thousands, hundreds and tens. The elite core was provided by Chinggis Khan's household troops, mostly drawn from the tribes who had been consistently loyal to him during his rise to power. Men from defeated peoples, such as Naimans and Merkids, were divided between different units to ensure that their loyalty was to Chinggis Khan rather than to their tribe. The troops were almost all mounted, and armed with short, powerful, composite bows; every man was obliged to provide his own equipment. The *Secret History* states that Chinggis Khan had an army of 30,000 when he fought the disloyal former companion of his youth, Jamuqa, and that in 1206 his commanders led 96,000 men. This would have been a huge force. Other sources give much larger numbers, even up to 800,000, but these cannot be credited.

The Mongols were skilled tacticians. Their nomadic way of life was good training for war. For them, 'the bowl of war to be a basin of rich soup'. The speed of their mounted troops meant that they could avoid hand-to-hand fighting. They were able to manoeuvre rapidly, to split up at times of danger and to recombine when the hammer-blow of a charge was needed. They would break up enemy formations with flank attacks, followed by encirclement, or by feigning retreat. They employed every kind of trickery, such as tying straw dummies onto spare horses to give the impression that their army was far larger than it actually was. Chinggis Khan and his commanders were quick to realize that they needed siege engines to capture cities, so they drew on Chinese and Persian expertise. Chinggis Khan was also well aware of the importance of logistics, telling Sübe'etei, 'Spare your soldiers' mounts lest they become too lean, husband your provisions lest they are used up.'

Chinggis Khan had the political skills to hold a vast empire together. His sons were important in this, but so also were the commanders and officials whose loyalty he obtained by a mixture of threats and rewards. Many decrees were issued, and probably a full codification of laws. A courier system linked the empire together. Merchants were under special protection, for the Mongols realized the benefits of allowing trade to flourish. Religious toleration was needed in such a disparate empire. The Mongol faith was a form of shamanism, but although Chinggis Khan often took the advice of shamans, his respect for them was limited. He declared of one, after he had been brutally killed, that 'he was not loved by Heaven and his life, together with his body, has been carried off'. He took little interest in other religions, thinking the mosque at Bukhārā was the sultan's palace.

Chinggis Khan was devoted to hunting, and to women. The Persian writer Juvaynī explained that he 'had much issue, both male and female, by his wives and concubines', even suggesting that 'the children and grandchildren of Chinggis Khan are ten thousand'. Genetic analysis has shown that a particular form of Y-chromosome is to be found in populations stretching from Uzbekistan to the Pacific. This originated some 1,000 years ago in Mongolia, but its spread came with the growth of Chinggis Khan's empire. It may well be that Chinggis Khan and his sons were responsible for the dissemination of a gene which is now to be found in some 8 per cent of the male population in much of Asia.

There are few individuals who have changed the world as much as Chinggis Khan. Even after his death, Mongol expansion continued. Under his son Ögedei, they threatened western Europe in 1241. By the end of the thirteenth century, Mongol domination of the world, from Asia Minor to China, seemed assured.

Simon de Montfort

LEADER OF THE ALBIGENSIAN CRUSADE

1165–1218

The chronicler Pierre des Vaux-de-Cernay described Simon de Montfort in glowing terms. Tall, with a good head of hair, broad in the shoulder and strong in the arm, he was handsome, agile, eloquent, prudent and chaste. However, Pierre failed to mention one very important characteristic: Simon's ambition.

A minor noble from the Ile-de-France, Montfort had an undistinguished early career. Through his mother, he had a claim to the lands and title of the earldom of Leicester. Conflict between England and France therefore put him in a difficult position, with his loyalties potentially divided. He did not go on the Third Crusade, but first came to prominence with the Fourth. Undoubtedly pious, he was appalled when the Christian city of Zadar in the Balkans was attacked in 1202, and he was not prepared to join in the next stage of the crusade, the assault on Constantinople. Clearly this was a man of principle and piety.

In 1209, he was presented with a quite different crusading opportunity, against the Albigensian heretics in Languedoc. They were Cathars, who were believed to deny baptism, resurrection of the body, and, naturally, the authority of the Church. They would not eat meat or eggs, or drink milk. Though their liturgies and practices were not those of the Church – 'good men', for example, took the place of the priesthood – they were Christian. For their opponents, however, it made sense to exaggerate the distinctiveness of their beliefs, to suggest a widespread conspiracy against the Church, and to claim that they were addicted to homicide, rape, perjury and every sort of crime. 'Attack the followers of heresy more fearlessly than even the Saracens, since heretics are more evil,' was the call of Pope Innocent III (see pp. 105–9). Religious zeal was combined with a desire to acquire land, and the preaching of the crusade met with an enthusiastic response in northern France, though the king, Philip Augustus, would have nothing to do with it.

After initial success in 1209, with the capture of Béziers and surrender of Carcassonne, Montfort was elected as leader of the crusade. 'Oh what foresight in the choice of the prince!' was Pierre des Vaux-de-Cernay's comment. When most of the crusaders departed, Montfort was left in a desperate situation, with no money and few troops. His wife, however, brought reinforcements from the north, and he gradually succeeded in taking stronghold after stronghold. The war was becoming as much one of conquest as of religion.

The seal of Simon de Montfort, showing him hunting rather than at war.

The Albigensian Crusade placed the Languedoc's leading magnate, Raymond VI, count of Toulouse, in an impossible position. Initially excommunicated, he had come to terms with Innocent III, and joined a campaign for which he can have had no sympathy. Desperate to preserve his lands, he looked to the king of Aragon, Pedro II, for assistance. In 1213, they were decisively defeated by Montfort and the crusaders at Muret. Pedro was killed, while Count Raymond fled; it was said that he had so exhausted himself with his mistress on the eve of battle that he was incapable of fighting. Despite his great success, Montfort continued to face stiff resistance. Raymond VII of Toulouse, a more redoubtable warrior than his father, successfully besieged the castle of Beaucaire in 1216, and the rising spread once again. Two years later, Montfort was killed when besieging Toulouse.

As a commander, Montfort had charisma. He had an excellent grasp of strategy, and the experienced, determined northern French knights who followed him were formidable in battle. He also had technology on his side. Trebuchets, operated by counterweights, bombarded Albigensian strongholds. At Lavour, his siege engines battered the walls for six weeks. The river was bridged, and a cat, or movable shelter, was brought up to the walls. The defenders, their morale broken, had no option other than to surrender. There was a poetic justice to his death: he was slain by a stone from a trebuchet operated by some of the women in Toulouse.

The war that Montfort conducted was astonishingly brutal and vindictive. It was total war, marked by massacres and the savage destruction of fields, villages and towns. At Béziers, the abbot of Cîteaux, when told that there were both Catholics and heretics among the townspeople, declared, 'Kill them all, for the Lord knoweth them that are His.' The mass burnings carried out by Montfort's troops, reported exultantly by Pierre des Vaux-de-Cernay, were acts of unimaginable horror. A firm conviction that God was with him no doubt helped Montfort justify his action in blinding ninety-nine men and cutting off their noses. A hundredth man was left with a single eye, so that he could lead the others away. At Lavour, the lady Giralda de Laurac was thrown alive down a well, with stones hurled after her. The townspeople were burned. Chivalry had no place in a holy war.

It can be argued that Montfort should not be judged by the standards of more recent times, and that, as he saw it, he was doing God's will as he watched the smoke from the burning pyres. The combination he displayed of pious righteousness with personal acquisitiveness, as he gained lands and titles, was not judged unacceptable by his contemporaries. Yet the fact that he, and others, thought that what he was doing was right surely cannot justify the horrors that he ordered.

Montfort's death did not end the Albigensian Crusade, although it took the heart out of the campaign. A settlement with Raymond VII of Toulouse was reached in 1229, but the Cathar heresy was not eradicated. There was a horrendous massacre at Monségur in 1244, and inquisitions continued to take place into the early fourteenth century.

Simon de Montfort's second son, also called Simon, used the family claim to the earldom of Leicester, and made his career in England. In his cause against the king, Henry III, he displayed a degree of righteousness, arrogance and conviction which was very reminiscent of his father.

A pyre for burning heretics, shown in a thirteenth-century universal history. The Albigensian Crusade was characterized by many such brutal acts.

Dominic de Guzmán

SAINT, AND FOUNDER OF THE DOMINICAN ORDER

c. 1170–1221

The establishment of the two orders of friars, the Dominicans and the Franciscans, in the early thirteenth century fundamentally transformed the Church. Believers in preaching and in poverty, the friars did not withdraw from the world as monks did, but were itinerant preachers who whipped up religious enthusiasm as they travelled. In many ways, they must have seemed little different from the heretics they combated, but they proved to be a powerful weapon in support of papal policies. The saints who founded the two orders were very different. Francis of Assisi, whose love of animals even extended to worms, is the best known; his Dominican counterpart was less colourful, but quite as influential.

Dominic de Guzmán was born in Castile, in about 1170. He was well educated in the schools of Palencia, studying the liberal arts and theology. According to his biographer Jordan of Saxony, 'he penetrated the arcane aspects of difficult questions, with the humility of his intelligence and his heart'. In 1191 he displayed a radical sense of values when, at a time of acute famine, he gave away all his treasured books and other possessions. He became a Benedictine canon, and in 1203, he accompanied his bishop, Diego of Osma, on a diplomatic mission to Denmark. They returned in 1206, visiting the great abbey of Cîteaux. At Montpellier, they met Arnaud Amaury, abbot of Cîteaux, and the other papal legates who had been commissioned to deal with the heretics of southern France. They were in some despair; Diego and Dominic urged a new approach. Heresy should be combated by preaching, and by matching the austere lifestyle of the Albigensian heretics. A letter from Dominic written in 1208 is indicative of his role in attempting to extirpate heresy. It explains that he was acting under commission from the abbot of Cîteaux, and in it, he set out severe penances for an Albigensian, Pons Roger, who had recanted. Regular floggings and frequent recitals of the Lord's Prayer were part of the recipe, while curiously part of what Dominic demanded was that Pons Roger should live in the manner of an Albigensian 'good man', abstaining from sex, and not eating meat, eggs and cheese, save at Easter, Whitsun and Christmas.

A detail of a fourteenth-century Florentine fresco, showing St Dominic preaching. Black and white dogs, representing Dominican friars, attack some unfortunate heretical wolves.

St Dominic's books springing miraculously out of a fire, in which heretical texts are blazing.

Dominic and Diego took poverty to extremes as they went out on foot, penniless, to preach the word of God. Their success, however, was limited. Dominic believed in taking on the 'good men' directly in intellectual debate; his arguments, however, did not always convince, nor had he developed the tricks of the popular preacher that were needed to whip up support. Matters took a very different turn when the crusade was launched against the heretics, and war replaced persuasion. In 1209, Simon de Montfort (see pp. 118–21) was chosen as the crusade leader. Dominic became a close associate of the fanatical Simon, though he continued to fight with the word rather than the sword. At Fanjeaux he preached amidst the ruins of the village, destroyed by crusaders. A terrified cat jumped up at one of the listeners. It was clearly a demon in disguise, the man obviously a heretic. He was duly burned at the stake. Dominic's role in the Albigensian Crusade is obscure, though he was present with Montfort at many sieges, and took part in the council of war before the battle of Muret in 1213. He may not have participated in the slaughter and many of the horrific burnings that took place, but he accepted and surely encouraged the actions of Simon de Montfort and the crusaders.

Dominic had a small number of close followers, and in 1215 he established a small community with them in a house he was given in Toulouse. This was, above all, a group of preachers, who adopted a rule of total poverty. Dominic received full papal approval early in 1216 for his new order. He sent seven of his followers to Paris in 1217, with instructions to set up a house there. Similar institutions at Bologna, Palencia, Montpellier and Oxford soon ensued. The Dominicans were linked in this way from the first to the leading schools and universities. A general chapter held in 1220 at Bologna was important in setting guidelines. Dominic stressed that the main role of the friars was preaching; at the same time, he emphasized that it was essential that they should have a proper academic education. Dominic's final preaching campaign against heresy took place in northern Italy, in 1220, and achieved little. When he died in 1221, his new order was on the brink of an astonishing expansion.

Although Dominic clearly had fulfilled an inquisitorial role, it was not until 1231 that inquisitions were established by the papacy on a more formal basis. The Dominicans were in the forefront as inquisitors; Robert le Bougre, responsible for the burning of some 180 alleged heretics at Mont-Aimé in Champagne in 1239, was a member of the order, as was Bernard Gui, active in southwestern France in the first quarter of the fourteenth century. By the 1270s there were some 400 Dominican houses in Europe. Members of the order provided some of the leading intellectuals of the age, most notably Thomas Aquinas (see pp. 146–48). Dominic had identified a need. With his advocacy of poverty, his order adopted much of the heretical criticism of the wealth and corruption of the Church. In preaching in ways deliberately designed to appeal to large audiences the Dominicans again used techniques employed by heretical movements. At the same time, total doctrinal orthodoxy, combined with absolute obedience to the papacy, ensured there could be no question of the friars being accused of possessing heretical beliefs themselves.

The Franciscans were not rivals or alternatives to the Dominicans, but emerged in the early thirteenth century alongside them. Their order was also characterized by poverty, preaching and orthodoxy, but it was not involved in the persecution of the Albigensians, and did not fully share the Dominicans' intellectual ambitions. Francis of Assisi lacked Dominic's organizational ability and scholarly rigour, but had a humanity and charisma which contrasted with the austere Castilian.

It is not easy to strip away the layers of eulogy in the sources to discern Dominic's true character. The earliest account of his life, by his successor as head of the Dominican order, Jordan of Saxony, presents a man too good to be true. He loved all the world, and the world loved him. Blessed with a superb intellect, disdainful of worldly trivialities, capable of spending all night in prayer, he was by this account a man of impeccable sanctity. He did, however, admit to preferring conversations with young girls rather than old women, though divine mercy had meant that he had never succumbed to their charms. The reality was surely more complex. The severity of the austere regime he required of his followers is an indication of the level of determination that drove Dominic; this was a man utterly convinced of the rectitude of what he did, who imposed strict discipline on himself and on his followers. At the same time, he was a man of vision, who saw how the Church could be transformed without challenging its fundamental beliefs, and who realized that the heretics could best be countered by adopting some of their methods. If, however, preaching failed, he was content to see heretics herded to the flames.

Robert of Wetherby

A REAL ROBIN HOOD?

d. 1225

In July 1225, a writ was issued authorizing the sheriff of Yorkshire to spend £2 to 'seek the outlaw and evildoer Robert of Wetherby, and to take and hang him'. Later, the sheriff claimed two shillings that he had spent on a chain to hang Robert. The cost of hiring men to capture him came to twenty-eight shillings. This was probably the same man whose name was given in a court record as Robert Hod. The trouble taken to arrest Robert suggests that he was no ordinary criminal. Wetherby is not far from Barnsdale, which was the location of Hood in the early tales about him, and it may well be that stories about Robert developed into the tales of Robin Hood.

Other candidates for a historical Robin Hood have been also suggested, such as an elderly porter with that name in Edward II's household in the 1320s. The early thirteenth century, however, fits far better as a probable date for Hood. By the last quarter of the century, there are records of a number of men with names such as Rabunhod, Robehod or Robynhod, which strongly suggests that the legend was current by that time. In 1282, a French poet had used the names of Robin and Marion for a pastoral romance. There was even a Robin Hood inn in London in 1294. Doubtless stories about the outlaw were told in the thirteenth century, but the earliest reference to tales of Robin Hood is much later, dating from 1377. By 1429, it was possible for a judge to quote the line, 'Robin Hood in Barnsdale stood.' In the early fifteenth century, a Scottish chronicler, Andrew Wyntoun, was the first to include Robin Hood in a historical narrative, placing him in the 1280s. The earliest surviving tale of Robin Hood is

Left *The title page of* A Mery Geste of Robyn Hoode, *printed in the mid-sixteenth century, when tales of the outlaw were very popular.*

Opposite *An archer stands at the top right of this page from the fourteenth-century Luttrell Psalter.*

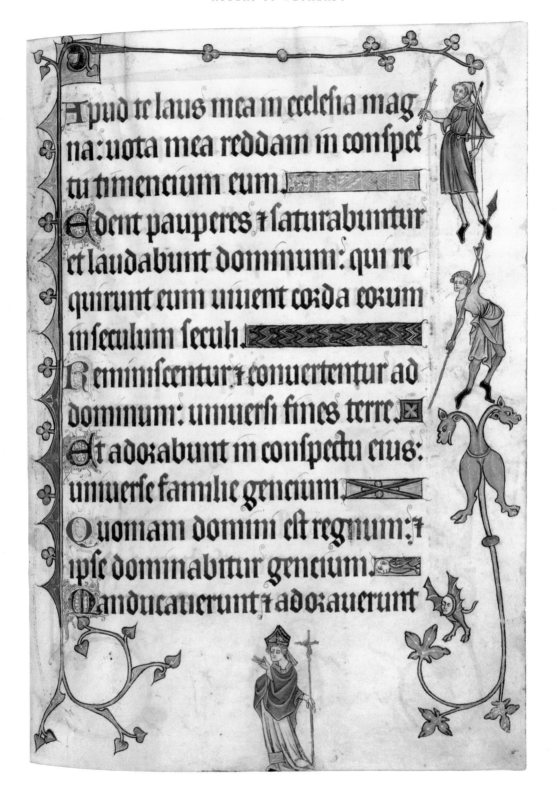

Apud te laus mea in ecclesia magna: uota mea reddam in conspectu timencium eum.

Edent pauperes ⁊ saturabuntur et laudabunt dominum: qui requirunt eum uiuent corda eorum in seculum seculi.

Reminiscentur ⁊ conuertentur ad dominum: uniuersi fines terre.

Et adorabunt in conspectu eius: uniuerse familie gencium.

Quoniam domini est regnum: ⁊ ipse dominabitur gencium.

Manducauerunt ⁊ adorauerunt

contained in a manuscript written in the mid-fifteenth century, and over the next hundred years many versions of the stories were produced.

Much of the content of these tales reflects the society of the fifteenth century, not that of a putative original Robin Hood of the early thirteenth. In the stories, the greenwood, expertise in the use of bow and arrow, the honest outlaws and the evil representatives of authority – above all, the sheriff – provide the unifying themes. Barnsdale provides the setting for the earlier versions of the tales; it was only later that they were placed in Sherwood.

One question about the stories of Robin Hood is whether they were meant to be subversive, offering a vision of an alternative society in which the wealthy oppressors of the time received their just deserts. There is no way of knowing what the audience for the tales was; indeed, there may well have been very different versions told in knightly households and in peasant dwellings. While they are highly critical of some elements of authority, notably the sheriff and the abbot, the stories do not attack the entire social hierarchy. The importance of archery might suggest the tales belonged to a yeoman class, but hunting also gave nobles and knights skills with the bow. Hunting was an upper-class activity, and the expertise in matters of the hunt which many of the stories display implies that it was an upper-class audience that enjoyed hearing about Robin Hood. Indeed, it was members of the upper echelons of society who were most likely to come into contact with the villains of the tales – sheriffs and their men – and to have delighted at stories of their downfall.

The tales of Robin Hood may have been fictional, but there was a real world not so far distant from them. In England, the first half of the fourteenth century in particular saw widespread activity by criminal gangs, often involving members of the gentry. The Coterel and Folville families were notorious in the Midlands for a string of crimes. Extortion and protection rackets were their stock in trade. Justices and jurors were intimidated. In Essex, John FitzWalter besieged the town of Colchester. Even the bishop of Ely used his retainers to subvert the course of justice. The romantic element of the tales also finds an echo in the menacing letter sent by one gang leader, who described himself as Lionel, 'king of the rout of raveners', and dated it at his 'Castle of the Four Winds'. It was against this kind of turbulent background that the original tales of Robin Hood were set.

Frederick II

EMPEROR, AND WONDER OF THE WORLD

1194–1250

According to his contemporary, the chronicler Matthew Paris (see pp. 133–35), Frederick II of Hohenstaufen was *stupor mundi*, the 'wonder of the world'. The last great medieval emperor, Frederick's dominions stretched from Germany to Sicily and even, for a time, as far as Jerusalem. A patron of learning, with a deep interest in science, he ruled a sophisticated state in Sicily and southern Italy, the Regno. Yet there is another side to the story. The chronicler Salimbene, who met Frederick, described him as both 'full of solace, jocund, delightful, fertile in devices' and as 'crafty, wily, avaricious, lustful, malicious, wrathful'. Matthew Paris also reported that 'It was asserted that he did not walk with a firm step in the law of the Lord, being a confederate of Saracens, keeping Saracen harlots as his concubines, and doing other things unfit and too numerous to mention.'

The emperor Frederick II, shown winning Jerusalem by negotiation with the Egyptian sultan al-Kāmil in 1229, from a fourteenth-century chronicle.

The emperor Frederick II, enthroned with a favourite falcon beside him, from a manuscript of his book on falconry,
De Avibus Venandis.

Frederick was the grandson of both the German emperor Frederick Barbarossa (see pp.
90–93) and Roger II, king of Sicily. Though he spent the years from 1212 to 1220 in Germany,
and was crowned king at a splendid ceremony at Aachen in 1215, he remained a child of
southern Italy and Sicily, where he had been raised as a boy. His imperial coronation took
place in 1220. He made every effort to restore royal authority to the Regno, recovering crown
lands that had been lost, establishing effective systems of taxation, and issuing a major law
code, the Constitutions of Melfi, in 1231. An elaborate bureaucracy exercised tight control.
In Germany, however, where royal power had been severely reduced by civil war, Frederick
made no attempt to create the kind of rule that he exercised in the south. A grant in 1220
formalized all the gains that the ecclesiastical princes had made; and, in 1231, a constitution
was issued which confirmed the rights and powers of lay princes. In peace legislation issued at
Mainz in 1235, he created an imperial justiciar for Germany, but Frederick's power north of
the Alps remained very limited.

Although Frederick had taken the cross at the time of his coronation in 1215, he did not set sail for the Holy Land until 1227. When he returned almost immediately, Pope Gregory IX refused to believe that this was due to illness, and excommunicated him. The emperor finally reached the Holy Land the next year. During the eight months he spent there, he succeeded in regaining Jerusalem, but by negotiation rather than by a glorious military victory. Consequently, his enemies claimed that he had said that what he wanted was to hear the call of the muezzins in the city. Rather than establishing much needed strong government in the east, Frederick brought division and distrust.

Meanwhile, papal hostility to Frederick continued to deepen. Alliance with the cities of northern Italy offered the best hope of preventing Frederick from completely encircling the Papal States. In 1237, it seemed that the emperor had triumphed, when he defeated the Lombards at Cortenuova, but Milan held out against him. A crusade was preached against the emperor, and in 1245 he was formally deposed by Pope Innocent IV. Frederick's forces were defeated at Parma in 1248, and by the time of his death in 1250 it had become clear that he could not succeed in northern Italy.

Frederick was the object of both admiration and suspicion, not least because of the exotic character of his court. When Richard of Cornwall, the emperor's brother-in-law, visited him in Italy in 1241 he was thoroughly entertained, with baths, music and, above all, two elegant Arab dancing girls who performed on rolling balls. It was only by Frederick's express permission that Richard was allowed to talk to his sister, for the women of the court were kept in a harem, in eastern style. A splendid zoo, with elephants and camels, accompanied Frederick as he travelled through his dominions.

Frederick's search for knowledge led him to enter into correspondence with the Egyptian sultan, the caliph in Morocco and Jewish scholars in Spain. He posed probing questions to his court scientist, Michael Scot. Where exactly was heaven? Where did salt water come from, and where fresh? What was the explanation for volcanoes? Frederick's scientific learning was demonstrated in the book he wrote on falconry and hawking. Though he used Aristotelian concepts, the book displays very considerable practical expertise and an interest in experimentation. For example, the emperor proved by sewing their eyes closed that vultures find their prey by sight, not smell. Astrology was also a subject of much interest to Frederick, for it had obvious practical political and military applications. Stories later circulated, which were intended to show the emperor in a bad light, satirizing his scientific concerns. Two men were fed dinner. One rested after the meal, the other went out hunting. Both were then disembowelled, to see which had digested his food better.

The Latin of Frederick's cultured court was much admired at the time, but far more remarkable was its lyric poetry in Italian. Dante recognized it an antecedent of his own use of the vernacular in poetry. There was a Provençal influence to the poetry of Frederick's court, which used a familiar framework of ideas about courtly love. Giacomo da Lentini, a royal official, and the most notable court poet, was probably the inventor of the sonnet.

The castles Frederick built in the Regno still reflect his court's grandeur. The finest to survive is Castel del Monte in Apulia. A remarkable and unique building, it is octagonal in plan, with polygonal towers standing at each corner. Its entrance gate, flanked by pilaster columns, reflects Classical forms. Intriguingly, there is no obvious distinction between any of the magnificently vaulted chambers; the castle has no great hall, or throne room.

Frederick is sometimes seen as following in the tolerant tradition of his grandfather Roger II of Sicily. He was prepared to allow his Muslim subjects their own faith, but his action in transporting them en masse from Sicily to Lucera in southern Italy is hardly evidence of enlightenment. Heretics received no sympathy from him. In the Constitutions of Melfi, he decreed that they should be burned. Unlike his son Henry he did not condemn the inquisitor Conrad of Marburg, a fanatical sadist. There was clearly a dark, cruel side to Frederick. When, in 1222, the defeated rebel Sicilian emir, Ibn Abbad, begged for mercy, Frederick viciously cut his side open with his spur. On Frederick's

A page from a French translation of Frederick II's book on falconry, showing owls and other birds, including a peacock.

instructions, over 100 cardinals and prelates captured from the Genoese fleet carrying them to Rome in 1241 were fettered and imprisoned in harsh conditions. In 1249, Frederick turned on his great minister, Piero della Vigna, accusing him of embezzling funds. Blinded and shackled, Piero committed suicide in prison by striking his head against a stone pillar.

Frederick died in 1250; the great, but ultimately unsustainable, Hohenstaufen empire had come to an end, for his son, Conrad IV, was never crowned emperor. Conrad died in 1254, and the Hohenstaufen line finally concluded with the death of his sixteen-year-old son, Conradin, in 1268.

Matthew Paris

CHRONICLER AND ARTIST

c. 1200—59

In 1257, King Henry III of England stayed at the abbey of St Albans for a week. The abbey's chronicler, Matthew Paris, seized the opportunity and spent every moment he could with the king. Henry described the election of his brother, Richard of Cornwall, to be king in Germany (with the title of King of the Romans), listed all the saintly kings of England and, in a prodigious feat of memory, went through the names of all the English baronies he could recall, about 250 of them. It was extraordinary that a king should spend his time like this with a chronicler, but Matthew Paris was no ordinary chronicler.

Matthew was probably about twenty when he became a monk at the Benedictine abbey of St Albans in 1217, and remained based there until his death in 1259. His great work is his

Chronica Majora, which includes much information about European affairs as well as providing an extensive account of events in England. He also wrote a shorter chronicle of English history, an account of the abbots of St Albans and some saints' lives. He accumulated a huge amount of information, and put it all together in a thoroughly readable way. He did not hold back from giving his own views: his account of English politics is thoroughly biased, and all the more interesting as a result.

Historians need evidence. Matthew obtained material from eyewitnesses; he knew a number of royal officials personally. He also relied heavily on documents, collecting as many as he could. He had considerable freedom to leave his monastery for London and elsewhere, and was present at

Matthew Paris drew himself, humbly kneeling in devotion, at the foot of this picture of the Virgin and Child.

grand occasions, such as the marriage of Henry III in 1236, and a grand feast at Westminster in 1247 to celebrate Edward the Confessor. In his entry for 1255, he noted that the French king had given Henry III an elephant as a present; Matthew must have gone to London to see it, for he drew it from life. His description of an extraordinary jewelled wash-bowl in the form of a peacock, presented to Henry III by the French queen, suggests that he had seen this piece of vulgarity in person.

Matthew left England once, when he was invited to Norway in 1248 to reform the island monastery of Nidarholm, in the Trondheimfjord. In some ways, this was the high point of his career. He had already acted on behalf of the house there in a financial matter, but why the Norwegians chose him is a mystery; he did not hold any administrative office at St Albans, and did not have any other obvious experience. Modestly, he had little to say about his Norwegian experience, apart from describing the dreadful fire that consumed most of Bergen, including the royal stone castle. During the fire, lightning struck the mast of Matthew's ship, reducing it to smithereens, but fortunately he was not aboard at the time.

Matthew did not set his *Chronica Majora* in a grand scheme of historical or philosophical development. He interlaced different strands and stories in a year-by-year account. He had an insatiable curiosity, and while political events were to the fore, he included a far greater range of topics in his work than most chroniclers. He provided regular information about the weather and the state of the crops. In 1258, for example, mild autumn weather continued to the end of January, but from then until the end of March a north wind brought freezing weather with frost and snow. At some points, he was more of a tabloid journalist than a historian; he had a good sense of what might appeal to a popular audience. He told of a child of two working miracles in Kent, and reported the discovery, in 1257, of an eight-year-old boy in the Isle of Wight who stopped growing at barely three feet tall, but was normally proportioned. The tale was balanced by one of a boy born in the Welsh borders with a full set of teeth, who grew within six months to the height of a seventeen-year-old. With his keen eye for the unusual, Matthew also noted the accident when workmen digging in London were overcome by a sudden gas explosion, which killed one of them.

A patriotic Englishman, Matthew's political views were strongly affected by his dislike of foreigners, in particular the king's half-brothers from Poitou. In his summary of 1252, he described the country as being under the heel of foreigners, bowing its head to many lords. He was critical of the papacy, which he regarded as exploitative. He suggested that the university of Oxford was quite the equal of Paris's. Of the Savoyard, Peter of Aigueblanche, bishop of Hereford, he wrote that his 'memory exhales a most foul and infernal odour.' However, as he grew older, Matthew became increasingly aware that some of what he wrote was unduly acerbic and provocative, and he went through one version of his chronicle marking some offensive passages. He changed his description of Boniface, archbishop of Canterbury, whom he had considered ill-educated and too young, to say that he was noble and elegant-looking. Regrettably, he did not live through the major political crisis of Henry III's reign, which began in 1258, though it is clear that his sympathies were solidly with the reformers.

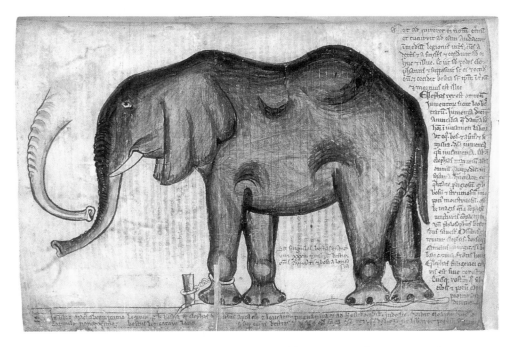

King Henry III was sent an elephant as a present from the French king Louis IX. This is one of two drawings of it by Matthew Paris.

Very unusually, Matthew wrote and illustrated his books himself. He was a self-taught artist of considerable skill. The idiosyncratic style he adopted, with pale colour-washes enhancing line drawings, looked back to Anglo-Saxon methods. His depictions of people are notable; and he had a gift for showing action in an almost cartoon-like manner. Matthew was also a cartographer. The four maps of England and Scotland in his chronicle are far more accurate and detailed than any previous ones. They have north at the top, and use signs for mountains, rivers and towns in a way that may seem obvious today, but which was revolutionary in the thirteenth century.

Gossipy, inquisitive, sometimes careless, always readable, Matthew stands beyond compare among medieval chroniclers.

King Håkon IV of Norway

AMBITIOUS NORWEGIAN RULER

1204–63

I f you came before the Norwegian king Håkon IV, your hair should be brushed, and your beard combed. You should address him politely, with 'God give you a good day, my lord king.' If spoken to by him, you should not say 'Eh', 'Hm', or 'What?' You should not appear wrapped in a cloak, and should not lean across the table towards him. At meals, you should not eat while the king is drinking. Nor should you get drunk, or tell dirty stories.

This was the advice of a remarkable book, *The King's Mirror*, written in the 1250s. It set out ideas about kingship, the royal court and much else in Håkon's Norway. It was intended to provide guidance for the king's heir, Magnus, whose main task as king would be 'to maintain an intelligent government and to seek good solutions for all the difficult problems and demands which come before him'. His rule should follow the fundamental principles of mercy, peace, truth and justice.

When Håkon came to the throne, the country was in a difficult state. From the 1130s until 1240, it had been riven by civil war. This was partly the result of dynastic issues, with rival claims to the throne from different factions, notably the Birchlegs (*Birkebeiner*) and the Croziers (*Baglar*), but there were deeper reasons for the malaise that followed the end of the age of Viking expansion. Although Sverre, the brilliant leader of the Birchlegs, and king from 1177 to 1202, owed much of his military success to recruiting followers from the lower strata of society, it would be wrong to analyse this as an age of class struggle.

Håkon was Sverre's grandson. The tale went that, in a dramatic escape from his enemies the Croziers, the young boy was carried through a blizzard by two Birchleg skiers in a dash over the mountains. He came to the throne in 1217, aged thirteen, on the convenient deaths of the kings of the two factions. His position was initially relatively weak, for Earl Skule Bårdsson, half-brother of the previous Birchleg king, had considerable power. However, by 1240, Håkon had overcome a number of rebellions, in the last of which Skule was killed. In 1247, his standing as king was confirmed in the clearest possible way, when he was crowned by a cardinal sent by Pope Innocent IV.

Håkon was keen to modernize his country. He was exceptional among rulers in having attended school. The saga account of his life suggests that the written word was extensively

The interior of the splendid Håkonshalle in Bergen, built in about 1260 by King Håkon IV in up-to-date Gothic style.

used in his administration, and while his was hardly a bureaucratic monarchy such as those of England or southern Italy, his rule marked a decisive change in the nature of government. There were important legal changes, notably with the New Law of 1260, in which traditional rules for the compensation of victims, and of kindreds, were radically simplified, so that only the closest heir was entitled to reparation. Royal justice, exercised by the king and his officials, increasingly came to replace local methods of resolving conflict. Håkon also strove to bring his court into line with those of other European monarchies. The fine hall of about 1260, the Håkonshalle, which overlooks the entry to the harbour at Bergen, symbolizes this, for it was

built in the style of the Gothic stone halls of England and France. Chivalric romances were translated into Norwegian, replacing the traditional culture of the sagas.

The King's Mirror included military advice, showing that the Norwegians were up to date with the latest technology. A section about siege warfare deals with the most modern engines, describing trebuchets for hurling stones, movable towers, and battering rams. Defenders might employ boiling water, molten glass or molten lead. The use of mines was explained. A touch of imagination was provided when it came to the most potent device of all: the 'stooping shield giant which breathes forth fire and flame'.

Håkon was eager to establish connections abroad. He had diplomatic links with many rulers, who no doubt particularly appreciated his gifts of gerfalcons, the most highly prized of all birds of prey. Henry III of England was even given a polar bear in 1252, which was kept in the Tower of London, and allowed to fish in the Thames, on a long lead.

Under Håkon, Norwegian sovereignty was extended far across the Atlantic, with Shetland, Orkney, the Faroe Islands, Iceland and Greenland all coming under his rule. However, the major overseas military expedition of his reign demonstrated that the Norwegians were no longer capable of emulating the achievements of their Viking predecessors. In 1263, a dispute with the Scots over the Hebrides, which were claimed by Håkon, led to war. As a poet put it:

Scenes of hand-to-hand fighting, depicted in a late fourteenth-century Icelandic manuscript, the Flateyjarbók.

The leader of his people unmoored the ploughers of
the ocean and raised aloft the expanded wings of his
sky-blue doves. Our sovereign, rich in the spoils of
the sea-snake's den, viewed the retiring haven from the
stern of his snorting steed, adorned with ruddy gold.

Fierce storms were a major problem, and the Norwegians achieved little apart from some pillaging on Bute. The expedition culminated in the inconclusive battle of Largs, in Ayrshire, after which Håkon withdrew to Orkney, where he died at the close of the year.

By the time of Håkon's death in 1263, it seemed that Norway was well set on a similar route to the monarchies of England, France and elsewhere. That, however, was not to be. Instead, complex dynastic issues eventually led to the Union of Kalmar of 1396, which saw Sweden, Denmark and Norway united under a single monarchy. As Danish influence over the union grew, Norway became overshadowed and slowly declined.

King Louis IX of France

CRUSADING MONARCH AND SAINT

1214—70

Military success was normally essential for a medieval king's reputation. With Louis IX, king of France, the contrary was the case, for it was his conspicuous failure in a noble cause that enhanced his standing. He led two disastrous crusading expeditions; he was taken prisoner on the first, and died on the second.

Louis succeeded to the French throne in 1226, at the age of twelve. He owed a great deal to his mother, Blanche of Castile, who successfully held the regency until 1236, and continued to exercise a strong influence over her son until her death in 1252. According to Louis's biographer, Jean de Joinville, she even did her best to control Louis's private life, for she 'would never, if she could help it, suffer her son to be in his wife's company, unless at night, when he went to bed with her'.

Louis took the cross in 1244, as he was recovering from a severe illness. In that year, the situation in the east was critical. Jerusalem, regained for Christendom by treaty in 1229, was lost. The Egyptians, allied with Kwārazmian Turks, then won a major victory against the crusaders and their Syrian allies. A new crusade was urgently needed, but it took four years to plan and prepare the expedition. There was a large-scale recruitment campaign, and massive fund-raising efforts. Louis had a grand new fortified harbour constructed on the Mediterranean coast at Aigues-Mortes. Ships were hired, and arrangements made to collect foodstuffs and store them in Cyprus. The force that eventually sailed in the summer of 1248 numbered about 15,000. It was probably the best organized of all the crusading expeditions.

The destination of Louis's crusade, after it had wintered in Cyprus, was not the Holy Land itself, but Egypt, repeating the

King Louis IX, as depicted in a sculpture in the lower chapel in the Sainte-Chapelle in Paris.

Louis IX about to sail for France from the Holy Land, in 1254.

strategy of the Fifth Crusade. It made sense to launch a direct attack on the main enemy of what was left of the crusader states. In 1249, all went well at the outset: Louis jumped from his ship into the sea, water up to his armpits, and strode ashore in Egypt. The Nile delta port of Damietta was soon taken. The first major battle took place at Mansoura in February 1250. Louis wore a golden helmet, and had a sword of German steel in his hand. When half a dozen Turks seized his horse's bridle, and began to lead him away, he bravely drove them off, slashing at them with his sword. The Egyptian forces were compelled to withdraw, but this was no decisive Christian victory. In the aftermath of Mansoura, the crusader army suffered badly from disease, particularly scurvy, and starvation. Louis himself was captured as the crusaders straggled back to Damietta, suffering appalling casualties. Despite his courage, he had shown little strategic or tactical skill; believing that faith alone would engender victory. His idea of protecting his men from incendiary ammunition hurled by the enemy's engines was to sit up in bed, weeping and praying, 'Gracious Lord, guard my people for me!'

After lengthy negotiations, Louis was ransomed. His sense of dedication led him to stay in the east, doing all he could to secure the crusader states. The failure of the crusade greatly affected him; humility became a keynote of his behaviour. In 1254, he finally returned to a France impoverished by the financial strain imposed by his expedition and captivity. He nevertheless remained devoted to the crusading cause. In the 1260s, the Egyptian sultan, Baibars, began to capture one crusader port after another. Once again, a new crusade was needed. Louis directed the crusade, which began in 1270. The destination was Tunis; Louis was probably misled into thinking it both nearer to Egypt and more important to Baibars than it was. The expedition was a disaster. Disease hit the crusader camp, and Louis himself. He died before it had become clear that the only option was to come to terms with the ruler of Tunis and withdraw. Of all the crusaders, it was only Edward of England, the future Edward I, who continued to the Holy Land.

Ships being loaded ready for a crusade, from the fourteenth-century statutes of the chivalric Order of the Knot.

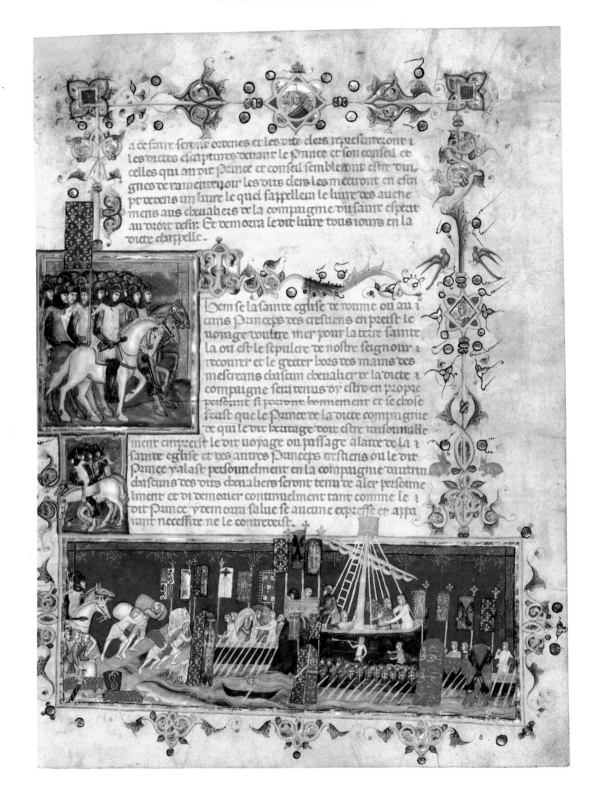

It was not the crusades alone that made Louis IX's reputation. Under him, the French monarchy was fundamentally reshaped. Royal administration was greatly improved by measures such as the introduction of *enquêteurs* (roving commissioners) in 1247 to oversee officials throughout France. The king expected high standards from all who served him, as was stressed in a major royal ordinance of 1254. The coinage was transformed, with the introduction of the silver *gros tournois* and the gold *écu*. Joinville stressed the king's reputation for justice; more and more cases came under royal jurisdiction, to be dealt with fairly and effectively. His verdicts were sought beyond the boundaries of France, as when he settled the issue of the succession to the county of Hainault, and arbitrated between Henry III of England and his political opponents, led by Simon de Montfort.

The religious elements of kingship were important to Louis. He was not the first to claim the power to heal scrofula, the 'king's evil', but he placed a far greater emphasis on this than previous monarchs. The Sainte-Chapelle, completed just before he went on crusade in 1248, was built to house relics of the Passion, and was at the same time a powerful visual representation of monarchy, with its stained-glass depictions of Old Testament rulers. The building of a new nave at Saint-Denis, and the construction of new royal tombs in 1264, further reinforced the image of the French monarchy.

Louis appears most vividly and at his most human in Joinville's biography of him. His book is a rarity, written as it was by a knight, rather than by a monastic chronicler or cleric. It depicts a king who was modest in dress, ate whatever was put in front of him, and watered his wine. He would happily wash the feet of the poor, to whom he gave generously. He did not like to hear people swearing, once punishing a foul-mouthed goldsmith by tying him to a ladder, with pigs' intestines wound round his neck, right up to his nose. In a celebrated passage, Joinville told of how, in summer, the king would sit in the forest of Vincennes, his back to an oak tree, hearing legal cases. Or he might do justice in the public gardens of Paris, simply dressed, hair well combed, seated with his companions on a carpet. Above all, Joinville describes a king dedicated to the crusading cause.

Louis raised the French monarchy to new heights of prestige with a combination on the one hand of personal humility and piety, and on the other a belief in his royal authority that he felt was a divine mission. He set an example – firmly cemented by his sanctification in 1297 – that was impossible to follow. At the same time, the failure of his crusades was a death knell for the kingdom of Jerusalem and the other Latin states in the east. Despite all the administrative skill and vast resources put into his expeditions, it was not possible to replicate the successes of earlier crusaders. Whether a different leader with greater military experience could have achieved more is an unanswerable question. There can, however, be no doubt that Louis, for all his religious faith and personal courage, was the wrong man in the wrong place as the crusaders struggled through the Nile delta in those awful days of 1250.

Alexander Nevsky

RUSSIAN HERO AND SAINT

1220–63

The legend of Alexander Nevsky, sainted by the Russian Church, is powerful. It has been enhanced by Sergei Eisenstein's great film, with its vivid depiction of the battle fought on the frozen surface of Lake Peipus in 1242. According to Alexander's medieval biographer, describing the prince's famous victory over the German Teutonic Knights, 'The clash of lances and the sound of breaking swords resounded in the still of the icy lake. No one could see the ice because it was covered with blood.' It led, during the Second World War, to Alexander becoming a powerful symbol of Soviet resistance to the Germans.

Alexander was born in 1220, the son of Grand Prince Yaroslav, ruler of the northern Russian principality of Vladimir-Susdal. Russia at the time faced many threats. Sweden was one; Swedish Vikings had traded and plundered along the Russian rivers since the ninth century. Lithuania had not been converted to Christianity, and from the 1230s under its ruler Mindaugas its armies frequently invaded Russian territory. The German Teutonic Knights were a crusading order, whose focus had shifted from fighting Muslims in the Holy Land to the Baltic. They spearheaded German expansion eastwards. The newest and most formidable threat came from the Mongols, or Tatars as they were usually called in Russia. There seemed to be no way to counter the swift mounted archers who came like a tidal wave in 1237. The Mongols had the capability to conduct siege warfare; the town of Vladimir was taken in 1238, its inhabitants put to the sword or burned alive in the cathedral. It was the death of Ögedei Khan in 1241, rather than Russian resistance, that brought the terrifying invasion to a conclusion. In southern Russia, however, the Mongols of the Golden Horde were now established as a major power.

A still from Sergei Eisenstein's great 1938 film, Alexander Nevsky, *showing the battle on the ice at Lake Peipus.*

A different type of threat came from the papacy. Russian Christianity was that of the Orthodox Church in Constantinople, the result of the missionary activity of Saints Cyril and Methodius in the ninth century. The papacy, though, was keen to see its influence expand to the east, and was happy to see the Teutonic Knights lead crusading activity not only against the pagans of the Baltic, but also against Orthodox Christians.

Alexander was a young man of twenty when his father gave him responsibility for defending the frontier regions of Novgorod and Pskov. In 1240, he campaigned against the Swedes with considerable success. His troops won a striking victory at the river Neva; he was apparently inspired when told of a vision in which the martyrs Boris and Gleb appeared. It was this success that, much later, earned Alexander his sobriquet Nevsky, from the name of the river where he had triumphed.

In 1242, the Teutonic Knights invaded. Initially, some of the Russian scouting parties were routed, but at the frozen Lake Peipus (also known as Chud), Alexander drew up his army ready for battle. His forces were substantial, for he was joined by his younger brother Andrey, who had brought reinforcements from Vladimir. The Teutonic Knights made the mistake of charging headlong at the Russian ranks, forcing their way through, only to be surrounded. A merciless rout followed. The Russian *Novgorod Chronicle*, anxious to make the most of the victory, held that 400 Germans were killed and fifty knights captured. In contrast, a German account explained that only twenty Teutonic Knights were killed, and six captured, in a battle where they had been outnumbered sixty to one. Whatever the true figures were, this was a great Russian triumph.

The Teutonic knights remained formidable after their defeat by Alexander Nevsky, as their fourteenth-century castle at Malbork in Poland shows.

Alexander's father, Yaroslav, died in 1246. A complex succession dispute was resolved when, thanks to Mongol intervention and support, Alexander became ruler of Kiev, and his brother Andrey received Vladimir. Alexander's interests, however, remained in the north, where his rivalry with Andrey was divisive. Political skill and good fortune saw him become Grand Prince of Vladimir in 1152, after Andrey and another brother, Yaroslav, had been defeated in battle by the Mongols.

Alexander did not oppose the Mongols as he had the Teutonic Knights. Rather, he was totally subservient to them. In 1257, his son Vasili, prince of Novgorod, took a different attitude when he opposed the taxes needed to pay off the Mongols. Alexander dealt with this savagely: 'He cut off the noses of some, and took out the eyes of others, of those who had led Vasili to evil.' In 1259, 'the accursed raw-eating Tartars, Berkai and Kasachik, came with their wives, and many others, and there was a great tumult in Novgorod, and they did much evil in the province, taking contribution for the accursed Tartars'. Three years later, there were widespread popular uprisings, and Alexander had to go to the Mongol court to explain his failure to control the country. He was held there for a time, and returned in the following year in very bad health.

Canonized in 1547, Alexander Nevsky was a man of considerable piety, as this seventeenth-century fresco suggests.

A deeply religious man, a firm defender of the Orthodox Church against the papacy, Alexander became a monk on his deathbed in 1263. His great victory on the ice of Lake Peipus marked the end of the Teutonic Knights' ambitions in Russia; it also deterred the Swedes and Finns from causing significant trouble. Other aspects of Alexander's career were less heroic. He backed the Mongols against his own brothers, and supported them in levying taxes in Novgorod. By the end of his life, he was little more than a puppet ruler controlled by the Mongols. This was a man whose immense reputation was deserved only in part.

Thomas Aquinas

PHILOSOPHER, THEOLOGIAN AND SAINT

c. 1225–74

The prostitute probably thought her task would be simple. She had been hired by a young man's family to seduce him, as a means of persuading him not to become a friar. The young man, however, was Thomas Aquinas, and she failed dismally in her task.

Thomas came from an aristocratic family in southern Italy. Born in about 1225, he was the youngest of nine children, and was sent at an early age to the great monastery of Monte Cassino. No doubt it was hoped that he would become a monk, but when he was about fifteen the abbot advised him to go to the university of Naples, founded by the emperor Frederick II (see pp. 129–32) in 1224. There, Thomas became a Dominican friar. His family was furious, and arranged for his kidnapping. No less a person than one of the emperor's chief advisers, Piero della Vigna, was involved. Thomas was held in the family castle of Roccasecca for a year. Every effort, including the hire of the prostitute, was made to dissuade him from his chosen vocation, but a life of study, teaching and poverty was what he wanted.

Paris was the next step. Thomas probably completed the initial stage of learning, known as the seven liberal arts, there. More

The apotheosis of Thomas Aquinas, painted at Pisa in the fourteenth century.

importantly, he began studying with the great German theologian and friar, Albertus Magnus. Albertus was commissioned by the Dominican order to set up a school in Cologne, and when he went there in 1248 he took Thomas with him. Four years later, Thomas returned to Paris to engage in the threefold activity expected of a friar at a university: to expound the Scriptures, to dispute and to teach.

In Paris, the university was in turmoil. The divisions were not simply a matter of secular teachers against the friars; there was also deep rivalry between the Dominicans and the Franciscans. When Thomas gave his inaugural lecture, the venue had to be protected by royal archers. The Dominicans were not popular; their action in breaking a strike at the university in 1231 had not been forgotten. On one occasion, a university beadle interrupted Thomas in the middle of a sermon, to advertise a book directed against the friars. Thomas was very clear in his views. One of his polemical works ended as follows:

A late fifteenth-century portrait of Thomas Aquinas by Fra Bartolomeo.

> If anyone would like to contradict this work, let him not go and babble to children,
> but let him write a book and publish it, so that competent persons can judge what
> is true and reject what is false according to the authority of truth.

The rediscovery of Aristotle's work, and the ideas of Avicenna (see pp. 29–32), Averroes and other Islamic scholars, presented a major challenge to established views. Thomas was eager to make use of Aristotelian knowledge, and to incorporate it into his theology. In his commentary on the work of the influential theologian, Peter Lombard, Thomas included over 2,000 quotations from Aristotle.

In 1259 Thomas left Paris, to return to Italy. He spent four years teaching in the Dominican priory in Orvieto; from 1265 to 1268, at the request of his order, he was in Rome, in a Dominican house of study. When he returned to Paris, he faced the arguments of, among others, the Franciscan opponent of Aristotelian ideas, John Pecham, later to become a difficult archbishop of Canterbury. In 1272, the university was once again at fever pitch, with a proposed strike looming, and ferocious arguments between the intellectual followers of Augustine of Hippo and Aristotle. Thomas departed, having been given the task of setting up a new Dominican theological centre wherever he chose. He returned, for the last time, to his homeland of Naples.

An initial 'D' from a fourteenth-century Italian manuscript, showing Thomas Aquinas teaching.

A large fat man with fair hair, Thomas was an extraordinarily productive scholar. In all, he wrote or dictated some two million words. His greatest work, the *Summa theologiae*, which he began in Rome in the 1260s, brought together faith and reason in complex philosophical argument. Much of his work reflects his role as a teacher, with arguments for and against propositions carefully worked through, and texts duly cited. His own handwriting was poor, and much of what he wrote was dictated to his secretaries. There is remarkably little in Thomas's work that relates to contemporary events or issues; he would have been all too well aware of the disputes between the papacy and the Empire under Frederick II, but such matters were not for him to explore. He operated on a higher intellectual and spiritual plane.

Thomas was not an easy person to relate to. Nicknamed 'the dumb ox', he could be taciturn. He would simply leave the room if the conversation drifted away from the serious matters that interested him. Often lost in thought, he was absent-minded, not noticing his surroundings. The story was told of how he was once at dinner with the French king Louis IX (see pp. 139–42) when he suddenly interrupted the conversation by thumping the table and declaring, 'That settles the Manichees!' The dedicated scholar did have a human side, though. He had a low pain threshold, and wanted good warning if he had to undergo bleeding. He was understandably nervous of storms; while still a boy, he had been sleeping close by when his young sister had been killed by lightning.

In December 1273, something happened to Thomas as he was saying mass. It is possible that this was a stroke, although a mystical experience brought on by overwork has also been suggested. He never fully recovered. His decline was exacerbated when he hit his head on a branch while not looking where he was going as he rode his donkey. In the last months of his life, following the incident in December 1273, he never wrote another word, saying: 'I cannot do any more. Everything I have written seems to me a straw in comparison to what I have seen.'

Villard de Honnecourt

ARCHITECTURAL DRAUGHTSMAN

MID-1200S

In contrast to most of those who feature in this book, virtually nothing is known of Villard de Honnecourt's career. He is known solely through the portfolio of drawings he left, which contains sketches and plans of buildings, machines and animals. It is a unique and astonishing work, and a considerable puzzle. Some have seen Villard as a medieval Leonardo; others as an incompetent draughtsman who did not understand the buildings he drew.

Villard came from Picardy, in northern France. To judge from the buildings he recorded, he produced his portfolio in the second quarter of the thirteenth century. He travelled

extensively, making drawings of the cathedrals at Cambrai, Chartres, Laon, Lausanne, Meaux and Reims. He wrote that he was sent to Hungary, but not who sent him, or why. He did not describe himself as 'master', and this, together with the inaccuracies in his drawings, implies that he was not a professional craftsman of any standing. A highly inquisitive man, he was concerned with the practicalities of how buildings were constructed, and how machines worked.

Villard was concerned to demonstrate the geometrical principles that underlay architectural design, though his descriptions of how this worked in practice are hard to comprehend. It is, however, very clear that sophisticated geometry was involved in planning the great cathedrals and churches of medieval Europe. At its simplest, circles, squares and triangles were manipulated to

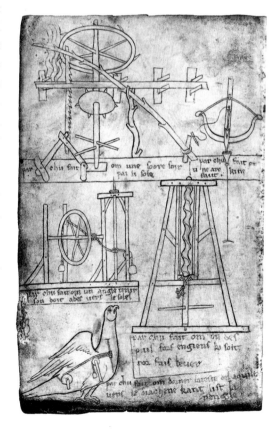

Mechanical devices in Villard's portfolio, with a water-powered saw at the top of the page, and a mechanical lectern at the foot.

149

Villard de Honnecourt intended this drawing of a lion to be particularly lifelike.

provide what were seen as the correct proportions. The principle of root 2 – the relation between the diagonal and the side of a square – was fundamental, yielding as it did the so-called golden section. Buildings could be set out using giant compasses and ropes. Templates were used so that masons could carve complex mouldings. Elaborate window traceries were drawn in full size. By Villard's time, architectural drawings were being used for design purposes; it seems that, rather than basing his depiction of Reims cathedral on his observation of the building itself, Villard used, or rather misused, just such a drawing. While his sketches may not have the accuracy of true plans, they do reveal the excitement of thirteenth-century building, with the ingenuity of features such as flying buttresses, extravagant carvings and elegant designs.

Villard's drawings of machines show a fascination with the curious. In one, a carved eagle forms a lectern, its head moving to face the reader. Another automaton was a device of ropes and weights, with a central spindle used to ensure that a statue of an angel always pointed towards the sun. The same page shows a mechanical saw, operated by a waterwheel. It is easy to see how a lifting hoist, or jack, operated by a screw, would have worked, but there was, of course, no chance that the perpetual motion device – a wheel with movable weights – drawn by Villard, could have functioned. An underwater saw to level off piles is also incomprehensible as he showed it. Villard's plan of a great siege engine, a trebuchet, is the only such to survive. Whereas most of the machines drawn by Villard would be difficult to reconstruct from his drawings, it has proved possible to build a trebuchet based exactly on his design.

Villard's work points to the technological changes that were taking place in the central Middle Ages, and to the enthusiasm that there was for the new. Methods of harnessing power were important. Windmills had first been developed in twelfth-century England. The use of camshafts enabled watermills to be used for tasks such as fulling cloth, as the shaft raised and lowered hammers. Mining was often hampered by underground flooding, and the process of draining was increasingly mechanized, with water and horse power used to keep deep mines open. Metal production was transformed as furnaces were improved. Large cranes, used to unload ships, were also an innovation of the thirteenth century. Horizontal looms enabled the production of wide pieces of cloth. As for Villard's frivolous automata, at the count of Artois's palace at Hesdin, in northern France, visitors in around 1300 were greeted by mechanical monkeys, before being squirted with water and, if they were not careful, covered with soot by ingenious water-driven devices.

Villard de Honnecourt's portfolio is unique and full of delights. One particularly splendid drawing of a lion was, according to Villard, done to show the beast alive, though it was in fact derived from a sculpture at Chartres; his account of how the trainer had two little dogs, which the lion hated to see beaten, however, was surely not an invention. Villard's drawings present many puzzles, although they certainly do not reveal him to be an early Leonardo. They do, however, demonstrate above all the inquisitiveness and inventiveness of the age, a period not of technical stagnation, but of innovation and experiment.

Villard's drawing of a rose window in Lausanne cathedral differs from the original, and was probably drawn from memory.

Benedetto Zaccaria

ENTREPRENEUR AND ADMIRAL

c. 1240–1307

The thirteenth century witnessed a commercial revolution, led by the great Italian ports and cities. It was fuelled by an ever-increasing demand for luxury goods: silks and spices from the east, and fine woollen cloth and other commodities from the Low Countries and elsewhere north of the Alps. Italian colonies flourished in eastern Mediterranean ports such as Acre, Tripoli and Constantinople, where agents bought and sold a bewildering range of items. Italian traders also exchanged goods at the fairs of northern Europe, particularly those held in Champagne. There was increasing specialization, with wealthy sedentary merchants providing the capital for ship-owners and active traders. New ways were developed to invest in trading ventures, with contracts and partnerships, and novel accounting methods were adopted. Bills of exchange provided a convenient means to transfer funds. They made it possible to profit from currency movements, and so avoid the Church's prohibition on interest payments.

This was a world where the bold entrepreneur could make huge profits, and a name for himself. Benedetto Zaccaria was one of the greatest of such men. He was probably born in 1240, to a notable Genoese family, and died in 1307. Operating in partnership with members of his own family, his trading interests extended from the Crimea to the Low Countries, his ships carrying furs from Russia, cloth from Flanders, arms from Italy and many other commodities. He pioneered the direct sea route from the Mediterranean to the North Sea, using a new type of ship, the Genoese *cocha*, or cog, a large sailing vessel that could carry far more cargo than a galley.

Benedetto's fortune was made by alum. Used to fix dyes, it was vital to the cloth industry; much of it came from mines close to Foça, in modern Turkey. In the mid-1270s, the Byzantine emperor Michael VIII Palaiologos granted the port and the mines to Benedetto and his brother, Manuel. They built a fleet to protect the trade from pirates, and kept costs down by using their own ships to take the alum to the west. A surviving contract from 1298 shows how Benedetto with his brother and son agreed a deal for the transport of 650 *cantari* of alum, originally from Foça, to be taken from Aigues-Mortes on the south coast of France to Bruges in the Low Countries. The arrangements were complex, providing

Merchants at work selling cloth in a market, from an Italian fourteenth-century manuscript.

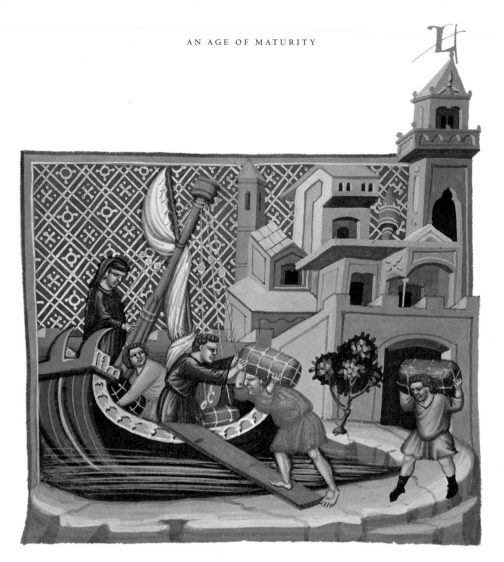

Loading a merchant ship, from an Italian manuscript of Benedetto Zaccaria's day.

various buy-back options, and insurance to cover the long sea journey. Every possible eventuality was considered in a highly sophisticated contract. Benedetto also cornered the market in another important commodity: mastic, a tree gum used in food and as a medicine, which was produced on Chios. In 1304, he was granted the island for ten years by the Byzantine emperor.

As well as establishing such long-term ventures, Benedetto was a great opportunist. On one occasion, he was even able to combine profit and patriotism. In 1276, there was a famine in his home city, and he was contracted to supply wheat from Romania. The famine was dealt with, and he filled his coffers. He regularly invested in other merchants' ventures, acquiring, for example, shares in a Florentine cloth business. In addition, he bought property widely, including a splendid palace.

Benedetto, however, was much more than a merchant. He was also an expert in naval warfare, as he demonstrated spectacularly at the battle of Meloria between the Genoese and the Pisans in 1284. By holding back his galleys until battle was joined, and then attacking the flank of the Pisan fleet, he achieved a decisive victory. His own great galley, the *Divitia* (*Wealth*), had three masts and 140 oars. Benedetto was available for hire as an admiral. He served Sancho IV of Castile for a time, defeated the Moroccans in a naval battle, and took the port of Rabat. In 1294, Philip IV of France appointed Benedetto as his admiral for a war against the English. Benedetto drew up a remarkably detailed and thoroughly realistic plan for raids on English ports, specifying the numbers of troops that would be entailed in the operations, the leadership they needed and the transport, financial and victualling arrangements required.

The negotiating skills that Benedetto learned as a merchant proved valuable to him in diplomacy. There was intense rivalry between the two great trading cities of Genoa and Venice. The conquest of Constantinople in 1204, in the Fourth Crusade, had been engineered in part by the Venetians. Genoa accordingly gave its support to the Byzantines, who retook the city in 1261. Three years later, it was Benedetto who negotiated with the emperor, Michael VIII Palaiologos. He married one of the emperor's relations, and named his son Paleologo in his honour. In 1281, the ruler of Sicily, Charles of Anjou, planned a great expedition to capture Constantinople with Venetian aid. Benedetto acted as one of Michael VIII's agents, negotiating with Charles' opponents, and disbursing funds to them. He was thus at least partly responsible for the rebellion against Charles in 1282 known as the Sicilian Vespers.

Not all of Benedetto's machinations were so successful. His fellow citizens were not impressed by his dealings over the Syrian port of Tripoli in 1288. A commune had seized power there, and Benedetto gave it formal recognition, using the opportunity to negotiate favourable terms for Genoese merchants. He then came to terms with Lucy, sister of the late count of Tripoli, Bohemond VII. He recognized her as countess, provided she acknowledged the commune and its Genoese *podestà* (the city's chief official). Meanwhile, Venetian envoys told the Mamluk sultan Qalā'ūn that the Genoese would destroy the Egyptian export trade if they were allowed to hold Tripoli. The outcome was the loss of Tripoli to Mamluk forces in 1289. The four Genoese galleys in the harbour departed before the end, laden with as many refugees as they could carry.

Trader, entrepreneur, naval commander and diplomat: Benedetto Zaccaria was a man of many talents. His career demonstrated the rewards that ambition and business acumen might bring. His technique of establishing monopolies so that he could buy cheap and sell dear, and his use of cleverly designed contracts, show how advanced — and ruthless — the business practices of medieval Italy were.

James of St George

CASTLE-BUILDER

d. *c.* 1309

In most cases, the identity of those who designed and built the great castles of medieval Europe is not known. An early exception is the sad case of Lanfred, who built a fine castle in the eleventh century at Ivry for a Norman lady, Aubrée. So pleased was she with his work that she had him killed once the castle was completed, lest he should built another as splendid for someone else.

Edward I of England made a surprising choice when he selected Master James of St George to mastermind the great chain of castles constructed to cement the conquest of Wales. After swift success against Llywelyn ap Gruffudd, the Welsh prince, in 1277, new castles were planned at Flint, Rhuddlan, Aberystwyth and Builth. The obvious choice for the work was Robert of Beverley, royal master mason at London and Westminster, but he was still engaged on great building works at the Tower of London. The initial planning of the new castles was therefore entrusted to Master Bertram, an expert engineer, but he too was needed at the Tower, to construct great defensive stone-throwing machines. The king therefore turned to Master James. He was a Savoyard, who came from Saint-Georges-d'Esperanche near Lyon. Edward had encountered his work, and presumably the man himself, when travelling back from crusade in 1273. After Edward's second Welsh campaign in 1282–83, further castles were begun under Master James's guidance, at Conwy, Caernarfon and Harlech. Beaumaris, in Anglesey, was added to their number after a major Welsh rising in 1295.

It is in their details that the castles betray the Savoyard origins of Master James and the masons who worked for him. The use of rounded rather than pointed arches was one characteristic feature, linking Harlech to castles such as Yverdon in modern Switzerland. Placing latrine chutes in the angle where towers abutted on to curtain walls was a method not used by English masons. Holes in the masonry show how the Savoyards used ramps and spiral scaffolds in place of the level platforms normally employed in England. However, the overall conception of the castles, with concentric defences and great twin-towered gatehouses, owed more to English practice than to Savoyard.

Master James did not build to a standard plan. At the first of Edward I's castles, Flint, there was a novel interpretation of a circular keep, which consisted in effect of one drum tower within another, a design that enabled comfortable chambers at the top level to be well lit. At both Conwy and Caernarfon, there was no space for concentric lines of defensive

Details of the design of Harlech castle in Wales, such as the method of scaffolding employed and the form of the windows, link it to the castles of James of St George's homeland in Savoy.

walls; instead, each had two wards, or courtyards, but no outer line of defences. Caernarfon, however, had elaborate gatehouses; Conwy did not. At Caernarfon, the innovative south curtain wall, built in the 1280s, had a shooting gallery running through it: three tiers of arrow loops presented a formidable aspect to any potential attacker. Caernarfon was also unusual in having polygonal, rather than circular towers. The castle was intended to put flesh on the bones of a Welsh legend, which celebrated it as the birthplace of the emperor Constantine. It is likely, therefore, that the castle's style was deliberately chosen to echo the buildings of the Roman Empire; the Roman walls of York, where Constantine was proclaimed emperor, also had polygonal towers.

It would not have been physically possible for Master James to exercise close supervision over the building of all of these castles. It is also likely that the king and his companions took a considerable interest in the overall plans, for they were men of immense military experience. Nevertheless, there is no doubt that Master James had a leading position in the castle-building project. He was termed 'master of the works in Wales', and was rewarded by Edward I with wages of three shillings a day, more than those of a knight, and three times those paid to Master Bertram. Abundant records show the way in which Master James organized his huge labour force and the supply of materials. Significantly, he was appointed as constable of Harlech castle in 1290. This was the kind of position that would normally have gone to a knight; it was wholly exceptional to put a castle in the charge of a master

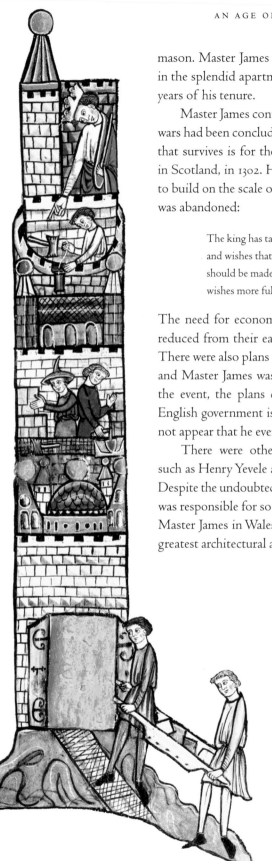

mason. Master James and his wife Ambrosia surely enjoyed residing in the splendid apartments of the great gatehouse there for the three years of his tenure.

Master James continued in Edward's employment after the Welsh wars had been concluded. The one contract between him and the king that survives is for the construction of new defences at Linlithgow, in Scotland, in 1302. However, the resources were no longer available to build on the scale of the past, and the initial plan to build in stone was abandoned:

> The king has taken counsel and has changed his proposal,
> and wishes that in place of these works good gates and towers
> should be made all of wood, as the king has explained his
> wishes more fully to Master James.

The need for economy also meant that Master James's wages were reduced from their earlier level, to one shilling and six pence a day. There were also plans for new castles to command the Firth of Forth, and Master James was doubtless involved in preparing them, but in the event, the plans came to nothing. His last payment from the English government is recorded in 1306; by 1309 he had died. It does not appear that he ever returned to his homeland in Savoy.

There were other great castle-builders in medieval England, such as Henry Yevele and John Lewyn in the late fourteenth century. Despite the undoubted splendour of much of their work, neither man was responsible for so grand a building programme as that headed by Master James in Wales, a man whose castles must rank as one of the greatest architectural achievements of the medieval period.

A thirteenth-century French manuscript illumination, showing builders at work on a tower.

Jacques de Molay

LAST MASTER OF THE TEMPLARS

c. 1244–1314

In the years following the capture of Jerusalem in the First Crusade, the Latin kingdom saw the establishment of several military orders – brotherhoods of knights who took monastic vows of service. The two greatest were the Hospitallers, whose original function was to care for the sick, and the Templars, created in about 1120 to protect pilgrim routes in the Holy Land.

Little is known of Jacques de Molay's career before he became Grand Master of the Temple at a time of crisis for his order. He was a Burgundian, and had joined the Templars in 1265. When he came into office, in 1293, the last remnant of the crusader states, the city of Acre, had fallen to Mamluk forces two years earlier. There were desperate hopes that the Christian position in the east might be re-established. Molay went to France, England and Italy in a futile attempt to try to gather support, men and materials. Raids on the Syrian coast in 1300, in which Molay took part, achieved nothing. Any further dreams that the Templars might play a leading role in recovering the crusader states were soon dashed.

By the beginning of the fourteenth century, the order had become, in effect, a major international bank. The network of Templar houses and properties across Europe, and the links that this provided, put it in an excellent position to transfer money easily across Europe and even beyond. The French crown made much use of the financial facilities the order provided, at a time of severe financial difficulties. King Philip IV had fought an expensive and inconclusive war with the English in the 1290s, and suffered a costly defeat at the hands of the Flemings at Courtrai in 1302. In 1303, the Templars were entrusted with collecting France's war taxation. But taxes were unpopular and difficult to negotiate; that of 1304 was the last major tax of Philip's reign. The currency was heavily debased as a means of raising money. In 1306, the Jews were expelled from the realm, and their property seized. The wealth of the Templars was a very tempting further target.

On 14 September 1307, orders went out in France to prepare for the arrest of all the Templars in the realm. Philip IV claimed to have discovered that newcomers to the order were forced to deny Christ, made to take part in homosexual activity and worshipped idols. Once arrested, in a dawn swoop on 13 October, the Templars were tortured. Of 138 who were questioned in Paris before the French Inquisitor, all but four confessed to some of the charges. Only three, however, assented that they had been forced to engage in homosexual acts;

A late fourteenth-century depiction of Jacques de Molay and Geoffroi de Charny being burned alive as heretics.

one of these claimed to have had sex three times in one night with Jacques de Molay. Molay himself admitted that the initiation ceremony included spitting on the cross, and he agreed to encourage all the Templars to make full confessions.

At the end of December 1307, two cardinals came to Paris. Molay appeared before them, revoked his confession, and ripped off his clothes to show the signs of torture on his body. In the following summer, at Chinon, in the presence of three cardinals, he changed his story again, making a limited confession, and denying that he had been tortured. In November 1309, however, before a papal commission, he said he was astonished at what the Chinon confession contained. He declared his beliefs were orthodox, and said that he would defend himself before the pope.

The issue was very difficult for Pope Clement V. The privileges of the Templars were such that the order was subject only to the papacy; Philip IV had no jurisdiction over them. Early in 1308, Clement suspended the French Inquisitor on whom Philip was relying. In the summer, he absolved the Templars. He was, however, in no position to combat the power and trickery of the French monarchy. His predecessor, Boniface VIII, had been attacked by Philip IV's most important minister, Guillaume de Nogaret, at Anagni in 1303, and Clement could not risk another direct confrontation. He suppressed the order of the Temple in 1312 at the Council of Vienne, and transferred its assets to the Hospitallers.

The end for Molay came in 1314. Along with three senior Templars he appeared in Paris before three cardinals and a number of theologians and canon lawyers. When sentenced to prison, Molay and Geoffroi de Charny, head of the Temple in Normandy, once again denied their confession. They were promptly handed over to royal justice. The king and his council acted with alarming speed; the two men were taken to an island in the Seine and burned as heretics.

It is not surprising that there should have been rumours about the activities of a somewhat secretive order such as the Templars. There was much suspicion about what happened behind the curtains in locked chapels. Most of the evidence, however, was highly suspect, obtained as it was through torture. Accusations about a denial of Christ and spitting on the cross may relate to ways in which the Templars were shown what might happen were they captured in the east. Worship of a mysterious head is most implausible, though charges of homosexuality against members of a male order are easier to credit. There was a plausible accusation against Molay himself:

> Brother Jacques, Grand Master of the Order, when overseas, committed the crime
> of sodomy with a certain servant of his, called George, who he cared for greatly,
> and who was drowned crossing a river.

In contrast to the Albigensian heretics, none of the Templars were prepared to die for the beliefs that they were charged with holding. Rather, they professed their innocence. Philip IV and his officials, however, were all too ready to believe every accusation, and had no doubts about the validity of evidence obtained under extreme pressure. Yet while his belief in the accusations against the Templars was almost certainly genuine, this does not by itself explain why Philip IV behaved as he did.

It is unlikely that Philip IV would have acted against the Templars had he not considered that there would be financial advantages, although the king and his ministers almost certainly overestimated what could be raised. A difficult, withdrawn man, Philip had a strong moral sense, as was shown in 1314 when he had the lovers of his two daughters-in-law brutally executed. He was also sure of his position and the power he possessed as an anointed king. The pope and the Templars could not possibly withstand him.

Jacques de Molay was a tragic figure. It is unlikely that anyone could have saved the Templars, but he was entirely the wrong man to lead them against Philip IV. He did not have a particularly notable career before he was chosen as master; certainly nothing in his experience had prepared him for the ordeals he was to suffer. An elderly man, he was thoroughly confused by his interrogations. He proved incapable of consistency, and unable to put up an effective defence. All he was able to do was show courage at the end.

The arrest of the Templars in 1307, from a late fourteenth-century French chronicle.

Marco Polo

TRAVELLER

c. 1254–1324

I n a Genoese prison at the end of the thirteenth century, a Venetian captive whiled away the time by telling stories about his extraordinary travels to a fellow inmate. The traveller was Marco Polo. His companion, no traveller himself, was an author, Rustichello of Pisa. Marco's tales provided him with fresh inspiration, and the work that resulted, usually known as *The Travels of Marco Polo*, was an enormous success. A form

The book of Marco Polo's travels was extremely popular. This illustration of merchants arriving at Hormuz is from a fifteenth-century manuscript version.

of travel guide, it covers not only China, but devotes many pages to India, places such as Sumatra and Zanzibar, and even extends as far as northern Russia. The book, however, is highly problematical. As a writer of fiction — he had written a book about King Arthur — Rustichello was not above embroidering on what he was told. It has even been suggested that Marco never visited any of the lands that are described.

Even if Marco Polo did not go to all the places mentioned in the book, he was a remarkable traveller. The difficulties in making a journey by land to China, and back to Europe by sea, were immense. Marco and his family were not, however, the first travellers to go to the east. The Mongol conquests had opened up the land routes across Asia to Christian travellers. In 1245, an elderly friar, John of Piano Carpini, led an expedition to Karakorum, and witnessed the enthronement of the Great Khan Güyük in the following year. In 1253, another friar, William of Rubruck, undertook the same journey. The Polos were not alone in seeking new trade routes for silk and spices. Pietro Vilioni, a Venetian, was in Tabriz in 1264. His family was committed to eastern trade; a tombstone at Yangzhou records the death of Catherine Vilioni there in 1342.

Marco Polo's father and uncle probably first set out for China in 1260. They reached Shangdu, the summer palace of the Great Khan Qubilai, and returned to Venice after some ten years. In 1271, they set out again, this time taking Marco with them. By his own account, Marco was entrusted with many missions by the Great Khan, travelling to India and elsewhere. He also claimed to have spent three years as governor of Yangzhou. In 1295, the Polos finally returned to Venice. Following his brief imprisonment in Genoa (he had been captured in a naval battle between the Genoese and the Venetians), Marco married, and spent the rest of his life in his home city. He died in 1324. By that time, there were significant numbers of Italian merchants operating in China, with the Genoese the most active. However, the fragmentation of the Mongol empire, and the eruption of the Black Death in the mid-fourteenth century, brought an end to European ventures across Asia.

Scholars have identified a number of difficulties with Rustichello's account of Marco Polo's travels. As long ago as 1747, it was pointed out that the Great Wall of China is not mentioned. Although the way that Chinese girls walk, placing one foot only just in front of the other, is described, the custom of binding their feet is omitted. Place names are given in a Persian, not a Chinese form. There is nothing about tea-drinking. It is not possible that the Polos were instrumental in introducing trebuchets at the siege of Xiangyang in 1273, as the book claims (other evidence shows that the trebuchets were the work of Arab engineers). It seems most unlikely that Marco Polo could have governed such an important Chinese city such as Yangzhou, and surprising that, if he did, he does not describe the place. It is such points as these that have led to the suggestions that Marco Polo never in fact went to China.

Yet, although there is much undoubted elaboration and invention in the book, many of its descriptions do ring true. The details of how paper money was produced and employed show first-hand knowledge, as does the expertise displayed about finance and taxation. It is not surprising that the Great Wall is absent; though there were various defensive lines, the stone Great Wall as it stands today was built after Polo's time. However, although Marco Polo in fact clearly did go to China, what he provided to Rustichello was in many ways limited to a Mongol view. He knew the Mongol language, but no Chinese dialects. Much of his information therefore was probably gleaned at the Mongol court.

There is a healthy scepticism in the book. Unicorns are identified as rhinoceroses, which, unlike the creatures of myth, are not susceptible to the charms of maidens. Preserved bodies alleged to be pygmies were in fact mummified monkeys. Tibetan magicians were capable of astonishing feats, but 'I will relate none of them in this book of ours; people would be amazed if they heard them, but it would serve no good purpose'. Strikingly, the book does not include accounts of the mysterious races thought to inhabit distant regions; there are no people with heads below their shoulders, or heads like dogs, or ears that hang down to their knees. It was perhaps part of the book's purpose to dismiss such accounts.

Marco Polo's personality is difficult to tease out. As a merchant, he was very interested in the exotic spices and other trade goods, and was clearly expert in financial matters. Animals intrigued him; there is a good description of a giraffe in the book. He was fascinated by sexual customs, explaining that in Tibet, prior to marriage, young women were expected to have at least twenty tokens given to them by men who had slept with them. In the province of Yunnan, 'they reckon it no matter for a man to have intimacy with another's wife, provided the woman be willing.' There was no suggestion, however, that Marco himself took advantage of such customs, though he certainly admired the beauty of many of the women he encountered. Those in Persia, 'in my opinion, are the most handsome in the world'.

Notable and successful as the book of Marco Polo's travels was, it did not meet popular demand as well as the *Travels of Sir John Mandeville*, written in the mid-fourteenth century in the Low Countries. Much of this was a nonsensical farrago, but in providing a lengthy description of the Holy Land, and much improbable detail about strange peoples inhabiting faraway islands, as well as explaining that the world was round, the author of these *Travels* knew just what his readers wanted. In the sixteenth century, it was believed that Columbus had been inspired by reading about Marco Polo's travels to try to reach China by sailing west. Sadly, there is no evidence to show that this was so.

Marco Polo setting out for the east from Venice in 1271, with his father and uncle, according to a late fourteenth-century manuscript.

4.

An Age of Plague

1300–1400

The Black Death of 1348–49 was a catastrophe on an extraordinary scale. It is probable that it killed half the population of Europe, with some regions, towns and villages hit even harder. Nor was this the only outbreak. The disease returned in 1361, and after that epidemics recurred frequently, preventing any significant recovery of the population. Doctors had no remedy, although the papal physician, Guy de Chauliac, identified the different forms the disease might take. Plague altered the age structure of the European population as life expectancy was lowered sharply. After 1348–49, there were social upheavals on a new scale. In France, the rising in 1358 known as the Jacquerie saw the nobility threatened as never before; in England, the Peasants' Revolt of 1381 menaced the accepted order.

Acre, the last crusader city to remain in Christian hands, had fallen in 1291. Crusading, however, did not end with the loss of the lands in the east. The Baltic in particular was a popular destination for those who took the cross, for not all the lands there had yet been converted to Christianity. In Spain, the *Reconquista* continued, though the various kingdoms were not all equally involved. In the north of the peninsula, Pedro IV of Aragon, who also ruled Catalonia, looked instead to expand his influence in the western Mediterranean.

In 1337, war broke out between England and France. This was nothing new; there had been four years of war in the 1290s, and conflict in Gascony in the 1320s. Yet 1337 marked the start of more continuous hostilities. The English king Edward III, who claimed the French throne, won a major victory at Crécy in 1346, and his son, the Black Prince, triumphed ten years later at Poitiers. By the 1370s, however, the pendulum had swung back towards the French, as another of Edward's sons, John of Gaunt, found to his cost. There were periods of truce, but what later became known as the Hundred Years War lasted until 1453. The war was chronicled by many contemporaries, but the most notable was Jean Froissart, whose gossipy, verbose, yet fascinating account, teems with insights into the chivalric world of the later Middle Ages.

Pedro IV of Aragon, the Ceremonious, sculpted by Jaume Cascalls in the fourteenth century, showing the king in the guise of the emperor Charlemagne.

The French war encouraged a new sense of Englishness; but there was an increasingly clear sense of national identity right across Europe in this period. When Petrarch visited Germany in 1333, he was surprised at the cultured atmosphere he found in Cologne, yet still he could not abandon the old stereotype that Germany was the home of the ferocious barbarian, the *Tedesco furor*. In Scotland, the Wars of Independence which began in the late thirteenth century, saw the emergence of powerful patriotic feelings. One of the most notable heroes of Scottish resistance against the English was James Douglas, a close associate of King Robert Bruce.

The election of a Gascon as Pope Clement V in 1305 led to the removal of the papacy from Rome to Avignon. It remained there until 1377. In the following year, two rival popes, Urban VI and Clement VII, were elected, heralding the start of the Great Schism. There was much criticism of the papacy in the fourteenth century; corruption among the clergy was an obvious target. Catherine of Siena, a remarkable young woman, bombarded the authorities with letters demanding reform. She was also anxious to bring to an end the incessant warfare between the rival cities of northern Italy, and even attempted to persuade one of the leading mercenary commanders, John Hawkwood, to leave the country and go on crusade.

Monarchies had style in the fourteenth century. None demonstrate this better than that of the emperor Charles IV in Bohemia. He blended together elements from France, Italy and Germany into a remarkable court in Prague. In Spain, Pedro IV of Aragon in particular was known for his love of ceremony. Grand and splendid as they seemed, however, monarchies were under heavy financial pressure, especially because of the growing costs of war. Kings now found it necessary to negotiate with their subjects in order to raise new taxes. In England and Spain in particular parliamentary institutions developed as subjects demanded redress of their grievances in return for the funds their rulers demanded.

It is invidious to single out the cultural achievements of one country, but what took place in Italy, especially in Florence, in this period was particularly significant. The use of the vernacular in poetry was raised to new heights. The standardization of the Tuscan dialect created a new language of literary expression, with Dante as its leading exponent. There was also a revival of interest in the Classical past among scholars. Manuscripts of ancient authors were collected in profusion, notably by Petrarch. There was a need to edit out the errors that had crept in over centuries of transmission. After a hard day in his Florentine office, the civil servant, Coluccio Salutati, would retire home to his books, and an evening of weeding out copyists' errors from Classical texts. In painting, pictures began to display a new realism, with a fresh characterization of faces quite different from anything seen before – none more so than in the works that brought Giotto such fame. For all its importance, however, late-medieval Italy did not have a cultural monopoly. In England, for example, Chaucer's poetry, above all his *Canterbury Tales*, was outstanding, with its vivid characters, occasional earthy bawdy, and insights.

The Middle Ages were no technological desert. Clockmaking had begun in the late thirteenth century, but it was in the fourteenth that clocks came to be widely used throughout

A detail of a fresco by Giotto in the Scrovegni chapel, Padua, showing the Lamentation of Christ. The faces are painted in far less stylized manner than was usual.

Europe. Timekeeping in cities was transformed, with major consequences for trade and industry. Highly sophisticated timepieces with elaborate gearing systems were developed, their prime purposes astronomical and astrological. In this, Richard of Wallingford was a pioneer. War was a significant driver of technological change. Whereas the thirteenth century had seen the development of huge stone-throwing machines, the fourteenth witnessed the advent of guns. Gunpowder was used in siege warfare in Scotland at the start of the fourteenth century as an explosive or incendiary, and soon after was being employed as a propellant. Edward III used guns in battle in 1346, and by the last quarter of the century large bombards were demonstrating their worth in siege warfare.

Dante Alighieri

GREAT POET, POOR POLITICIAN

1265–1321

Poets do not make good politicians, as Dante Alighieri demonstrated. He was born in Florence in 1265. The city was riven by many disputes; this was a factious world, in which the wheel of fortune turned fast. The main division was between the Guelfs, supporters of the papacy, and the Ghibellines, who backed imperial claims to rule in Italy. A further complication was the division of the Guelfs into a White and a Black faction. Dante was unfortunate to be a Guelf at a time of Ghibelline supremacy, and a White when the Blacks were more powerful.

Dante's family was not aristocratic, but was wealthy enough. His mother died young. His father remarried, and died in 1283, leaving him to look after his half-brothers and sisters. Two years later Dante married Gemma Donati; the couple had four children. Politically ambitious, he became one of the seven priors of the city in 1300. In 1302 he was sent to Rome as one of ambassadors from Florence. While he was out of Florence, the Black Guelfs came into power, and Dante was sentenced to death for corruption, almost certainly a trumped-up charge. He had no choice but to go into exile, and he spent the rest of his life wandering from city to city. There was a moment when he could have gone back to Florence, but the conditions, including as they did public penance, were too severe for such a proud man to accept. Curiously for someone brought up in a Guelf tradition, Dante saw the German emperor, Henry VII, as a possible saviour; in his *Monarchia* he set out his political philosophy, in which he argued for the emperor as supreme ruler. The failure of Henry's Italian campaign in 1313 demonstrated the futility of such views. Neither in practical politics, nor in political theory, did Dante appreciate the realities of power in Italy. He was able, however, to find service with various patrons. Cangrande della Scala of Verona was one, but Dante found his court too frivolous, and in his final years he settled in Ravenna, where he died in 1321.

Political disaster led to poetic triumph. Dante's greatest work was his *Divine Comedy*, a complex allegorical poem which describes in turn hell, purgatory and heaven. He wrote this during his years of exile; the many difficulties he faced as he 'wandered, a pilgrim, almost a beggar displaying against my will the wounds of fortune' proved an inspiration. In the poem, he met figures from the past in the course of an epic journey, while there are many references to contemporary politics. There are high words of praise for Brunetto Latini, from whom

A mezo del camin di nostra uita

Dante, accompanied by Vergil as his guide, explores the underworld, where sins are punished. This illuminated initial 'N' is from a fifteenth-century Italian manuscript.

Dante had learned much, but nevertheless he is placed receiving punishment among the sodomites. Numerological theories run through the work, with each of the three realms divided into nine circles or rings. The verses, linked by rhyme, are each of three lines, symbolizing the Trinity. The poem, which can be read on many levels, shows the punishment of sinners, and the way towards salvation.

A fifteenth-century Italian manuscript illustration of Dante and Vergil being rowed across the river Acheron by the unwilling boatman Charon.

According to the poet himself, a key moment in his life occurred when he was nine, and met Beatrice Portinari, who was a year younger. He encountered her again nine years later, and she became the unattainable object of his adoration. She married in 1287, and died in 1290; even though Dante apparently met her no more than twice, the memory of her was a constant source of inspiration. In the Divine Comedy she takes over from Vergil as his guide, wearing a crown of olives, and a red gown under a green mantle. Dante's wife Gemma, on the other hand, is never directly mentioned in his poetry.

It was remarkable that Dante chose to write so serious a work as the *Divine Comedy* not in Latin, but in his local Tuscan Italian dialect. This was an important moment in the development and standardization of the Italian language. It was Dante, above all, who turned Italian into a great literary language. His influence was swiftly noticed, and by the late fourteenth century Boccaccio was even giving lectures on the subject of Dante's poetry.

Dante was a great man, but not an easy one. His near contemporary, the chronicler Giovanni Villani, who died in 1348, praised him as a great scholar, but at the same time, described him as rather difficult, 'somewhat haughty and reserved and disdainful, and after the fashion of a philosopher, careless of graces and not easy in his converse with laymen'.

In 2008, the Cultural Committee of Florence finally pardoned the poet, and conferred the city's highest honour on his family, by way of compensation for the way he had been treated 706 years earlier.

William Lene

SUCCESSFUL PEASANT FARMER

d. 1329

ot all peasants were poor. When William Lene, of Walsham le Willows in Suffolk, died in 1329, he possessed thirty-seven acres of arable land, as well as some meadow and woodland. He owned a substantial amount of stock: a couple of oxen, eight cows, a bullock, three calves, three horses and a filly. There were 120 sheep, a couple of pigs and eight piglets, as well as geese and chickens. He had two ploughs and a cart. He was married, with three sons (one illegitimate) and two daughters. In his house, he had five brass pots and pans, a jug and basin, cooking implements, a trestle-table with three benches, and a chair, as well as sheets, bedcovers and a couple of tablecloths. His clothes were worth thirteen shillings. Despite the fact that he had three times more land than the average for Walsham, he was a villein, not a free man, and so was obliged to work on his lord's land, as well as tending his own holdings.

Like many villages in East Anglia, Walsham was complicated in its organization. It consisted of two distinct manors and possessed three main open fields, divided into separately owned strips, three woods, and three commons for grazing. Peasants owed rent for their lands; if they were unfree, they also performed labour services. Thus, in 1327, two brothers, John and Adam de Angerhale, owed almost two shillings in rent, as well as half a chicken. They were also obliged to work for twelve days on the lord's land at harvest time, and on ten occasions

Preparation of a meal, from the Luttrell Psalter of about 1340. William Lene's funeral was the occasion for a grand village feast.

during the winter. It was possible to exchange labour services for cash; for example, Emma Stronde paid six shillings to be quit of those she owed on one of her holdings in Walsham.

Manorial courts kept the villagers under tight control. Fines were levied for offences such as selling land without permission, letting pigs root in the meadows, allowing animals to damage the lord's crops or selling ale contrary to the regulations. Payment of debts was enforced; thus Thomas Kyng brought Ralph Wybert to court for not paying the thirteen shillings he owed for an ox. William Lene, however, was one of the more law-abiding villagers, though he was fined on one occasion for damage to the lord's woods, and on another for digging on the common.

The manorial court rolls detail many acquisitions of land by William Lene, who must have made good profits from his farming. East Anglia was the most advanced region of England for agriculture, and it was the peasants, not the lords, who were at the forefront of innovation. One of William's ploughs was shod with iron so that it cut through the ground more easily. Horses were more productive than oxen, and were increasingly favoured by the peasants for ploughing. There was a system of crop rotation, with one field left fallow every year. In addition to cereals, beans and peas were grown, which helped enrich the soil. Crop yields, however, were very low by the standards of later centuries. In a good year, farmers might hope to harvest six times as much wheat as they had sown.

William Lene lived through some tough times. The weather was appalling in 1315 and 1316, with constant rain. Fields were flooded, and crop yields fell to half their normal level. Disease followed on from the rains. Undernourished people lacked resistance, while cattle succumbed to diseases such as rinderpest and sheep died of murrain. Recovery came fairly quickly in the 1320s, and William did not live to see the full horrors that might overcome

A plough, with a team of oxen, from the Luttrell Psalter. William Lene probably used horses for ploughing, as well as oxen.

a village. In 1349, Walsham was hit by the Black Death. The court rolls indicate an overall death rate of at least 50 per cent, with the young and the old particularly hard hit. The village population did not recover to pre-plague levels until the mid-nineteenth century.

It was rare for peasants in William Lene's day to take violent collective action in defence of their rights. After the Black Death of 1348–49, however, times changed. As labour became scarcer with the fall in population, wages rose. Authority was not accepted as easily as in the past, and tension rose between the peasantry and their lords. In Walsham, the 1350 court roll records that some villeins had left, and some services were not performed. Three years later, the peasants refused en masse to do autumn works; they were promised that, if they did agree to work, their fines would be waived. Suffolk was one the counties hit by the Peasants' Revolt in 1381. The rebels were led by a renegade priest, John Wrawe, who helped to whip up hostility to the abbey of Bury St Edmunds in particular. The abbey's prior, a fine musician, was 'condemned to death by the award and judgment of his own serfs and villeins', because of his harsh policies as a landlord. This was a rising not so much of the completely downtrodden, as of those who felt that they could be doing much better were it not for government taxation, and attempts to enforce labour services and keep wages down to pre-plague levels. Further, some peasants bitterly resented their unfree villein status.

Peasants in a village such as Walsham, however, were not solely concerned about purely local matters. Taxation and the requisition of foodstuffs for royal armies brought national affairs home to them, and they were well aware of political events. William Lene must have felt strongly about Edward II's appalling and tyrannical government, for he specified in his will that a pilgrim should be paid to go to the shrine in Yorkshire of Thomas of Lancaster, the greatest earl in England, who had paid with his life in 1322 for rebelling against the king.

William Lene's is ultimately a sad story, for he was in the prime of life when he died in 1329, probably in an accidental fire. His eldest son was only ten at the time. The funeral was a great event in the village. One bullock, six sheep, four piglets, a dozen geese and twenty cockerels were roasted. The bread cost nine shillings. Salt and spices enhanced the meal, and there was ample ale to wash it down. A man such as William deserved a good send-off.

James Douglas

HERO OF SCOTTISH INDEPENDENCE

1286–1330

On Palm Sunday in 1308, a small band of men led by James Douglas burst into the church at Douglas in Lanarkshire. Then and there, they killed some of the English garrison of the local castle, who were attending the service. Others they led back to the castle and down into its cellar. They broke open the barrels of grain and wine, and then slaughtered their prisoners. Blood and brains, grain and wine, were mashed together in a horrific scene.

This tale of the Douglas Larder may be a myth, but it shows the bitterness and brutality of the Scottish Wars of Independence. The origins of the wars lay in the death of the heiress to the Scottish kingdom in 1290. The right of succession was unclear, and the Scots turned to the English king Edward I, for help. After lengthy hearings, the verdict went in favour of John Balliol, rather than his main rival, Robert Bruce, earl of Carrick. Edward I was determined to establish his lordship over Scotland, and when the Scots allied with his enemy, Philip IV of France, in 1295, he moved swiftly. In a rapid campaign in 1296, he secured the abdication of John Balliol. The following year, William Wallace, a man of gentry origin, led an astonishingly successful popular rising against the English. William Douglas, James's father,

Little now remains of Douglas Castle in Lanarkshire, captured by James Douglas in 1308.

and a brutal, violent man, was one of the first nobles to join in. He was also one of the first to be imprisoned by Edward I, dying in custody in 1298.

Edward I further ensured the enmity of James Douglas when he granted the Douglas lands to one of his captains, Robert Clifford. Initially, there was little Douglas could do. He spent a few dissolute years in Paris, and then joined the household of the bishop of St Andrews, William Lamberton. He was one of the first to join Robert Bruce when he seized the Scottish throne in 1306. John Barbour's life of Bruce, written in the 1370s, suggests that it was Douglas who did most to comfort the new king in the difficult days that followed his enthronement. The book emphasizes the role of James, known as the Black Douglas, almost as much as that of Bruce; a life of Douglas was probably one of Barbour's sources. Douglas is described as grey-faced, with black hair, lean, big-boned and broad-shouldered, and he had a slight lisp. Even at the end of a life of conflict, his face was unscarred.

James Douglas was a master of guerrilla warfare. He ambushed one English captain by sending some men to seize a herd of cattle within sight of the enemy. The English pursued them, and were led straight to where Douglas lay hidden, and were massacred. He seized the border castle of Roxburgh early in 1314 in a daring night attack. Pretending to be cows — by going on their hands and knees, with black cloaks over them — Douglas and his men were able to approach the castle undetected, scale the walls with ingenious ladders, and overrun the garrison.

The Douglas monument in St Bride's Church, Douglas. James Douglas died in Spain, but his bones and heart were brought back to Scotland for burial.

The turning point came at Bannockburn in 1314. The Scots had been steadily reducing English-held castles one by one. The great fortress of Stirling was a major obstacle, almost impossible to take by assault. Robert Bruce's brother Edward accordingly reached an agreement with the garrison. If the castle was not relieved by midsummer, it would be surrendered to the Scots. Edward II, who had succeeded to the English throne in 1307, met this challenge with a huge relieving army, which was comprehensively routed in two days of fighting at Bannockburn. The Scottish infantry phalanxes, the schiltroms, held the field. Douglas, who had been knighted on the eve of battle, distinguished himself in the fight. At the end of the battle, he asked permission to pursue the English king. He harassed Edward's troops for sixty miles, all the way to Dunbar, but had too few men to risk attempting to capture him.

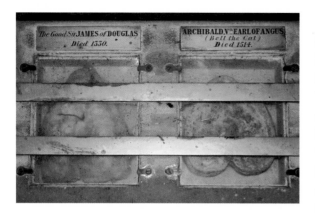

The sealed burial vault, containing James Douglas's heart.

Following Bannockburn, the Scots took the war to the English. Bruce himself took little part in the savage raids in the north of England, but Douglas led many of them. The conventions of chivalric behaviour were not for him, unlike Bruce, who treated those he captured at Bannockburn with courtesy. Villages were burned, crops destroyed and hostages seized as far south as Yorkshire. In 1319, Douglas and Thomas Randolf, earl of Moray, defeated a motley force close to York. Douglas's brutality was revealed when he surprised an English force at Lintalee in 1317; he decapitated a cleric called Elias and stuck the head in the corpse's bottom. In 1327, on his last campaign in England, Douglas almost succeeded in seizing the young Edward III in a daring surprise attack on the English camp at night.

In 1329, as Robert Bruce lay dying – the English claimed he had leprosy – Douglas promised to carry his heart into battle against the Saracens. The king's heart was duly embalmed, and placed in a silver holder for Douglas to wear around his neck. On his way to the Mediterranean, Douglas put in at the port of Sluys in the Low Countries. There was astonishment at the scale of his retinue, which consisted of a banneret (a knight commander), six knights and twenty fine squires, and at the quantity of sumptuous silver plate he used for entertaining guests. Douglas then sailed for Spain, where he joined Alfonso IX of Castile in a campaign against the Moors. In the course of the battle, he and his companions charged as the Castilians stood by, amazed at the rashness of the Scots. Douglas was duly slain, having hurled Bruce's heart at the Moors. It was, however, recovered, to be buried at Melrose abbey.

The Scottish Wars of Independence were not a simple patriotic fight against oppression. Bruce's rising in 1306 began, not with an attack on the English, but with the murder of a Scottish rival, John Comyn. There was an element of civil war to the struggle, as well as resentment of the English. For James Douglas, as Barbour makes clear, a central motive was his determination to recover his family lands. Patriotism, however, cannot be denied. It developed as the war continued, and found lasting expression in the Declaration of Arbroath of 1320:

> As long as a hundred of us remain alive, we will never on any conditions be subjected to the lordship of the English. For we fight not for glory, nor riches, nor honours, but for freedom alone, which no good man gives up except with his life.

Giotto di Bondone

CELEBRITY ARTIST

c. 1267–1337

A ten-year-old boy tending his family's sheep one day passed the time by drawing a picture of them on a convenient flat rock. The painter Cimabue happened to see it and, astonished by the boy's skill, asked if he could take the child as his apprentice to Florence. Soon the boy equalled and surpassed his master, 'introducing the drawing from nature of living persons, which had not been practised for two hundred years'. One day, when Cimabue was out of the workshop, Giotto painted a fly on the face of an unfinished picture. It was so realistic, that on his return, Cimabue tried several times to swat it.

This story is told by Giorgio Vasari in his *Lives of the Painters*, written in the mid-sixteenth century. Once the myth constructed by Vasari is stripped away, there is surprisingly little left to be gleaned from the historical record. Giotto di Bondone was born in the late 1260s. The family did not live in the country; his father was a blacksmith in the parish of Santa Maria Novella, in Florence. In 1301, Giotto owned a house in the same district. He lived for a time in Rome; in 1313, he was attempting to recover goods he had left in a house there. Back in Florence, records show that he was a man of means, employing six lawyers to recover debts he was owed. In the 1320s, he was buying and renting rural property. His renown was such that, in 1334, the city authorities in Florence made him superintendent of works, both of the city and of the cathedral. He should, his letters of appointment stated, 'be welcomed as a great master in his native land and should be held dear in the said city'.

Giotto's Ognissanti Madonna *shows the influence of Byzantine tradition, as well as a new three-dimensional realism.*

Giotto was widely acclaimed by his contemporaries. Soon after his death, the chronicler, Giovanni Villani praised the realism of his art, for he 'more than any other drew each figure and action to the life'. Before Giotto's time, figures with stylized faces had appeared against flat backgrounds – often splendidly gilded – in the Byzantine manner. The start of the move away from this tradition can be seen in Cimabue's work, in which he began to explore the representation of three-dimensional space. Giotto, however, went much further than his master. There was a new realism to the figures he painted, a solidity brought out by the skilled treatment of drapery. The human form is still more sculptural than animated, but Giotto's faces are those of real people. The many scenes in the Arena chapel are set against imaginary rocky landscapes and buildings. Though not painted from life, these provide a far more realistic background than Giotto's audience was accustomed to. Even in the formal *Ognissanti Madonna*, with its traditional gilded background, the throne on which a rather severe Virgin Mary sits with a podgy Christ child on her lap appears fully three-dimensional, as do the draperies of the angels looking on.

Giotto's genius is revealed in his paintings. There has, however, been much argument among art historians over the attribution of work to his brush. In some cases, there is no doubt. Giotto was certainly commissioned by the Scrovegni family to paint the frescoes in the Arena chapel at Padua. The great merchant banking firms, the Bardi and the Peruzzi, turned to Giotto to decorate their chapels in the church of Santa Croce, in Florence. There is, however, considerable doubt over Vasari's statement that Giotto was responsible for the St Francis cycle of frescoes in the upper church at Assisi. Some paintings, such as the *Ognissanti Madonna*, were also certainly by his hand, but in his later years Giotto had a large workshop, with the result that it is often difficult to distinguish his works from those of his apprentices.

The poet Boccaccio, who knew Giotto, described him as ugly. He was also witty. Vasari recounted a conversation he had when he was employed by the king of Naples, Robert of Anjou. 'Giotto, if I were you, now that it is hot, I would give up painting a little,' said King Robert. Giotto replied, 'And so would I, certainly, if I were you.' Dante (see pp. 170–72) visited Giotto when he was working on the Arena chapel, and rudely remarked that it was a pity that the painter's skill at depicting beautiful figures was not matched by his ability to produce beautiful children. Giotto's riposte was that he painted in the light of day, but fathered children in the dark of night.

Giotto was the first celebrity artist. The genius of this small, ugly artist was immediately recognized by his public, as he set painting in a new direction. In contrast to many painters who achieved fame in their lifetime, his reputation has remained intact through all the subsequent changes of style and vagaries of artistic fashion.

Giotto's Last Judgement, *occupying one wall of the Scrovegni chapel at Padua. In it, Enrico Scrovegni is shown presenting a model of the chapel to the Virgin Mary.*

Richard of Wallingford

CLOCKMAKER AND LEPER

c. 1292–1335

In a world without clocks, timekeeping relied upon the sun. Time was particularly important in monastic communities, with their routine of services throughout the day. As the duration of daylight was not constant, the length of the divisions of the day varied through the year. With a clock, the day was divided into equal divisions, without regard to the sun's movements. The change from one form of time to another was revolutionary.

The first mechanical clocks driven by weights appeared in the late thirteenth century. There are references to a *horologe* at Norwich cathedral priory in 1273, and to one at Dunstable priory ten years later. Bartholomew the Clockmaker was employed at St Paul's, London, in 1283. England was ahead of the game; Italy was not far behind. There was a clock in Milan in 1309, and Dante (see pp. 170–72) referred to them twice in his *Divine Comedy*. By the late fourteenth century, clocks were to be found all over Europe, with seventy known in France alone. The rhythm of urban life was being transformed, as clocks came to define hours of work.

In 1302, the prior of Wallingford, in Oxfordshire, adopted a ten-year-old boy mourning the death of his blacksmith father. A few years later the boy, Richard, was sent to university in Oxford. He then entered the monastery of St Albans, later returning to Oxford, where he spent nine years studying and, as he hinted later, enjoying himself. The university, and in particular Merton College, was a major centre for mathematics. Richard wrote a commentary on the astronomical tables collected by John Maudith, a fellow of Merton, and a treatise on trigonometry. Other works followed. He was later said to have regretted not spending more time on the study of theology and philosophy, but that was not where his abilities and interests lay.

Richard was no purely theoretical scientist; he was both a scholar and technician. In 1326, he described two intricate instruments which he had made. One was a complex device of jointed rods for observing the stars and calculating their movement. The other was his 'Albion', which provided a means of calculating the position of the planets by turning a series of disks. Extremely sophisticated mathematics underlay the device. Richard hoped that if the movement of the stars and planets could be observed and calculated accurately, it would be possible to produce reliable astrological predictions. He was particularly interested in the use of astrology in weather forecasting, and wrote a treatise on the subject.

Richard of Wallingford working on an astronomical instrument, his 'Albion'. His books lie on the floor, and a quadrant hangs in a cupboard.

It was said that his astrological skill enabled Richard to predict the death of the abbot of St Albans in the autumn of 1326, and that this was why he returned to the abbey. There, he gave a sermon on the theme that the best man should be elected abbot, and was duly selected himself. As abbot, Richard faced tough challenges. The monks were lax, the abbey's estates were run down and the local townspeople hostile. Richard was not a man for compromise; he had the rigid mind of a mathematician. A stringent financial regime was introduced, and order restored to the abbey's finances; in an extreme measure, thirty-two volumes from the library were sold. Poorly performing estate officials were removed from office. There were no concessions to the townsmen; among other things, they would now have to pay to have their grain milled in the abbot's mills, and could not use their own handmills.

Despite the pressures of administration, Richard continued his scientific work, writing a treatise explaining the mathematical principles behind gears, and designing and supervising the construction of an extraordinary astronomical clock. Unlike a modern clock, it had no hands, but it struck a bell every hour. The huge dial, probably six feet across, was a rotating star map, around which the sun moved on a separate pointer. The clock also gave the times of tides at London Bridge, and displayed the phases of the moon, while a wheel of fortune turned. One of the main problems facing clockmakers was how to make an escapement to regulate the movement, as the pendulum had not come into use. Richard used an ingenious mechanism, known as a verge and foliot, in which a pivoted oscillating beam engaged the clock's cogs. The sun was driven by another clever invention, an oval contrate geared wheel. The clock cost a great deal; even the king, Edward III, criticized Richard for spending so much when the abbey church needed a great deal of rebuilding after years of neglect. Richard, however, was adamant. The money was well spent, for his clock was unequalled in the world.

There were parallels to Richard of Wallingford's clock. In Italy, between 1348 and 1364, Giovanni de Dondi, son of a noted clockmaker, designed and built his own magnificent astronomical clock. This showed the time, the movements of the planets and provided a calendar

that even gave the date and time of eclipses. Clocks such as Richard's and Giovanni's demonstrated the extraordinary technological skills that existed in the fourteenth century, with highly complex systems of gearing demanding remarkably precise metalworking.

Richard's state of health made his achievement all the more remarkable. In 1327, he was struck with acute pain in his left eye, which lasted two years, and left him blind in that eye. Worse followed, for he contracted leprosy. This reduced to him to a state where he could hardly speak. His affliction led an ambitious monk, Richard of Ildesley, to seek to have him removed from his position as abbot. A papal commission reported that he was indeed unfit. The community would not accept this; some large, tough monks even threatened to kill Ildesley, who fled. Richard died in office,

A reproduction of the St Albans clock built by Richard of Wallingford.

This illustration from a mystical treatise by Heinrich Suso, The Clock of Wisdom, *shows the range of clock types that had been developed by the mid-fifteenth century. At centre right is one similar to that built by Richard of Wallingford.*

in 1335, without having suffered the humiliation of ejection and isolation that was so often the fate of lepers.

Richard of Wallingford was an extraordinary genius. In modern terms, he was both an applied mathematician and an engineer. Like many academics, he found himself thrust into an administrative role, in his case as abbot of one of the greatest abbeys in England at a difficult time in its history. The way he carried on his work when afflicted with an appalling disease, half-blind and barely capable of speech, marks him out as truly heroic.

Jean de Lamouilly

GUNPOWDER PIONEER

EARLY 1300S

E dward I, king of England, had no hesitation when it came to recruiting foreign experts. The Savoyard mason, Master James of St George (see pp. 156–58), masterminded his castle-building programme in Wales; Italian bankers provided him with credit; and moneyers from Marseilles provided the technical knowledge to run the mint during his great recoinage of 1279. In 1299, he hired a Frenchman from the county of Bar, Jean de Lamouilly, to be a squire in his household and to assist the siege operations in his Scottish wars.

Jean was an expert in explosives. For the siege of Stirling, in 1304, he acquired sulphur, saltpetre and cotton. Once he added charcoal, he had the three vital components of gunpowder, and cotton to make fuses. The mixture was put into clay pots, to be hurled into the castle. His work was clearly effective, for he was rewarded by the king with £20 'for making Greek fire for burning the houses of the said castle'. The incendiary pots, however, did not bring the siege to an end; that came when the terrified garrison sued for terms at the sight of the king's great siege engine, the Warwolf, long under construction, at last being ready for action.

Jean's use of gunpowder presaged a major development in military technology. In China, gunpowder had been known from the eighth century as an incendiary. The Mongols encountered gunpowder weapons of some kind, probably incendiaries and rockets, during their conquest of the southern Song dynasty in the mid-thirteenth century. Guns were possibly known in China as early as the mid-thirteenth century, though clear evidence for their use in warfare there does not come until a century later. In Europe, the city authorities in Florence ordered the manufacture of guns in 1326. The first known illustration of a gun is in an English manuscript of 1327. This was a treatise written by a minor civil servant for presentation to Edward III. The picture shows a vase-shaped weapon, which fired a dart-like projectile. By the onset of the Hundred Years War in the late 1330s, the English were supplying significant quantities of saltpetre and sulphur for the guns they had installed to defend their castles in Gascony. Guns were used by Edward III at the battle of Crécy in 1346, and by the 1370s the French were employing large siege guns with considerable success. There was

This page from Walter Milemete's treatise on kingship, completed in 1327, contains the earliest picture of a gun. The artist had no understanding of the carriage on which it rests.

no sudden revolution in warfare, however, for it took time to develop the technology for casting reliable gun barrels, and for manufacturing powder and ammunition on the scale that was needed.

Jean de Lamouilly remained in English service after 1304, at least until 1312. The Scottish war went badly for the English, notably with their defeat at Bannockburn in 1314, and it is not surprising that Jean went back to France. In 1317, the earl of Pembroke was returning to England, after taking part in an embassy to the papacy in Avignon, when Jean ambushed him and held him to ransom, demanding £10,400 (about three times his annual income) for his release. Jean was angered because he had not been paid his wages by the English government; one debt to him was for the large sum of £711. Pembroke's discomfort did not last too long; Antonio Pessagno, Edward II's Italian banker, paid £2,500 as a first instalment of the ransom, which was enough to secure the earl's release.

Jean de Lamouilly is little known today, but he deserves to be remembered as a pioneer of military technology. His clay pots at Stirling provide the first documented evidence of the use of gunpowder in warfare in western Europe. Although he did not make the connection, it was not long before it was realized that gunpowder could be used as a propellant – giving birth to the weapon of the future: the gun.

Petrarch
(Francesco Petrarca)

OBSESSIONAL POET

1304—70

One day in church in Avignon, in 1327, a young Italian spotted a beautiful blonde, and was immediately infatuated. He barely knew the woman; they may have exchanged a few words, and she was probably unaware of his adoration – but this was an obsession, not a love affair. The woman was called Laura; the young man was the poet, Petrarch; and the sequence of sonnets he penned expressing his feelings about her is one of the greatest, and most influential, collections of love poetry ever written:

> Twas on the morn, when heaven its blessed ray
> In pity to its suffering master veil'd,
> First did I, Lady, to your beauty yield,
> Of your victorious eyes th' unguarded prey.
> Ah, little reck'd I that, on such a day,
> Needed against love's arrows any shield.

Although it is the poems about Laura that have done most to give Petrarch his lasting fame, his life reveals a far wider range of achievement. He was born in Arezzo, in Tuscany, after his father, a notary, had been exiled from Florence. When he was eight, the family moved to Carpentras, close to Avignon, which had recently become the seat of the papacy. Petrarch studied law at Montpellier for four years, followed by three years at Bologna. However, he did not want a career in law, for he felt that lawyers were dishonest and that, given his scrupulousness, he could not have been successful. Instead, he considered the Church as a profession, taking minor orders. However, friendship with the wealthy Cardinal Colonna provided

Petrarch, as shown in a mid-fifteenth century fresco by Andrea del Castagno.

him with the patronage he needed to fulfil his real ambition, as a man of letters. Petrarch had soon established his literary reputation. In 1341, at the invitation of the Roman senate and with the backing of Robert of Anjou, king of Naples, he was crowned with laurel, as poet laureate, in a ceremony which aped the Classical past. He spent most of the 1350s in Milan, despite attempts by the emperor Charles IV (see pp. 203–6) to persuade him to reside in Prague. Subsequently, Petrarch spent time in Padua and Venice, finally settling near Parma, where he died in 1370.

Petrarch was a compulsive writer: 'I find myself always in a sad and languishing state when I am not writing.' He wanted to equal the authors of the Classical past, whom he revered, so he wrote a lengthy epic poem in Latin, *Africa*, about the defeat of Hannibal by Scipio the Elder. No doubt he hoped to achieve fame with this, but it has deservedly been little read. Of his other Latin works, it is his many letters, which he carefully collected, that became well-known. His style was clear and Classical, avoiding the baroque elaborations of thirteenth-century style exemplified by the letters of Piero della Vigna, minister of the emperor Frederick II (see pp. 129–32). Writing to Boccaccio, Petrarch acknowledged that Latin was a noble language, one that he felt could not be improved. The vernacular, on the other hand, still had great scope for improvement, as he demonstrated in the numerous sonnets that he wrote in Italian, not least the many he wrote about his love for Laura.

The object of Petrarch's obsession was probably Laura de Noves. She was younger than Petrarch, married, had ten children, and died from the Black Death in 1348. Petrarch's

Love aiming an arrow at Laura, while Petrarch looks up from his book. A scene from a fifteenth-century fresco.

Pallida non ma piu che neue biancha
Che senza uenti in un bel colle fiocchi
Parea possar come persona stancha
Quasi un dolce dormir ne suo begliocchi
Essendo il spirto gia da lei diuiso
Era quel che morir chiaman li scioechi
Morte bella parea nel suo bel uiso.

An illustration from a late fifteenth-century manuscript of Petrarch's poetry, showing him in conversation with the dead Laura.

love-struck attitude, however, did not prevent him from having a mistress and two children of his own. In none of his voluminous writings did he reveal his mistress's name or express any affection for her. His view was probably that which he put in an imaginary dialogue with St Augustine of Hippo, in which the latter declared: 'Few indeed there be who, having once imbibed the sweet passion of desire, manfully endeavour to grasp the truly foul character of woman's person.' At the age of forty, soon after the birth of his daughter, Petrarch gave up sex, 'a disgusting slavery which had always been hateful to me'. In a letter of 1352 to his brother, who had become a monk, he wrote that 'although I am still subject to severe and frequent temptations, I have but to recollect what woman really is, in order to dispel all temptation and return to my normal peace and liberty'. Petrarch thus exemplified two quite different contemporary attitudes to women. In one, they were seen as inferior and lecherous, a temptation responsible for man's downfall. The other, characterized by the cult of the Virgin, idealized and honoured women, emphasizing their beauty and chastity. Petrarch, confused and guilty about sex, expressed one view in his sonnets, and the other in his letters, apparently without realising the contradictions involved.

Petrarch was an avid reader and an obsessional book collector. He built up a vast library of manuscripts, mostly Classical texts, some of which he had rediscovered. Cicero and Vergil were his particular favourites. He abhorred anything written later than the early Christian fathers; for him, there was a dark age from the end of the Roman Empire to his present day. He had a deep distaste for the scholastic theology of figures such as Thomas Aquinas (see pp. 146–48).

Petrarch described himself as 'comely enough in my best days', with a complexion neither dark not fair, good eyesight – until he had to start wearing glasses after he turned sixty – and good health up to his old age. He also recorded his 'deep-seated and innate repugnance to city life'. He had a house in Vaucluse, in Provence, where he lived for several periods until the early 1350s. He described his life there, where 'the only sounds are the occasional lowings of cattle and bleatings of sheep, the song of the birds, and the ceaseless murmur of the stream'. The food was simple. 'Grapes, figs, nuts and almonds are my delicacies. And I thoroughly enjoy the little fish which abound in the river.' The most famous example of his awareness of his surroundings came when, in 1336, he climbed Mont Ventoux, in Provence, 'to see what so great an elevation had to offer'. Once at the summit, however, he soon tired of the vistas, took out his copy of St Augustine's *Confessions*, and began to read.

Petrarch was much more than a sad, if eloquent, victim of unrequited love. Remarkably self-aware, he has justifiably been seen as the pioneer of a new humanism, and as a man prepared to disclose his inner thoughts in a new way.

John Crabbe

NOTORIOUS PIRATE

d. 1352

Piracy pays. It may not always do so, but it certainly did for the Fleming, John Crabbe. In 1306, he lay in wait near La Rochelle, and seized a ship sailing close to the French coastline as it returned from Gascony to Dordrecht with a cargo of 160 tuns of wine. Crabbe burned the ship, and kidnapped its crew. Attempts by the ship's owner to obtain compensation from Robert, count of Flanders, lasted four years, but Crabbe was never brought to court. In 1310, he struck again when he attacked an English ship in the straits of Dover. Crabbe was clearly something of an embarrassment to the count of

The English victory at the battle of Sluys in 1340, in which John Crabbe played a leading role, from a manuscript of Froissart's Chronicles.

Flanders, and he moved his base of operations to Scotland, England's bitter foe. In 1311, he was quick to snatch a couple of ships belonging to Newcastle merchants.

The years 1315–16 saw northern Europe in the grip of a famine of unprecedented scale. Fields drenched by incessant rain were incapable of providing the crops that were so desperately needed. The count of Flanders reacted by recalling Crabbe, appointing him admiral of a fleet, and commissioning him to purchase food, or seize it from any enemy ships. He duly captured three English vessels. A chronicler in the Low Countries commented: 'He wrought great damage on the seas, showing mercy to no one. Now he appeared here, now there. Now he served one person, next he turned against him and sought the favour of another.'

When Crabbe returned to Scotland, he revealed new talents. In 1319, the English besieged Berwick, and Crabbe took charge of the construction of war machines, even using Greek fire (probably an oily combustible mixture) to defend the town. In 1332, an English force invaded Scotland in a private act of war, with tacit government approval. Crabbe assembled a fleet and attacked the English ships as they lay in the Firth of Tay. He took one English ship, but the wind changed and so did his fortunes. Although he escaped, his ships were all sunk. Worse followed when he was taken prisoner by Walter de Mauny, a knight from Hainault, who was to provide King Edward III with distinguished service in the Hundred Years War. A chronicler rejoiced at the capture of 'that worst pirate John Crabbe, who had wrought carnage at sea against the English for many years'. Crabbe, however, was not a man to tolerate imprisonment for long. Perhaps persuaded by Mauny, he changed sides. In 1333, he assisted Edward III in attacking Berwick, the town he had once protected. He received a full royal pardon for all his past activities, and was made constable of Somerton castle in Lincolnshire.

In 1335, Crabbe was back at sea, this time with a squadron of ten ships in English service. With the outbreak of war with France in 1337, Crabbe proved to be of immense value to Edward III. The high point of his career came in 1340, when he was employed to organize the English fleet. News had come that the French had assembled a huge navy in the Low Countries, in the Zwyn estuary. Crabbe's advice was that it was too dangerous to challenge the French, but Edward III took a different view. In a dramatic sea battle the English fleet destroyed the French as they lay at anchor off Sluys. Naval tactics in this period largely consisted of crashing ships together, boarding and fighting hand to hand. The way that the French, under the command of a Genoese admiral, Pietro Barbavera, had chained their ships together made the English task easier and their longbowmen proved highly effective. Late in the battle, one group of enemy ships succeeded in making their escape. It was Crabbe who was ordered to make chase. Much of the credit for Sluys must go to Crabbe, whose knowledge of the difficult waters of the Zwyn estuary was essential. The victory, in which French losses were probably three times as great as the total of those at the battle of Trafalgar, was one of the great English triumphs of the Hundred Years War. However, it marked the end of the active career of this turncoat pirate, who had become a respected servant of the English crown.

Guillaume Cale

PEASANT LEADER

d. 1358

In late May 1358, the peasantry of the Beauvaisis region to the north of Paris, turned on the local nobility in what became known as the Jacquerie. Mob violence spread like a forest fire. Castles and lordly residences were stormed by enraged peasants. They killed any nobles they could find, slaughtering their wives and children. Everything possible was set ablaze. The chronicler, Jean Froissart (see pp. 229–31), told of a knight roasted on a spit. His wife was gang-raped, forced to eat his flesh and then killed.

Charles of Navarre supervising the execution of the peasant leader, Guillaume Cale, as shown in a late fourteenth-century French chronicle.

Cy puse de la bataille a meaulx
en brye ou les Jacques fuct
desconfitz par lecote de foix
z le captal de bens. z est
xvº.xvº. Chapitre.

Nce temps que ces
meschans gens
couuient reuin
drent de prince
le conte de foix z le captal
de bens son cousin. si enten
dirent en leur chemin ainsi
comme ilz deuoient entrer
en france la pestilence qui
estoit sur les nobles homes.
Si entendirent en la cite de

chalons que la duchesse de
normandie z la duchesse
dorleans et bien .iii. dames
z damoyselles et le duc dor
leans aussi estoient en
meaulx en brye retraitz pour
celle Jacquerie. Lors saccor
derent ces deux cheualiers
quilz yroient voir ces da
mes z les conforteroient
a leur pouoir combien q
le captal estoit anglois.
mais treues estoient entre
les roys de france z dagletre.
Si pouoient estre en leur
route enuiron .lx. lances.

The speed with which the rising spread strongly suggests that it was premeditated and planned, with messages sent from village to village. Once it started, a leader soon emerged among the peasantry, in Guillaume Cale. A well-built, eloquent man, he came from Mello in the Beauvaisis. He possessed a seal, which suggests that he was reasonably wealthy, and he clearly had military experience. His forces, said to have totalled some 5,000 men, bore banners patriotically bearing the fleur-de-lys.

Cale was quick to make common cause with the people of Paris, where Etienne Marcel, provost of the merchants, had whipped up popular hostility to the government. In February 1358, the mob had forced its way into the palace of the Louvre. Two marshals of France had been killed in the presence of the terrified dauphin. This was a revolution. The crimson and blue colours of Marcel's supporters were everywhere. Paris was put into a state of defence, fearing attack from the dauphin's troops. On 14 May, the government ordered all castles around Paris to be garrisoned and put into a state of defence, a highly inflammatory move. Marcel may not have instigated the initial rising in the Beauvaisis, but he gave the Jacques — as the peasant rebels were known — every encouragement. He commissioned one peasant leader to destroy all the castles and noble residences between the rivers Seine and the Oise. At Ermenonville, Cale's peasants and Parisian militias combined to take the castle held by the royal chamberlain, Robert de Lorris. He and his family were spared; the Parisians did not indulge in the orgies of killing that characterized the actions of the peasants.

The rising lasted no more than a month. Charles the Bad, king of Navarre and count of Evreux, soon began to restore order. In June, his forces confronted the peasant army at Mello. Cale had drawn his men up carefully, interestingly much as the English had done at the battle of Crécy in 1346. Archers and crossbowmen were in front, and baggage carts formed a defensive enclosure to the rear. The armies faced each other for three days. Then, on 10 June, Cale was invited to discuss a truce. Contrary to the conventions of war, he was seized and put in irons. The peasant army was routed, and Cale was beheaded.

Cale's death was followed by further scenes of bloody revenge by the nobility, who committed many atrocities equalling those of the Jacques. In one, some 300 peasants were burned alive in a monastery where they had taken refuge. In village after village, the cry was heard: 'Death to the villeins!' At Meaux, a group of Jacques had joined forces with some Parisians. The mayor had opened the city gates to them, while the dauphin's wife and children, her sister, various other ladies and a small garrison were in the castle, along with the Gascon lord, Jean de Grailly, and the count of Foix. These two were returning home after crusading in the Baltic, and had chivalrously come to Meaux to rescue the ladies. At the head of a troop of about twenty-five men, the two crusaders charged into the peasant ranks. What followed was brutal butchery. Froissart put the death toll at 7,000.

The massacre of the peasant rebels at Meaux by troops led by Jean de Grailly and the count of Foix, from a manuscript of Jean Froissart's Chronicles.

Pardons issued later suggest that the Jacques were keen to force men of rank and experience to lead them. Germain de Réveillon, a member of the count of Montfort's household, had been compelled to lead a group for thirty-six hours. As a result, his property was devastated in revenge once the rising was over, and he and his family had to go into hiding. A man called Colart du Four had been compelled to join the Jacques by threats that his house would be burned and his head chopped off. He had managed to escape from them, and had not 'pillaged, set fires, or committed other evils', but the nobles sacked his lands, and he and his wife had to take refuge in the woods.

There were many similarities between the Jacquerie and the Peasants' Revolt of 1381 in England. Like Cale, Wat Tyler emerged from obscurity to lead the peasants. Like the Jacques, some of the English rebels tried to force knights to join them. Like the Parisians, the Londoners had links with the peasants. Cale was seized when trying to negotiate, and Tyler was slain by the mayor of London when he appeared before the young King Richard II. Weakness of government and failure in war were important causes of both risings. When the Jacquerie occurred, the French king John II was a prisoner in England, having been captured at the battle of Poitiers in 1356. In England in 1381, the king was a minor. The peasants of the Beauvaisis felt betrayed by the nobility, which proved incapable of providing protection from the freebooting mercenary companies ravaging France. For the English rebels of 1381, recent French raids on the south coast had brought the war home as never before. In Kent, in particular, the peasantry felt ill-protected. The wider economic and social changes that followed the Black Death also formed part of the longer-term background to both peasant risings.

While political, military and social circumstances can explain in part why the peasantry of the Beauvaisis and those of southeastern England turned so savagely on the authorities, the human element of leadership should also be considered. In Guillaume Cale and Wat Tyler the peasants of France and England found that leadership. For all that both men failed, they must have possessed considerable qualities. Cale, in particular, was a persuasive man, who knew how to whip up support for his cause. He had organizing ability, and realized the importance of gaining the support of the Parisians. Yet, although the rising appeared at first to show how flimsy the mechanisms of social control were, in the end, the Jacquerie, like the Peasants' Revolt in England, was crushed. Aristocratic power was not to be broken.

Guy de Chauliac

PIONEERING DOCTOR

c. 1300–68

During the Mongol siege of the Genoese trading outpost of Caffa in the Crimea, in 1347, the besiegers lobbed corpses infected by a strange and deadly disease into the city. The plague was then brought to Italy on Genoese ships fleeing the Mongol onslaught; within a couple of years it spread through all of Europe, and even reached distant Iceland. People had no immunity; death rates varied from place to place, but overall it is likely that half of the European population died.

The plague, or Black Death, presented doctors with an impossible challenge. The most notable medical expert of the day was Guy de Chauliac, the pope's personal physician. He came from a humble family in central France. The local chatelaine sent the talented boy to study medicine, first at Toulouse, and then at Montpellier. A desire for further learning took him to Bologna in the mid-1320s. There, Chauliac was taught by Niccolo Bertuccio, who explained that an alternative to studying anatomy in books was to dissect executed criminals. Chauliac also went to Paris, but nothing more is known of his career until 1344, when he became a canon at Lyon. In 1348, he moved to Avignon, the seat of the papacy at that time, where he was a papal chaplain and physician, first to Innocent VI, and then to Urban V. He remained in post until his death in 1368.

Chauliac observed the plague closely, perhaps too closely, for he caught the disease, but was fortunate enough to recover from it. He criticized his fellow doctors:

> They do not dare to visit the sick, for fear of being infected. And if they do visit, they do nothing and gain nothing from it, for all the sick die, except for a few at the end who escape after the buboes had run their course.

He explained that there were two distinct forms of the illness: one invariably fatal, in which the lungs were affected; the other, characterized by black abscesses and swellings. In his view, with which the Paris medical faculty concurred, the overall cause was astrological, the result of the conjunction of Saturn, Jupiter and Mars. He prescribed cordials, purging and bleeding as preventatives, and also advocated lighting fires to improve the quality of the air; this was duly done in the papal apartments. While his treatments made little sense, Chauliac's analysis of the disease was remarkable, for no one else registered the distinction between the pneumonic and bubonic forms of plague.

Guy de Chauliac, with three patients, who present problems with an arm, an eye and the genitals. An illustration from a fifteenth-century manuscript of Guy's Chirurgia Magna.

In 1363, Chauliac completed his great, encyclopaedic work on surgery, the *Chirurgia Magna*. Immensely successful, it continued to be used as a standard medical textbook until the seventeenth century. It was heavily dependent on writers from the Classical past, notably Hippocrates and Galen, while also relying on Avicenna (see pp. 29–32). A more immediate source was the early fourteenth-century work of the French doctor Henri de Mondeville. Chauliac did not follow his authorities blindly, but showed a keen critical sense.

For Chauliac the doctrine of the humours (choleric, melancholic, sanguine and phlegmatic) was of central importance, for a proper balance was essential for health. A sufferer from elephantiasis should, for example, avoid meat that was considered melancholic, such as beef and venison. His discussion of how he dealt with a ruptured hernia using a curved knife shows that he was far from being a theoretical academic. He operated on cataracts, and described the procedure in detail. Invasive surgery, however, was dangerous, and the scale of intervention that he advocated was limited. Personal observation led him to note the different herbs that women in Montpellier, Paris and Bologna used to dye their hair. Predictably, obstetrics did not feature at any length in his work; these were matters to be dealt with by expert women.

There has been much argument over the nature of the plague that swept through Europe in the mid-fourteenth century and which Guy de Chauliac described so well. The high level of mortality and details of the symptoms do not tally with twentieth-century outbreaks of plague. Nor is there archaeological evidence for a widespread population of rats; these are normally thought to have carried the fleas that bore the disease. Furthermore, the Black Death spread far faster than any recent plague. DNA analysis of the remains of plague victims, however, has shown that the pathogen was indeed *Yersinia pestis*, the plague bacterium.

Victims of the plague, showing the characteristic buboes and abscesses, in an illustration from the early fifteenth-century Swiss Toggenburg Bible.

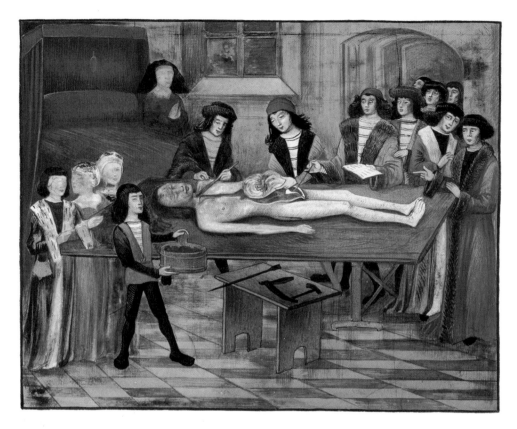

A fifteenth-century illustration of the dissection of a corpse, from a manuscript of Guy de Chauliac's Chirurgia Magna.

The impact of the Black Death was immense. The demographic dynamic of Europe had slowed by the fourteenth century, but was transformed by the epidemic. The first outbreak of plague was followed by many others, preventing any recovery of the population for at least a century. The psychological effects must have been profound. Chroniclers varied in their views of the immediate reaction to the epidemic. In Florence, according to Boccaccio, some decided 'to drink heavily, enjoy life to the full, go round singing and merrymaking, gratify all one's craving whenever the opportunity offered'. In contrast, a French chronicler, Jean de Venette, reported that men became more miserly, and more quarrelsome, resulting in fights and lawsuits. He also noted that those born soon after the plague had fewer teeth than was normal. Yet society survived. While the plague had enormous repercussions throughout Europe and beyond, the resilience of society faced with an unimaginable disaster was astonishing.

Charles IV of Bohemia

EMPEROR AND CREATOR OF A CAPITAL

1316–78

At the battle of Crécy in 1346, during the Hundred Years War between England and France, the blind and elderly John of Luxembourg, king of Bohemia, insisted that his knights should lead him into battle against the English. When the fighting was over, with the French and their allies defeated, John and his men were found slain. His son Charles, however, showing more sense and less chivalry, had fled the field.

Born in 1316, Charles had been educated at the French court. Given his father's incapacity, his rule in Bohemia effectively began in 1334. John of Luxembourg had acquired Bohemia through marriage, and Charles was therefore able to present himself through his mother as the heir of the Přemyslid dynasty. He acquired some estates in Germany through purchase and inheritance, but it was the Bohemian lands that were his powerbase. Soon after his father's death at Crécy, Charles was crowned King of the Romans, the title accorded to a future emperor. In 1355, he was crowned emperor in Rome. His main qualification for the imperial throne was the weakness of his position; he offered little threat to the powerful German principalities and towns that had dominated the country after the collapse of Hohenstaufen rule in 1250. In Italy, Charles had even less power. He died in 1378, with no great military victories to his name, but having successfully built up his wealth and power, doubling the territory he ruled.

The emperor Charles IV, shown with the relic of the Holy Thorn, in a fresco at his castle at Karlštejn.

According to Charles himself, when he first came to Prague:

> We had nowhere to live, save in houses in the town like any other citizen. The castle
> in Prague was completely desolate, destroyed and ruined, for it had been levelled
> to the ground since the time of King Ottokar. We had a beautiful large palace built
> at great cost there, as you can see to this day.

The new palace was built in French style, with a splendid entrance reached by a great staircase, opening on to a magnificent hall. The building of St Vitus's cathedral, inspired if not paid for by Charles, began in 1344, when the bishopric was elevated to an archbishopric; the first architect hailed from Arras, and on his death in 1356 the celebrated Peter Parler, a master mason from southern Germany, took over. In 1348, the complete transformation of Prague was begun, with the foundation of the New Town. The walled circuit stretched for two miles. Nine churches and religious houses were founded by Charles himself. In 1357, building of the Charles Bridge began, replacing an older structure destroyed in 1342. The dominating Old Town Tower at one end was started later, in about 1370. A further important development was the foundation of the university, by means of a papal bull in 1347 and a royal charter in the following year.

Not far distant from Prague, Charles rebuilt Karlštejn castle, remarkable not for its fortifications, but for the astonishingly lavish interior. The staircase to the Holy Cross chapel was decorated with scenes from the lives of St Wenceslaus and St Ludmilla. Within, the walls gleamed with gold and semiprecious stones. Relics gave a special sanctity, while paintings set out a complex religious message. This chapel glorified not only the heavenly kingdom, but also the Empire and the Luxembourg dynasty. The mastermind behind all this magnificent display was Charles's court painter, Theodoric, who was rewarded with a tax-free estate.

Charles was not physically impressive. He was of medium height, slightly bent in posture as he thrust his head forward. He was bald, had a broad face with full cheeks, protruding eyes and a black beard. Towards the end of his life, he suffered badly from gout. He had considerable linguistic gifts, being fluent in Czech, French, German, Italian and Latin. Rare among monarchs, he was an author. He wrote a life of St Wenceslaus, and contributed extensively to a chronicle; he considered that it was important that there should be a proper history of Bohemia. Above all, he wrote an autobiography, which covers dynastic matters and his military exploits in Italy, as well as providing a tale about things that go bump in the night. Regrettably, it closes in 1346.

A man of great piety, Charles was an exceptionally avid collector of relics. St Vitus's cathedral in Prague benefited from this; Charles was devoted to Saint-Denis and gave the cathedral part of the saint's head, and a portion of an arm. He was prone on occasion to

In this votive panel Charles IV is shown in the top row of figures, kneeling before the Madonna.

visions; in one, as he reported to the pope, an angel castrated the dauphin of Vienne with a sword, because of his sins.

Charles's autobiography provides insights into his religiosity, but, perhaps because it only deals with his early career, there is no hint in it that he had artistic interests. An account of his visit to Paris in 1378, however, suggests that he was an eager collector. He received a great many splendid gifts, but asked in addition for a book of hours. Offered a choice of two by the French king, one large, one small, he decided to keep both. He was so impressed by a new crown that he asked to meet the goldsmith responsible.

Charles was not, of course, single-handedly responsible for the cultural achievements of his reign; others also deserve credit. One of Charles's chancellors, Jan ze Středa, and Arnošt z Pardubice, Prague's first archbishop, who had spent fourteen years in Italy, were both important patrons of manuscript painting. Under such men, influences from France and Italy, as well as from Germany, were combined in the development of a truly international style, with work quite the equal of anything produced in Italy at the time.

By bringing together courtiers, officials, advisers and artists from across the Empire and beyond Charles developed a new style of monarchy. Architecture and art were used not only to demonstrate his piety, but also to enhance his prestige and authority in a new way. He presided over the transformation of his capital, making Prague one of the finest cities in Europe, as it remains to this day.

The Charles Bridge and the Old Town Tower at Prague. The reconstruction of the city of Prague was one of Charles IV's major achievements.

King Pedro IV of Aragon

A CEREMONIOUS MONARCH

1319—87

On 1 January 1354, Pedro IV, king of Aragon, stood on a high platform in the main square of Barcelona wearing his royal robes, his crown upon his head. Flanked by the barons and knights of his household, he addressed the assembled crowd about the need for a military expedition to Sardinia. 'We spoke many appropriate words about it, both from Holy Scripture and other ancient deeds which were worthy of retelling.'

Pedro took the tasks of kingship seriously, and composed his own speeches, carefully correcting his initial drafts. He also had a detailed account of his reign written. Known simply as the *Chronicle*, it takes autobiographical form. In fact, the writing was done by a secretarial team, but the king planned and supervised it carefully. It gives an insider's view of kingship, and reveals much about Pedro, on one occasion even giving details of his bedtime reading. Pedro emerges as a pragmatist who balanced the pros and cons of any action carefully. He consulted his councillors and others extensively, but at the same time was a tricky politician capable of devious decisions. Though he made much of biblical examples in his speeches, and likened himself to King David, he did not always attribute success to divine intervention. He did, however, suggest that on one occasion God gave him a nasty spot so that he would not have to go to see his sister.

Pedro succeeded to the kingdom of Aragon and the county of Catalonia (in the latter as Pere III) in 1336. His rule saw the conquest of Majorca, conflict with Genoa, and war against Castile for almost ten years. His interests lay in the Mediterranean, particularly Sardinia; he was not much concerned with the *Reconquista*, the war to drive the Moors out of Spain. Pedro's eventual achievement lay not in large-scale conquests, but in the maintenance and consolidation of his lands with the limited resources available to him. His reign saw many administrative reforms, starting with a reorganization of the royal household and the chancery. He faced many internal difficulties and rebellions, as a result of the ambitions of his brother-in-law Jaume, and of the nobility in Aragon, Catalonia and Valencia.

Pedro claimed that he was ready to risk his life in war, telling his men, 'I will ask you one favour, that I shall be the first in battle and the front hooves of your horses should be with the rear feet of my horse, for this is enough for me.' On one occasion in Sardinia, he charged, but quickly lost his lance and was unhorsed. Then, on foot, with drawn sword, he drove the enemy back. It was not, however, by acts of heroism or chivalry that Pedro achieved military

The interior of the Cistercian monastery of Poblet, much favoured by King Pedro IV. The altarpiece dates from the early sixteenth century.

success. Rather it was by consultation with the nobles in his armies, by careful preparation and through a realistic appreciation of what was possible given his limited resources. Sieges, not battles, characterized his campaigns.

At home, Pedro faced a serious crisis in 1347, when the *Uniònes* of Aragon and Catalonia saw nobles and towns united against the crown in defence of what they saw as their traditional liberties. The *Unión* of Aragon demanded the expulsion of any in the royal household who would not swear to their terms, and imposed councillors on the king. In Valencia, the mob burst into the palace, playing horns and kettledrums, and forced Pedro and the queen to dance. Later, the ringleaders of this major affront to the royal dignity were executed by having molten metal from the bell they had used poured down their throats, and Pedro had to be dissuaded from ordering the destruction of the entire city. Military force, and the Black Death, brought the rebellion to an end.

As well as open revolt, Pedro faced determined constitutional opposition. In Spain, there was a long tradition, going back to the twelfth century, of representative assemblies known as *cortes* (or *corts* in Catalonia), which involved townsmen as well as nobles. At them, taxation was approved, and grievances addressed. Pedro faced many challenges from these assemblies in both his realms, and had to sanction many new rights. By the later years of his reign, he had been forced to concede control of war finance, army recruitment and logistics in Catalonia to the *corts*.

A highly intelligent man, Pedro had wide cultural interests. His court astronomers were instructed to draw up new tables, based on their celestial observations. He had various works, including the great thirteenth-century Castilian compilation of laws and other matters, the *Siete Partidas*, translated into Catalan. He attempted to revive troubadour poetry, even writing some himself. Scholarship was encouraged, with universities established at Huesca and Perpignan. The dynasty was celebrated with grand new royal tombs at the monastery of Poblet. Pedro took a keen personal interest, on one occasion objecting to the design he was shown and visiting Poblet in person to put it right. He also had a royal library built there, to house his impressive collection of books.

Known as 'the Ceremonious', Pedro enjoyed the pageantry and dignity of kingship. His *Chronicle* carefully recorded that, when he was crowned in Majorca in 1343, he wore a green silk shirt, a scarlet dalmatic, and a scarlet stole on his left shoulder, which then went round his waist. Oddly, he wore stockings, but no shoes. He processed out of the church under a golden canopy, and then mounted a horse led by long white silk reins. He expected to be treated with due respect, and was clearly surprised when, in the same year, 'We entered Barcelona and the people did not make Us any welcome, rather it seemed they were discontented that We had not taken Perpignan and Roussillon.' He was not pleased when, on one occasion during his travels, the royal bed did not arrive, and he had to sleep on the linen provided by a local inn.

Many parallels to Pedro's rule can be found among other European monarchies in the fourteenth century. The increasing bureaucracy, the dependence on negotiation with representative assemblies for grants of taxation, the growing emphasis on ceremonial, can all be observed elsewhere. Other kings, however, did not compose speeches in their own hand, or deliver scholarly sermons. Learned and hard-working, self-important and cunning, Pedro IV of Aragon was a remarkable ruler.

Pedro IV depicted in one of the initial letters of the Book of Privileges of the monastery of Val de Christo.

Coluccio Salutati

CIVIL SERVANT AND HUMANIST

1331–75

Italy, in the fourteenth century, was a society governed by paper. Legislative acts and state committee minutes were recorded on a massive scale. Deeds and contracts were needed to keep businesses running and to make property deals. For an ambitious young man such as Coluccio Salutati, a career as a notary offered excellent prospects.

Coluccio was born in 1331 in Stignano, a village in the Tuscan district of Valdinievole. The family soon moved to Bologna, where Coluccio gained the legal training needed to be a notary. In 1350, political upheaval forced the family back to Stignano, and he began work as a minor local official, serving in various roles across Valdinievole. His fortune seemed to change in 1367, when he became chancellor of Todi. Yet success refused to materialize either here or in a similar appointment at Lucca, and he returned to Stignano, an apparent failure. In 1374, however, he obtained a position in Florence, and in the following year became one of the city's two chancellors, taking responsibility for external affairs.

In Florence, Coluccio was astonishingly successful, riding the storms of factional disputes and popular uprisings. The city soon discovered that, in him, they had a powerful weapon in their conflicts both with the papacy and with Milan. The official correspondence that Coluccio wrote was superbly argued. Gian Galeazzo of Milan went so far as to say that one letter from Coluccio could do more damage than a thousand Florentine horsemen. Coluccio's reputation was partly built on this ability, but there was more. He was honest, fair, hard-working and devoted to Florence. Charges of treason brought against him were rightly dismissed as concocted. He had his own opinions, emphasizing the liberty and freedom the city offered, but he did as a civil servant should, and provided the state with the service it required, irrespective of who was in control. He was often overwhelmed by its demands:

> Imagine me trying to satisfy everyone, when I am surrounded all the time by citizens, many of them not knowing what they want so that I have to work it out, and then decide how to put it in writing. Nor do I have quiet to do this, for I am frequently interrupted with calls to attend the lords of the city.

A fifteenth-century portrait of Coluccio Salutati, showing him in a typically scholarly pose.

At the end of the day, Coluccio would leave his workplace in the grand Palazzo della Signoria and return to his rented house in the Piazza dei Peruzzi. There, he would turn his attention to his other calling: the world of scholarship. An excellent teacher at Bologna, Pietro da Moglio, had first introduced Coluccio to the Classics. During his years as an obscure local official, he had expanded his knowledge, buying books he could probably ill afford; in 1355, he spent four florins, about two months' salary, on four manuscripts of Priscian, Lucan, Vergil and Horace. By the end of his life, he had built up a library of some 800 books. A meticulous scholar, he was determined to restore the texts of Classical works that had often been corrupted by poor copying. With his pernickety mind, he was insistent on points of punctuation and spelling, and enjoyed correcting mistakes that others made. French spelling and grammar appalled him.

Coluccio was instrumental in bringing the Greek scholar, Manuel Chrysoloras, from Constantinople to Florence. Although Chrysoloras did not remain in the city for long, his coming marked the revival of Greek studies in the west and was a key moment in the development of Italian humanism. Coluccio's own attempts at learning Greek met with very limited success. His scholarly output was characterized by a shift from exclusively Classical ideas, in his early years, to their growing integration with Christian thought in his later writings. His importance, however, lay less in the impact of his treatises and letters, and far more in his role in improving Classical texts and the encouragement he offered to other scholars, such as his successor as chancellor, Leonardo Bruni.

Coluccio was a great admirer of Petrarch (see pp. 189–92), although he was not the sort of man to be distracted by an unrequited passion or by idealized concepts of courtly love. When he was young, he canoodled with a local girl a thousand times, or so he said, but he went no further than eager embraces. Instead, he married another girl, Catarina, in 1366, and was shattered by her death some five years later. To judge by his correspondence, he was not as devoted to his second wife, Piera. He often worked late. If not busy with his official duties, he would be immersed in his books, or discussing issues of scholarship with his followers. Much as he appreciated the physical charms of women, he did not believe they possessed the mental capacity for such learned matters. He employed a female slave, and doubtless saw no contradiction between this and his praise of the freedom Florence offered.

Plague shadowed Coluccio throughout his life. His father, four of his brothers and sisters, both his wives and two of his sons died of the disease. Coluccio's fatalistic attitude – it was God's decision when death struck – meant that he insisted on remaining in Florence as the disease raged, although he did let his children go away into the country. He was prepared to carry an aromatic dispenser during epidemics, but only because he liked the smell, not for any protective value it might have.

Coluccio, ever conscientious, remained at work until the very end of his life. The last letter in his hand was written on 23 April 1375; he died eleven days later. He was rightly honoured with a grand funeral ceremony by the city of Florence, to which he had contributed so much.

Catherine of Siena
(Catherine Benincasa)

DIFFICULT BUT REMARKABLE YOUNG
WOMAN AND SAINT

1347–80

There can be a narrow line between insanity and sanctity. Catherine Benincasa was born in Siena, in 1347, to a reasonably well-off family. She had visions from the age of six, and vowed chastity at seven. As a teenager, she gave away her clothes, and became a vegetarian, passing her meat to the cats. She bitterly regretted being persuaded by her sister, Bonaventura, when she was about twelve, to dye her hair and wear attractive clothes. On Bonaventura's death in childbirth, she rejected her family's demands that she should marry. She cut off her hair, and began a hunger strike. When she was taken to a spa, she deliberately scalded herself in the boiling water. She was convinced that a young, half-clad man she met was Jesus. He asked her for clothes; she happily handed over all she could, including some of her parents' garments, and those of their maid. She only stopped when she realized how difficult it would be to maintain her modesty if she gave him her one last dress.

Catherine eventually left home and joined a group of Dominican women, the *Mantellate*, whose mission was to look after the poor and sick. She vomited up anything she was made to eat. She scourged herself for an hour and a half three times a day, and wore a steel chain which cut into her flesh. For three years, she confined herself to a small cell, with nothing but her confessor and her visions for company. She went to even further extremes. She kissed the open sore of a victim of breast cancer, and drank the water in which she had washed an open wound, declaring it sweet and agreeable. An

A fifteenth-century portrait of St Catherine of Siena experiencing a mystical trance.

St Catherine of Siena, depicted by her near-contemporary Sienese artist Andrea Vanni.

erotic element can be read into a famous letter by her recording the way she held a prisoner's head on the block, and was duly spattered by blood as the axe fell: 'I have just received a head in my hands, which was to me of such sweetness as heart cannot think, nor tongue say, nor eye see, nor the ears hear.' She claimed that, in 1366, she entered into a mystical marriage with Christ; in her visions, he would often bring saints with him. In later life, 'her ecstasies became so frequent, that she could scarcely recite the Lord's Prayer without being ravished out of her external senses, by a heavenly favour'. She asked her secretaries 'to hear and commit to writing what she would say during her ecstasies'. The result was her *Dialogo*, a book taking the form of a dialogue between God and the human soul.

There were suspicions that Catherine was a heretic, but in 1374 her opinions were declared orthodox. This gave her the confidence to begin travelling through Italy, attempting to start a new crusade, and to advance Church reform. In using letters to put forward her views she was adopting a genre which perhaps owed something to Petrarch and Coluccio Salutati (see pp. 189–92, 210–12). Unlike them, she dictated in Italian, in an informal style, often at considerable length. She sent many letters to the pope, Gregory XI; she also wrote to the kings of France and Hungary, and to Joanna, queen of Naples. She pulled no punches with the latter:

> You who were a lady have made yourself a servant, and slave of that which is not, having submitted yourself to falsehood, and to the devil, who is its father; abandoning the counsels of the Holy Spirit and accepting the counsels of incarnate demons.

Catherine was deeply involved in Italian politics. Her advocacy of peace was undertaken in the interests of the papal cause. The War of the Eight Saints in the late 1370s, between Florence and the papacy, saw her working to prevent Pisa and Lucca joining the Florentine coalition. She wrote to the pope: 'I have been at Pisa and at Lucca, up to now, influencing them as much as I can not to make a league with the decaying members that are rebelling against you.' Her political efforts were not universally appreciated. 'Take that wicked woman and burn her alive; let us cut her to pieces,' was one cry in Florence.

Catherine's many protestations and demands had relatively little effect. She helped to influence Gregory XI to bring the papacy back to Rome from Avignon, but on his death in 1378 the election of Urban VI was swiftly followed by the election of a rival, Clement VII, who set himself up in Avignon. This appalled Catherine, but she was powerless to prevent what would become known as the Great Schism, which lasted until 1415. Nor did Catherine succeed in inspiring a new crusade, while her pleas for Church reform had little effect. The bitter rivalries between, and within, the great cities of northern Italy could not be quietened by the activities of a single woman. She died, disappointed, in Rome in 1380. She was only thirty-four.

A fifteenth-century illustration of St Catherine dictating her Dialogo *to Raymond of Capua, who later wrote her biography.*

Remarkable as Catherine was, she was not unique. Bridget of Vadstena, a Swedish widow, was also much given to visions. Bridget's husband died in 1344, and from 1350 she spent most of her time in Rome, agitating for the return of the papacy from Avignon. She died in 1373, and in her visions, mysticism and desire for reform of the Church, she paralleled Catherine in many ways.

It was hard for a woman to enter into public affairs as Catherine did. When young, she had even considered disguising herself as a man, and becoming a friar, so that she could spread her message. One reason for her acceptance was that her visions gave her a special mystical authority. Nor was she alone; the support of a small group was very important to her. This included some of the *Mantellate*, such as Fat Alessa and Crazy Cecca (as they were affectionately termed in some of Catherine's letters). There was also the Dominican, Raymond of Capua, who would write Catherine's biography. A number of well-born young men from Siena were devoted followers, calling Catherine their Mamma. There can be no doubt, however, that it was Catherine herself who was the driving force.

How far it is possible to diagnose Catherine in modern medical terms is a moot point. Merely to say that she suffered from anorexia and bulimia is not sufficient; her neuroses and self-hatred surely went much deeper. She undoubtedly suffered physically; her biographer wrote of constant headaches, a pain in her side and another in her breast. She herself wrote:

> I wish pains to be food to me, tears my drink, sweat my ointment. Let pains make me fat, let pains cure me, let pains give me light, let pains give me wisdom, let pains clothe my nakedness, let pains strip me of all self-love, spiritual and temporal.

Her physical torment may provide part of the explanation of Catherine's driven character, but there was much more to this extraordinary woman than any medical diagnosis can suggest.

One of St Catherine's fingers, preserved in a reliquary in the church of San Domenico, Siena.

John Hawkwood

SOLDIER OF FORTUNE

c. 1320–94

For any man seeking a rapid route to fame and fortune, late fourteenth-century Italy offered rich pickings. War was endemic, with bitter rivalries among the cities of the north. Florence was opposed by Siena and by Pisa. Milan controlled much of Lombardy, but had many enemies. Padua and Verona were at daggers drawn. These were all wealthy states, and it made sense for them to hire experienced soldiers rather than rely solely on their own militias. The age of these great *condottiere* (mercenaries) began with the German, Werner of Urslingen, who led what he called the Great Company in Italy in 1339. One of the most remarkable exponents of the trade was an Englishman, John Hawkwood. He rose from relatively humble beginnings to become one of Florence's most noted military captains, commemorated in a splendid fresco by Uccello, which shows him on horseback and wielding a baton of command.

John Hawkwood was born in Essex in the 1320s, one of seven children. His family was of some standing in village society. He is said to have worked for a time as a tailor in London, but the lure of Edward III's wars in France soon attracted him. Although a few men rose through the ranks of Edward's armies to achieve command, Hawkwood was not one of them. He must, however, have learned much from these campaigns. When the French war came to a temporary close in 1360, Hawkwood's career as a mercenary began. He joined what became the White Company, whose activities were so brutal that the pope preached a crusade against it. After ravaging in France, the Company moved to Italy early in 1361. Along with other English mercenaries, Hawkwood brought a new style of fighting to Italy. The basic unit of their forces was the 'lance', which consisted of two mounted men-at-arms and a squire or page. In battle, however, the English lances fought as they had done in France, dismounting to fight on foot, with archers in support.

Hawkwood had many masters in Italy. As well as Florence, he fought for, and often also against, Pisa, Milan, Padua, the papacy and the rulers of Naples. For all his skills, he was not always victorious in battle. He was still learning his trade as a commander in the 1360s, and was defeated on several occasions. However, he soon began to show his mettle. In 1369, when in Milanese service, he used a feigned retreat to excellent effect against a Florentine force at Cascina. In 1373, he won an unexpected victory against the Milanese at Montichiari, where he rallied his outnumbered forces when they seemed to be routed. In 1380, he became captain

Fourteenth-century Italian warfare. This fresco by Lippo Vanni shows the Sienese army setting out in 1363 to defeat mercenary forces at the battle of Val di Chiana.

general of war for Florence, and remained loyal to that city for the remainder of his life. He obtained his most resounding triumph at Castagnaro, in 1387, having been hired by Padua to fight Verona. His careful choice of ground, good use of archers and timely deployment of his mounted reserve routed the Veronese. In his final campaign, in 1391, he adroitly led his Florentine army to safety after the Milanese thought they had him at his mercy. Hawkwood had long hankered for a return to England, but his death, in 1394, intervened to prevent it.

Hawkwood possessed all the instincts a great commander needed. He looked after his men, who never mutinied. He was cunning and skilful, surprising his opponents with swift winter campaigns, knowing when to withdraw and when to attack. Spies and secrecy were an important part of his armoury. He had tactical and strategic skills; the one aspect of warfare that he did not engage in on any scale was siege warfare, for that demanded resources and time which were not available to him. A soldier, he understood much more than the art of war. He knew how to negotiate with his various employers, and was a capable diplomat, acting as such on two occasions for the English king. He was, however, no orator, and the two surviving letters he wrote in English, though remarkable for being among the earliest in the language, are no more than business-like. Though an outsider, he had little difficulty in integrating into Italian society – helped, no doubt, by his marriage, in 1377, to the illegitimate daughter of Bernabò Visconti of Milan.

War was brutal, and it is not surprising that mercenaries gained a bad reputation, especially given the activities of men such as Werner of Urslingen, who declared that he was the 'Enemy of God, Pity and Mercy'. In Hawkwood's case, the massacre at Cesena in 1377, when he was in papal service, has done most to blacken his name. The citizens had risen against the Breton troops of Cardinal Robert of Geneva (in 1378, elected pope as Clement VII in opposition to Urban VI). The cardinal ordered Hawkwood to do his worst, and three days of slaughter followed. However, the extent of Hawkwood's responsibility is unclear; one chronicler partly exonerated him, stating that he sent 1,000 women to Rimini for safety.

Sir John Hawkwood served the city of Florence well. This memorial in the cathedral, showing him carrying a baton of command, was painted by Paolo Uccello.

Another allegation made against Hawkwood is that, during the sack of Faenza in 1376, he found a couple of his soldiers squabbling over a pretty nun, and ended the argument by stabbing her. The tale reveals more about Hawkwood's reputation among his enemies, than about the reality of his conduct. There is no doubt, however, that Hawkwood's troops ravaged the land, extracted protection money from towns and villages and terrorized the populace. His men would not have accepted his leadership had he not allowed this, nor would his employers in Florence and elsewhere have contracted for his services had he held his men back.

For Hawkwood, war was always a business. His earnings reached a peak in 1377 of 82,600 florins (about £14,000), a sum far greater than the annual income of an English earl. Money quickly acquired, however, was just as quickly lost. Hawkwood faced heavy expenses; much of his salary had to be passed on to his men: in 1387, his personal following comprised eighty-two lances, forty archers and two trumpeters The end of his life was troubled by such severe financial problems that there was no money even to buy a wedding dress for his daughter, Catherine. Hawkwood sold much of his property, collected debts owing to him and commuted his pensions for cash. Even so, the Florentine authorities accepted that the family had no money, and paid for Hawkwood's lavish funeral. There was certainly no fortune for his children to inherit.

Hawkwood was the last of the foreign mercenaries to make his name on a grand scale in Italy. The next generation of *condottiere* were Italian. Alberigo da Barbiano, born in 1349, was one of the first to achieve fame when he defeated a Breton mercenary force in 1378. One of the leading *condottiere* at the start of the fifteenth century was Musio Attendolo, known as Sforza, who founded the dynasty which ruled Milan until the early sixteenth century.

John of Gaunt

SOLDIER AND STATESMAN

1340–99

At first sight, the career of John of Gaunt appears a catalogue of failures: unsuccessful in war, unable to make good his claims to the Castilian throne, an object of hatred in the Peasants' Revolt of 1381, an elder statesman who found it hard to prevent his nephew King Richard II's political follies. The reality, however, is far more interesting.

Gaunt was the second son of King Edward III. Henry II's reign had shown how difficult it could be for a king to manage a brood of ambitious sons, but Edward III succeeded with astonishing little difficulty. Gaunt was introduced to war at the age of only ten, when he was aboard the royal flagship in battle against a Castilian fleet in 1350. His first experience against the French came in 1355, with a short and ineffective campaign.

In 1359, Gaunt married Blanche, daughter of the duke of Lancaster. This brought him vast estates much sooner than he could have expected. With the deaths of his father-in-law in 1360 and his sister-in-law in 1362, Gaunt acquired all of the Lancastrian lands, as well as the ducal title. Sadly, Blanche died in 1368. Geoffrey Chaucer (see pp. 225–28) mourned her in *The Book of the Duchess*:

> I saw her dance so comelily,
> Carol and sing so sweetly,
> Laugh and play so womanly,
> And look so debonairly,
> So goodly speak and so friendly,
> That certes I trow that nevermore
> Was seen so blissful a treasure.

In 1367, Gaunt campaigned in Spain alongside his elder brother, the Black Prince, and led the vanguard with distinction in the battle of Nájera. When war with France reopened in 1369 after almost a decade of truce, the Black Prince was in a poor state of health, and the king too old to campaign as he had done in the 1340s. Leadership of the English war effort fell increasingly to Gaunt. He led an ambitious raid in 1373, which left Calais, swung across northern France, then down through Burgundy, finally reaching English-held territory in Gascony. The expedition lasted five months and marched almost a thousand miles, during

John of Gaunt, on the left, dining with the king of Portugal, with whom he later quarrelled. From a late fifteenth-century Flemish manuscript.

which Gaunt's men were constantly harassed. Food supplies were inadequate, and it was a dispirited force, which had lost many of its number, which eventually straggled into Bordeaux. The raid may have achieved little, but Gaunt had at least managed to prevent it becoming a total disaster.

In England, the 1370s was a difficult decade. The government came under attack in the Good Parliament of 1376, with leading ministers impeached for corruption. Even the Edward III's mistress, Alice Perrers, was charged. The Black Prince died, leaving Gaunt as the leading active representative of the crown, for the king was in his dotage, and the Black Prince's son, Richard, a mere boy. When the acts of the Good Parliament were reversed in 1377, at Gaunt's instigation, he could hardly have been more unpopular. During the Peasants' Revolt, in 1381, his property in London was targeted and his great palace of the Savoy sacked.

In 1386, Gaunt embarked on an attempt to enforce the claim to the Castilian royal title that he had gained through his second marriage, to Constance of Castile, in 1371. Though Gaunt had Portuguese support, the small force with which he landed at La Coruña had little success, disease severely reducing its effectiveness. In the next year, a brief invasion of León, together with João I of Portugal, achieved little as the two allies quarrelled. The main benefit of Gaunt's fruitless Spanish adventure was that it took him out of England at a particularly difficult period.

Gaunt returned to England in 1389 as an elder statesman. He was able to exercise some restraining influence on his nephew, Richard II, whose exalted concepts of his royal status sat ill with many of the nobles, and with the representatives in parliament. In 1388, there had been a major political crisis, with threats of deposition. With Gaunt's return, the situation was calmed. It was not until after his death that the king's despotic inclinations led to renewed crisis in the autumn of 1399. Gaunt's son, Henry Bolingbroke, had been forced into exile in October the year before. He returned after his father's death and, in a rapid revolution, Richard II was finally removed from the throne. Gaunt's son thus gained the crown as Henry IV.

Three years before he died, Gaunt married his mistress, Katherine Swynford. He had first turned to her over twenty years before, in the early 1370s, when his marriage with Constance proved unsatisfactory. To have a mistress was not unusual. Much earlier in the fourteenth century, Earl Warenne's career had been dominated by his desire to rid himself of his wife; but after he succeeded, he did not marry his mistress, Maud de Nerford. Nor did Edward III marry Alice Perrers, who comforted him in his declining years. Katherine Swynford, however, was successful where others had failed.

John of Gaunt added lavish domestic apartments to Kenilworth Castle. This view shows, in the centre, the windows of his hall.

Such matters aside, Gaunt was remarkably conventional. He was personally impressive, being tall and well spoken. 'Good lordship' was important in such a man, and Gaunt was generous and loyal towards those who served him in his household. He took full part in the chivalric world of the tournament. Though he did not boast of any exceptional skill himself, his sportsmanship was impeccable. He was not given to extravagance in dress, but he liked to live in splendour, and could afford to do so, as the richest magnate in the land. He built on a large scale, refurbishing the castles of the duchy of Lancaster. At Kenilworth, in Warwickshire, he constructed a magnificent new hall and grand apartments, which were no doubt decorated with the French tapestries of which he was particularly fond. He lived a busy life, and had little time for literary interests; there is no evidence that he built up a library. His support of Geoffrey Chaucer, whose wife was Katherine Swynford's sister, was not because of the latter's skill as a poet. Chaucer's *The Book of the Duchess* may have been written for Gaunt, but not at his behest. Though Gaunt provided John Wycliffe with some protection, he had no truck with his views, or those of his fellow Lollards, once their heretical character became clear. He had a particular devotion for the Virgin Mary, and had a close relationship with the confessors who served him. His father-in-law had begun to build a collegiate church at Leicester, which Gaunt continued to finance. He also founded a chantry in memory of his duchess, Blanche, in St Paul's cathedral.

John of Gaunt may not have succeeded in many of his ventures, but he does not deserve to be condemned as a failure. He served his country well in a difficult period.

Geoffrey Chaucer

CUSTOMS OFFICIAL AND POET

c. 1340–1400

Geoffrey Chaucer was a moderately successful civil servant, one of a great many officials who flourished in royal service. His son, Thomas, had a far more distinguished career. As a royal councillor, diplomat, skilled politician and administrator, Thomas achieved far more than his father did. Yet, because Geoffrey wrote great poetry, it is the father who is still remembered.

Chaucer was a Londoner, and was probably born in the early 1340s. Although the records yield many details of his various appointments, they provide few personal insights. In 1359, he took part in a large-scale, but ultimately futile, expedition to France; he was captured at Reims, but was ransomed within a few months. His first employment had been in the household of the countess of Ulster, but in the 1360s he joined the royal household as a squire. Around this time, Chaucer married one of the countess of Ulster's ladies, Philippa Roet, the daughter of a knight herald from the Low Countries. His marriage brought Chaucer an unexpected connection, for Philippa's sister, Katherine Swynford, was first governess to the children of John of Gaunt (see pp. 221–24), and then his mistress. This brought him some favour from Gaunt, but suggestions that Philippa, like her sister, provided sexual favours to Gaunt, and that he was the father of her son, Thomas, are unwarranted. Marriage, however, often offered means for the ambitious to gain wealth and standing.

An early fifteenth-century portrait of Geoffrey Chaucer, an inkhorn hanging round his neck, and a rosary in his left hand.

Chaucer showed promise as a diplomat and, in 1372, he was sent with two Italian merchants as a royal envoy to Genoa, spending several months in Italy. Other missions followed, including another to Italy in 1378. That same year, his career went on a very different route when he was appointed controller of the London customs, a post in which his task, at least in theory, was to check the accounts of the collector of the customs, and write a duplicate set. Chaucer was surely appointed because of his family background in London trade; had it not been for this, the appointment of a royal squire with diplomatic experience as a customs official would have been strange.

In 1380, Chaucer was accused of rape by one Cecily Champain. She was later paid £10, a substantial sum, in return for her releasing him from prosecution. The incident has caused embarrassment to some literary scholars, though this is perhaps surprising given the character of some of his poetry. Chaucer's guilt, however, cannot necessarily be taken for granted; it could be that Cecily brought the charge as a means of forcing him and his associates into paying debts owed to her. Whatever the truth of the matter, the case shows that it was no simple matter to obtain the conviction of a well-connected royal official.

Chaucer had interests in Kent, and in 1385 was appointed as one of sixteen justices of the peace there. In 1386, he was elected as a member of parliament for the county. He must have been alarmed during the proceedings when a petition was presented asking that controllers of customs should no longer be appointed for life. He took the hint, and later that year gave up his post at the customs.

In 1389, Chaucer became clerk of the king's works. There were no major building projects at this time: over £100 worth of stone was bought to repair St George's chapel at Windsor, but no work took place. Chaucer's accounts reveal, among many other details, the sale of 104 oaks from the king's park at Eltham, in Kent, which had been blown down in a storm. As befitted a man with accountancy experience, his receipts and expenses were almost in balance. Chaucer retired from this office in 1391, and was granted an annuity of £20 in 1394. Three years later, he was promised a tun of wine every year, enough to have provided him with about five bottles a day. He died in 1400.

Although Chaucer possessed strong links to the royal court, he was not primarily a court poet. His greatest work, *The Canterbury Tales* — which purports to be a collection of the stories told by a group of pilgrims as they travelled from London to the shrine of Thomas Becket (see pp. 83–86) at Canterbury — looked to a much wider audience, particularly perhaps the London merchant society from which he came. He wrote at a time of extraordinary change in language, when English was taking over from French in aristocratic circles. In 1362, the opening speech at parliament was delivered in English for the first time, and a statute authorized the use of English in the courts of law. The war against France was one reason why English was becoming more acceptable, and Chaucer made a huge contribution

A portrait of Geoffrey Chaucer, from a facsimile of the early fifteenth-century Ellesmere manuscript of The Canterbury Tales.

The poet John Lydgate imagined himself as one of Chaucer's pilgrims, shown here leaving Canterbury. From a mid-fifteenth century manuscript.

to the development of the language. The English he used was that of the southeast; this would eventually develop into 'standard' English.

Chaucer drew on a vast cultural heritage; he was familiar with a great deal of French literature, and while his travels to Italy may not have brought him face to face with Boccaccio or Petrarch (see pp. 189–92), he surely acquired copies of their works, as well as those of Dante (see pp. 170–72). In writing *Troilus and Criseyde*, he had access to French and Latin versions of the story, but based the lengthy poem primarily on Boccaccio's *Filostrato*. *The Canterbury Tales*, which he probably began in the late 1380s, drew on a remarkable range of sources. He used indecent French *fabliaux*, translations into French of Ovid and of Petrarch, sermons and the Bible, all in a framework which owed much to Boccaccio's *Decameron*. The result was a masterpiece, not a derivative miscellany. Chaucer's sophisticated adaptation of his source material, his ingenious use of language and his earthy sense of humour ensured that he created one of the great works of English literature.

Jean Froissart

CHRONICLER OF CHIVALRY

c. 1337–c. 1404

In 1388, the chronicler, Jean Froissart, was staying in the Hôtel de la Lune in Orthez, in southwestern France. There he met a Gascon, the Bascot de Mauléon. The two had a lengthy conversation, and doubtless a good deal of wine. The Bascot reminisced about his experiences as a soldier of fortune. He told tales of sieges and stratagems, profits and losses, love and betrayal. As well as fighting in France, he had campaigned in Spain and in the Baltic during a thirty-year career in arms. Froissart knew a good story when he heard one, and duly included the Bascot's memories in his *Chronicles*.

Froissart came from Hainault in the Low Countries. In 1361, already known as an author, Froissart travelled to England, where he joined the household of Edward III's queen, Philippa, his compatriot. He remained in her employment until her death in 1369. He then settled in Brabant, began his *Chronicles* and took holy orders. He found a number of patrons in the Low Countries, notably Robert de Namur, who had married Queen Philippa's younger sister, and Wenceslaus of Bohemia, duke of Luxembourg.

It is the *Chronicles* that have made Froissart famous. The book was a best-seller, with more than 150 surviving manuscripts. It was primarily an account of the wars between England and France, with a strong emphasis on the individual feats of arms performed by noble combatants. Despite its length, and detail, it is not a comprehensive history. Froissart skipped over the Black Death, for example, no doubt considering that this was of no interest to his readers. Battles, sieges and tournaments, with tales of personal valour, fill his pages. The values are those of the chivalric world on which Froissart focused.

Jean Froissart presenting a copy of his Chronicles *to King Richard II, from a fifteenth-century manuscript of the work.*

Plagiarism, for a medieval chronicler, was no sin. Froissart lifted most of the first part of his chronicle, up to 1360, from the work of an older Hainaulter, Jean le Bel. Thereafter, he used some written sources, such as a life of the Black Prince, but he relied mainly on interviews that he held with participants in the events that he described. On a visit to England, in 1395, he rode from Rochester to Dartford alongside the Gascon knight, Jean de Grailly, and wrote that 'I eagerly listened to all he said, and treasured his words in my memory'. He was irritated that he could not attend a session of parliament; but he had dinner with an old friend, Sir Richard Sturry, who told him what had happened. As his fame grew, people brought him information, such as an Anglo-Irish squire who approached Froissart to tell him about Ireland and Richard II's recent expedition there.

Remarkably, Froissart probably never witnessed a battle or a siege in person. His accounts were therefore based largely on hearsay, but he had the skill to make them come alive. For his description of the battle of Otterburn, in 1388, he took care to obtain accounts from

Jean Froissart shown kneeling before the count of Foix, from a late fifteenth-century manuscript. A servant behind him carries his book.

both Scots and English, and concluded that 'there was not a man, knight or squire, who did not acquit himself gallantly'. He understood the kind of details about tactics that would interest an experienced soldier, and realized that his vivid accounts of single combat in jousts needed to be enhanced with technical minutiae. While there is a chivalric gloss to Froissart's work, he did try to show both sides of war. He justified a long excursus on the career of a far from exemplary soldier of fortune, Aymerigot Marcel, saying that 'in such a history as this both good and bad must be spoken of, that they may serve as an excitement or warning in times to come'.

Froissart's extensive use of oral testimony inevitably led to some inaccuracy. His chronology was sometimes confused, and names were sometimes mistaken. It has even been suggested that the Bascot de Mauléon was a product of his imagination, dreamed up to add colour and drama to his work; the charge, however, is unwarranted, for the Bascot was a real individual. Nor were all stories accepted credulously by Froissart. He was puzzled by a tale about the rape of the countess of Salisbury by none other than King Edward III himself, which he drew from Jean le Bel's chronicle. Though he included it, he wrote a sceptical chapter in one version of the *Chronicles*, showing that he had the good historical sense to doubt so bizarre a tale.

Froissart's *Chronicles* was far from straightforward. The work was sophisticated, skilfully constructed and carefully revised. Rather than tell the story of the crusade of 1396, which ended in defeat at Nicopolis on the Danube, in one section, he divided it up, adding to the tension by interspersing it with accounts of other events, such as the marriage of Richard II. His explanation of the defeat of the crusader army was not expressed purely in conventional terms of divine judgment. Rather, it was caused by the Hungarians' lack of courage and, above all, by the arrogance and presumption of the French.

Froissart probably died in 1404. His view of his own life had been set out in a poem he wrote in 1389. It had not been profitable, for he had acquired no riches, no houses or ships. Yet he had travelled widely, on a good horse and well dressed, and was not in debt. Above all, he had written books that would see his name live for centuries. As he explained in the *Chronicles*: 'I well know, that when the time shall come, when I shall be dead and rotten, this grand and noble history will be in much fashion, and all noble and valiant persons will take pleasure in it.' How right he was.

5.

An Age of Transition

1400–1500

The Middle Ages, as they drew to a close, continued to be dominated by warfare. The fifteenth century saw Christian Europe threatened by the relentless advance of the Ottoman Turks. An attempt to halt them inspired the last large-scale crusading expedition to the east, only for it to be decisively defeated at Nicopolis in the Balkans in 1396. The victorious Ottoman sultan, however, proved no match for the latest nomadic conqueror of much of Asia, Temür, perhaps better known as Tamerlane. The Ottomans' setback was to be temporary. Temür's evanescent empire imploded after his death in 1405, and it was Turkish forces, not steppe tribes from central Asia, that captured Constantinople in 1453 and brought the thousand-year Byzantine Empire to its end.

That same year also witnessed the end of the Hundred Years War. The astonishing English victory at Agincourt in 1415 saw the capture of one of the survivors of Nicopolis, a hero of French chivalry, Boucicaut. The conquest of Normandy by Henry V soon followed, but his premature death and the succession of his infant son, left the English unable to maintain their hold on France. How far the French resurgence was due to the inspiration provided by one peasant girl, Joan of Arc, is open to debate; her achievements were brief, but the motivation she provided was immense and lasting.

By 1453 England had lost all her continental possessions, save Calais. Such a demoralizing defeat undoubtedly contributed to the litany of problems faced by Margaret of Anjou, queen to the feeble King Henry VI. Above all, she faced the dynastic conflict between the rival houses of York and Lancaster, known as the Wars of the Roses, which began in 1455. This period of turmoil was only brought to an end in 1485 with the triumph of the Lancastrian faction in the guise of a new, Tudor dynasty.

Rebellion in the fifteenth century, however, was not confined to England. Perhaps its fiercest outbreak was in the imperial heartland of Bohemia, where the Hussite revolution of the 1420s combined radical ideas of religious reform – many of which foreshadowed the rise of Protestantism in the early sixteenth century – with Bohemian nationalism in a potent mix. An extraordinary leader emerged to command the Hussite rebels, the one-eyed Jan

A flattering portrait of Charles the Bold of Burgundy, the work of the Flemish painter Rogier van der Weyden.

Žižka, who proved to be a military genius. He died in 1424, but the Hussite wars continued for another decade, with crusade after crusade launched against the heretics.

As Žižka demonstrated with his near-impregnable war-wagons, military methods were changing fast. Charles the Bold, last Valois duke of Burgundy, had prescient ideas about the way to reorganize his army, which anticipated the military revolution of the sixteenth century. However, his professional standing army was shown to be too small and ineffective when faced with the pikes and halberds of the Swiss infantry levies that hacked Charles himself to pieces at the battle of Nancy in 1477. His death was followed by the division of the great late-medieval state of Burgundy between the French king and the Habsburg emperor, which sowed many of the seeds of conflict that were to flourish in Europe over the next 200 years.

The seemingly endless wars and conflicts of the fifteenth century did not prevent this from being a period of major artistic and intellectual achievements. In France and the Low Countries, magnificent illustrated manuscripts were produced, while the Flemish painter Rogier van der Weyden's skills were envied by his Italian contemporaries. Court culture reached new heights of grandeur and sophistication in Charles the Bold's Burgundian state. In Italy, this was the age of the early Renaissance, with astonishing developments across the cultural spectrum. In painting there were many great names; Piero della Francesca was particularly remarkable for combining mathematical learning with artistic ability. Architecture broke away from the Gothic mould with the development of a Classical style. One of the most striking architectural and engineering achievements was the vast dome of the cathedral at Florence, designed by Brunelleschi. Like so many of the great Renaissance figures, he was a man of many parts; his explanation of perspective was especially notable. His friend from Siena, Taccola, displayed a fascination with ingenious engineering

The earliest known terrestrial globe, made by Albert Behaim in 1492, shows the world just before the discovery of the Americas.

This woodcut of 1499 from a danse macabre *is the earliest known illustration of a printing press. In it, the printers and a bookseller are carried off by Death.*

solutions, which anticipated some of Leonardo da Vinci's work. There was also a very different side to Italian society, as the career of the abbess, Clara Sanuto, demonstrated. Her convent provided somewhat unorthodox services to the young men of Venice.

In the late fifteenth century, many changes were taking place that can be seen as presaging the end of the Middle Ages. Two were to be particularly significant: the discovery of America and the invention of printing. The expansion of the known world came about through Portuguese exploration by sea, which revealed much of the coast of West Africa, and above all with Columbus's expedition of 1492 across the Atlantic. Columbus's achievement was in part made possible by the continuing improvements in the technology of shipbuilding. The most important technological change, however, was the development of movable type, pioneered by Johannes Gutenberg in Mainz. Printing would transform the availability of knowledge, and bring forth a new age.

Temür
(Tamerlane)

THE SCOURGE OF GOD

1336–1405

In 1403, a Spanish nobleman, Ruy Gonzalez de Clavijo, was sent from Castile as an envoy to the great conqueror Temür, eventually reaching him at his court in far-off Samarkand. At their first meeting, Temür was seated on silken carpets and wearing a silk robe and a tall, bejewelled, white hat. In front of him was a fountain with apples floating in it. His eyesight was very poor, so the ambassadors were brought close up. At dinner, after the audience, there was a squabble over whether the Spanish or some rival Chinese ambassadors should sit closest to Temür: the former won. Boiled and roast mutton and horsemeat were dragged in on great leather platters, then cut up and served in basins with some sauce and thin biscuits. Melons, grapes and nectarines followed. When the Spaniards' interpreter was late at another feast, Temür was furious. He ordered that a hole be bored through the man's nose and a rope put through it so that he could be dragged through the ranks of the

army. However, he soon forgave him, and the punishment was not carried out. There was a great deal more feasting and drinking in a tented camp set up outside the city; on one occasion, trained elephants entertained the ambassadors. In Samarkand itself, the palaces were splendid, decorated with glazed tiles, carpeted, and hung with silk, while the gardens were adorned with tents and silk awnings. There was a great mix of peoples brought there by Temür, and a vast range of merchandise, from Chinese silks and satins, and spices from India and beyond, to furs from Russia and the north. Clavijo's account of all this shows just how astonishing he found it.

Left *A twentieth-century bust of Temür, made using measurements of his skull by Mikhail Gerasmov, pioneer of facial reconstruction.*

Opposite *Temür's troops in action. A battle scene, as imagined in a sixteenth-century Persian manuscript.*

The entrance gate to Temür's mausoleum in Samarkand. Under him, the city was transformed with splendid palaces and mosques.

Temür, popularly known as Tamerlane, was reaching the end of his life when Clavijo met him. Born in 1336, in modern Uzbekistan, he saw himself as a new Chinggis Khan (see pp. 114–17). He was of obscure Turkish-Mongol origins, and is said to have been convinced of his own greatness by the time he was twelve. In the century since Chinggis Khan's death, the Mongol empire had splintered into different khanates, whose political rivalries presented opportunities to the arrogant and ambitious Temür. He began as little more than a brigand, who acquired the sobriquet 'the Lame' (*Tīmūr-I lang*, in Persian) when he was injured sheep-rustling. Over the course of about a decade, he reduced the Chagadai khans of central Asia to puppet status and took their throne for himself at Samarkand in 1370, calling himself *amir* rather than claiming the title of khan.

Raid after raid into Kwārazm was followed by campaigns in Persia and Iraq. Temür then faced the Mongol Golden Horde to the north. In 1395, he was victorious in battle at the Terek river, in modern Chechnya. Following this, he sacked the Golden Horde's capital on the Volga. In 1398, Temür's incessant campaigning took him to India. In the next year, he sacked Aleppo and Damascus in Syria. His opponent was now the Ottoman sultan Bāyazīd, victor over a large crusading force at Nicopolis on the Danube in 1396. At Ankara, in 1402, Temür outmanoeuvred and defeated the sultan, taking him prisoner. When 'the butler of death gave him to drink a bitter cup' in 1405, Temür was about to embark on a campaign in China.

Temür was the last of the great nomadic conquerors. He had undoubted genius as a military commander. The core of his armies was organized in traditional Mongol fashion. The troops were mounted, and marshalled into units of thousands and hundreds. Toughened by nomadic life, they could, according to Clavijo, survive cold and hunger to a remarkable degree. The supreme mobility of Temür's mounted troops meant that surprise flank attacks and feigned retreats were part of his tactical armoury. His campaigns were well prepared and planned; his victory at Ankara was largely due to the secret negotiations that had taken place with the Tatars in Bāyazīd's army, who duly deserted their lord when battle was joined.

Atrocities were hardly unusual in medieval warfare, but the scale and nature of the horrors inflicted on captured cities by Temür's troops were astonishing. In 1400, the people of Siwas in Anatolia were promised mercy, but when the town was stormed, the troops of the garrison were buried alive on Temür's orders. At Aleppo, the moat was filled with corpses, forming a roadway. At Baghdad, in 1402, Temür ordered every soldier to bring him two heads. The skulls were then heaped up in towers to serve as a lesson to future generations, and the Tigris ran red with blood. On his travels, Clavijo passed through Damghan in Persia, where Temür had ordered the destruction of an entire people, the White Tatars. The towers of skulls were so tall that it was barely possible to throw a stone to reach the tops.

There was another side to the fierce warlord. Though illiterate, he had intellectual interests, and indeed arrogance. 'I am intimate with learned men, to whom I am greatly devoted and in whose company I delight and I have the ancient zeal for learning.' In 1400, he met the great historian Ibn Khaldūn, and had many discussions with him. Ibn Khaldūn's verdict was that 'he is highly intelligent and very perspicacious, addicted to debate and argumentation about what he knows, and also about what he does not know'. Among other matters, the two disagreed over whether Nebuchadnezzar was the last of the kings of Babylon, or the first of Persia. Ibn Khaldūn was fortunate; it was not wise to contradict Temür. To sharpen his mind, Temür played chess, in particular a variant with additional squares and pieces such as the camel, giraffe and vizier.

Temür was a city-builder on a grand scale. He reconstructed Samarkand with magnificent palaces and mosques, which glittered with ornate tiles. Domes shone in iridescent blue. Fruit trees and fountains filled many a shady garden. Clavijo was extremely impressed by the palace being built at Kesh. Temür took an active personal interest in work on the mosque there, complaining that the door was not high enough and demanding that it be raised.

Governmental structures were of little interest to Temür. He made use of existing Persian administrative traditions, while relying to a great extent on members of his family and his close followers among the Chagadai people. Abuses of power, particularly by Persian bureaucrats, were investigated and the guilty executed. There was, however, little integration across the lands Temür ruled; his empire was held together by not much more than his personal authority and military power. On his death, it fell apart amidst a welter of localized power struggles. Although Temür had defeated Bāyazīd, it was the latter's Ottoman Empire that lasted, while Temürid rule collapsed.

There was little understanding of Temür in the west. His victory over Bāyazīd led some to rejoice that the Tatars had rid the world of the Ottoman threat. Others, though, were wiser. The French chivalric hero, Boucicaut (see pp. 240–43), realized there was no prospect that Temür would be any more a friend of Christendom than Bāyazīd had been. Clavijo may have enjoyed the feasts and gardens in Samarkand and been well treated, but his embassy was in vain.

Boucicaut
(Jean II le Maingre)

CHIVALRIC HERO

1366–1421

Jean le Maingre, known as Boucicaut, appreciated the importance of a good image. His biography, almost certainly written at his own request, firmly established him as one of the great chivalric heroes of France. Behind the spin, however, lies a tale of failure and unfulfilled promise.

Boucicaut was born in 1366, son of the marshal of France. He had great athletic prowess, the result of hard training. Among his feats, he could climb the underside of a ladder using only one hand, or two if he was wearing a steel breastplate. He could do a full somersault in armour. He was expert in handling weapons, particularly the lance and his sword; he was also a formidable tennis player. His military career began young; he first went on campaign at the age of twelve, and took part in his first battle at sixteen.

A true knight should fight in the service of Christendom. Boucicaut chose to go the Baltic, in 1384, on the first of three campaigns against the heathen of Lithuania. The third of these crusading ventures was especially 'grand, and very honourable and fine, with a great company of knights, squires and gentlemen'. Boucicaut also fought on many occasions in Spain and the eastern Mediterranean. In 1396, along with several thousand other Frenchmen, he joined the major crusade in the Balkans intended to reverse the advance of the Ottoman Turks. At Nicopolis, in modern Bulgaria, the Christian host was crushed by the Turkish sultan Bāyazīd's army. Boucicaut distinguished himself in the battle, charging right through the enemy ranks, sword in hand. He then turned back to help his companions, only to be taken prisoner. Many of the crusaders were executed, much as Boucicaut himself had massacred Muslim prisoners, but in his case a ransom secured his release.

To demonstrate prowess in the use of arms, knights were expected to compete in tournaments. In 1390, during a truce in the war between England and France, Boucicaut and two other French knights set up camp near Calais. They challenged any who dared joust with them. Though badly bruised – he had to take a week off – Boucicaut triumphed in the contests. The event was a great success, marked by much festivity.

Boucicaut kneeling in prayer before St Catherine of Alexandria; above him, an angel holds his shield. The illustrator of this Book of Hours is known as the Boucicaut Master.

Orders of knighthood, of which the best known was to be the English order of the Garter, were also an important feature of chivalry at this time. In 1399, Boucicaut set up his own order, that of the Green Shield with the White Lady. This combined the idea of an order with the chivalric obligation to protect ladies, for Boucicaut and his dozen companions vowed to assist noblewomen who found themselves in difficulty. As the poet, Christine de Pisan, put it:

> Those who, without faltering
> Bear the green shield with a beautiful lady,
> Wish, with sharp cutting swords
> To protect her against evil-doers.

The order was established for a trial period of five years; no more was heard of it.

Piety was another quality expected of a true knight. As the mid-fourteenth century treatise on knighthood written by Geoffroi de Charny explained, those who performed fine

deeds of arms 'to gain God's grace and for the salvation of the soul' would see their souls 'set in paradise to all eternity'. Boucicaut's biographer duly stressed his piety. He would get up early and pray for three hours; he attended mass twice a day. His approach to religion was not wholly austere; he had a magnificent book of hours produced for him in the leading Parisian workshop by one of the most notable artists of the day, whose identity regrettably remains a mystery. This book was at one and the same time an expression of religious faith and a display of wealth and taste.

Boucicaut was appointed as marshal of France in 1391. The post gave him an important voice in military command, and it was he who drew up the French battle-plan before the battle of Agincourt in 1415. The scheme was sensible, with dismounted men-at-arms positioned in the centre, two cavalry wings, and archers in front. In the event, it proved impossible to implement Boucicaut's plan on the narrow battlefield. As the French advanced at the start of the battle, they had no answer to the English longbowmen, and their cavalry was ineffective in the muddy conditions. The hand-to-hand fighting was brutal. Boucicaut was wounded, and dragged out from one of the horrific piles of bodies on the battlefield. He was taken to England, where he died, a prisoner of war, in 1421.

Boucicaut was not, if his biographer is to be believed, particularly good company. He forbad anyone under his command to play dice, and threatened to punish severely anyone who swore. His reading matter consisted, not of chivalric romances, but of saints' lives or histories of Classical heroes. He was frugal, insisting on being served only one kind of meat, and disdaining any elaborate sauces. He would use only wooden platters, not gold or silver plate, and he drank his wine well watered-down. All this, of course, was set out by his biographer in order to emphasize his hero's upright, chivalrous character, and perhaps should not be taken at face value. What seemed admirable at the start of the fifteenth century may have less appeal today.

In many ways, Boucicaut epitomized the chivalric knight. He was brave, courteous, pious and highly skilled in the use of arms. Yet he was a failure. He was on the losing side in the two battles he fought as an adult, Nicopolis and Agincourt. His many crusading ventures, particularly those in the Mediterranean, did not secure any significant advances for Christianity. His attempt to set up a new order of chivalry came to nothing. His reputation, however, could hardly have been higher. Heroism, even in a lost cause, was thoroughly admirable.

The Jousts of St Inglevert took place in 1390 near Calais. Boucicaut and his colleagues distinguished themselves in combat against all comers. From a late fifteenth-century Flemish manuscript of Froissart's Chronicles.

Jan Žižka

BLIND HUSSITE GENERAL

d. 1424

I n the 1370s, an Oxford scholar, John Wycliffe, began to develop ideas that were regarded as heretical. This was an occupational hazard for theologians, but Wycliffe went far further than most, attacking the papacy, the Church's hierarchy, monasticism and the friars. Popular preachers spread his ideas, and in 1414 they inspired an ineffective rising led by Sir John Oldcastle. However, these Lollards, as they were known, never posed a real threat to state and society in England. The story was very different in Bohemia, where Jan Žižka provided the Hussites with military leadership of a kind the Lollards never had.

At the university of Prague, another theologian, Jan Hus, had taken up Wycliffe's ideas. Hus also was an ardent critic of the clergy, the papacy and the sale of indulgences. He raised many doctrinal issues, notably over transubstantiation and the mass; and, like Wycliffe, he believed in predestination. The connection with the Lollards was close; in 1410, Oldcastle offered Hus encouragement and, in the same year, Wycliffe's works were publicly burned in Prague on the orders of the archbishop.

In 1414, Hus was summoned to attend the Council of Constance, which had been convened in Switzerland to try to resolve the Great Schism and bring to an end the embarrassment of rival papacies. Hus agreed to attend under the aegis of a safe-conduct provided by the emperor-elect, Sigismund, son of Charles IV (see pp. 203–6). Despite this protection, he was arrested in the Swiss town in June 1415. He was tried, refused to recant, and was burned for heresy.

Hus's execution spurred on his followers. No fewer than 452 Bohemian and Moravian nobles endorsed a letter of protest. Increasingly, however, radical views were put forward in what was becoming as much a popular as a religious rebellion. Church reform and nationalist feelings combined in a heady revolutionary mix. Different branches of this Hussite movement soon emerged. The Utraquists held that all should take both bread and wine at communion; more radical were the Orebites and the millenarian Taborites; most extreme of all were the anarchic Adamites, who believed in nudism and free love. Sigismund, who had succeeded his brother, Wenceslaus IV, as ruler of Bohemia in 1419, was determined to put down the rising. In 1420, at his instigation, a crusade was declared against the Hussites, who were described in a papal bull as 'a vile and venomous serpent's egg'.

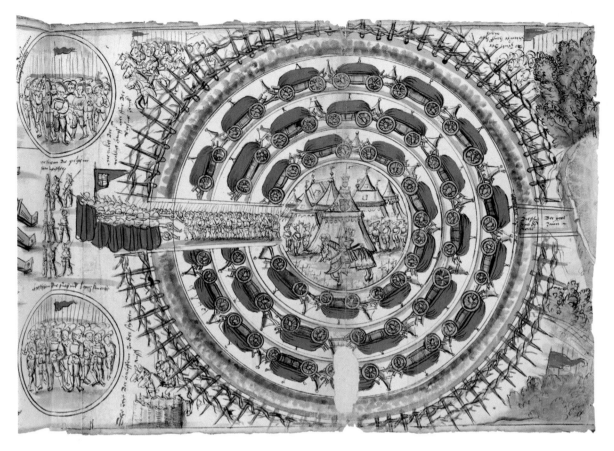

A representation of the Hussite wagenburg, *a powerful defensive ring of armoured war-wagons.*

In 1419, a Hussite mob stormed the city hall in Prague and threw the councillors from the window. Among those who took part in the attack was Jan Žižka, a member of the palace guard. Žižka came from Trocnov, near Budějovice, where his family was of the minor gentry. At some point in his childhood, he was blinded in one eye. In the 1380s, he sold his lands and sought a career at court, initially as a huntsman. His first military experience came in 1410, when he fought with the Poles against the German Teutonic Knights, and probably took part in the battle of Tannenberg. When the Hussites seized one of the royal castles that commanded Prague, he emerged as one of their leaders.

Žižka soon revealed his qualities as a commander. In 1420, he defeated royalist forces at Sudoměř, where the power of his war-wagons against cavalry attack was first demonstrated. Later in the same year, he broke Sigismund's siege of Prague. At the siege of Rábí, in 1421, an arrow hit Žižka in his good eye, completely blinding him. He was not deterred, but continued in command, winning further victories. Žižka fought other Hussites, as well as Sigismund's royalist armies. He destroyed the Adamites and, in 1424, was victorious in

Hussite troops shown as the army of Christ, tearing down the banner of their crusading opponents, from the remarkable contemporary manuscript known as the Jena Codex.

two battles over the Utraquists. In October that year he died, not fighting in battle, but of disease, possibly plague.

Žižka's achievement was extraordinary. He built a new kind of army, and equipped it with new weaponry, including guns. Few of those he led were professional soldiers; some were women. He needed 'everyone capable of swinging a club and throwing a stone'. He believed in strong discipline, as his military regulations of 1423 showed. No one was to go ahead of the army to set up camp or find a billet without proper orders. Fires could be lit only by those appointed to do so. Before starting any march, the troops should fall to their knees to beseech God 'that we may carry on His holy fight to His holy glory'. No personal plunder was to be taken, and quarrels, fights, desertion and other such offences were strictly forbidden, on pain of 'flogging, slaying, decapitating, hanging, whipping, burning, drowning'. The Hussite battle song reflected this code. One verse went:

> Everyone must remember the password
> Just as it was given to you
> Always obey your captain
> Each one should help and guard his companions
> Everyone must stay in his own battalion.

The Hussite war-wagons, defended with iron plate and equipped with gun loops, were a novelty on the battlefields of the early fifteenth century. When they were linked together in a circle it was almost impossible to breach their defence. Žižka aimed to set them on high ground, and to repel any attacks with gunfire. When the moment came, the wagons were opened, and infantry armed with flails and clubs rushed out. Nor were the wagons purely defensive. At Malešov, in 1424, he had them loaded with stones and launched downhill on a terrified enemy. Unlike most medieval commanders, Žižka sought battle rather than avoiding it, and he campaigned in winter when his enemies least expected to be attacked.

Žižka was a stout, strong man of middling height, with a Polish-style moustache. He possessed intensely strong religious feelings, describing himself as 'seeking the law of God and the good of the commonwealth'. It was, no doubt, his convictions rather than motiveless cruelty that led him to order the massacre and burning of the Adamites. He was a man of enormous courage, a leader who believed in fighting in the front rank. The power of his personality was shown to the full when, astonishingly, he did not give up his command after he was blinded. The problems he faced in trying to hold together a popular movement were immense, his achievements extraordinary. He created a new army, developed new tactics, and never lost a battle. His death did not mark the end of the movement he had led with such charisma. His mantle was taken up by a priest, Prokop the Bald, and it was not until 1434 that the Hussites were finally defeated.

Hussite guns were notably advanced. This reproduction of a tarasnice has an easily adjustable elevation mechanism.

Joan of Arc

THE MAID OF ORLÉANS AND SAINT

c. 1412–31

There are no good contemporary descriptions of Joan of Arc's appearance. This suggests her looks were unremarkable. If so, that was surely all that was ordinary about her. A pious, poorly educated peasant girl from Domrémy, in northeastern France, she claimed to have heard 'voices' from the age of thirteen, and to have been directed by God to inspire a recovery by the hard-pressed French in the war against the English.

Joan left her home late in December 1428, and emerged four months later, at the siege of Orléans, as a fully fledged and highly effective military leader. The many surviving records give no hint as to what assistance Joan received in acquiring military skills and constructing her identity as the saviour of France, although it is inconceivable that she had no training at all. The French commander, the Duc d'Alençon, said later that she had the ability of a captain of twenty or thirty years' experience: 'She was very expert in war, both in bearing a lance and recruiting an army, in planning a battle and setting up artillery.' She rode in style, sword in hand, ready to give 'hard clouts and buffets'. She took a full part in councils of war, and determinedly put forward her ideas, usually advocating swift surprise attacks. It is almost unbelievable that hardened soldiers were prepared to listen to, and argue with, a totally inexperienced peasant girl.

Men were prepared to accept Joan's advice because it appeared that divine authority underlay it. She claimed the help she provided came 'from God, who at the request of Saint Louis and Saint Charlemagne, felt pity for the city of Orléans'. There had been prophetic tales that an armed virgin on horseback would rescue France from her enemies, and these provided Joan with an agenda to follow, and gave her unanswerable arguments. She told one critic, 'Have you not heard the prophecy that having been destroyed by a woman, France will be saved by a maiden from the marches of Lorraine?'

As a military leader, Joan had great courage. Bold and determined, she was the first to plant a scaling ladder in the capture of a fortress at Orléans. When wounded by an arrow she cried, but, once bandaged up, returned to lead the fight. She was adept at encouraging and giving heart to her men. They did not object even when she did all she could to stop their swearing. Her one weakness as a commander was occasional indecision. The advice of the 'voices' she heard, those of St Michael, St Catherine and St Margaret, was not always

An idealized image of Joan of Arc in gilded armour, from an early sixteenth-century manuscript.

sufficiently specific; on one occasion at Orléans she woke in the night: 'In God's name, my councillor says I should go against the English, but I don't know if I should attack their forts, or Fastolf, who is revictualling them.' One chronicler described her as 'perpetually changing her resolutions; sometimes she was eager for conflict, at other times not'.

Joan's impact on French morale and on the war was extraordinary. It took her nine days to drive the English away from Orléans and relieve the seven-month siege of the city. Following this triumph, 'The country now resounded with praises of the Maid, and no other warrior was noticed.' After her victory at the battle of Patay, in June 1429, her ambition of seeing the dauphin crowned at Reims was fulfilled. However, further military success eluded Joan. She failed in her assault on Paris in the following September, and was wounded. The bubble was burst. When she was captured by the Burgundian allies of the English in March 1430, her French supporters made no efforts to rescue her.

Joan was transferred to the English-held city of Rouen, in Normandy, where she was tried for heresy. Her trial, which began in January 1431, presented her with very different challenges from any she had faced previously. Alone, she confronted an array of learned French clerics, headed by the bishop of Beauvais, anxious to trip her up and get her to contradict herself. She was clever and determined, and did not make it easy for her questioners, avoiding their attempts to catch her out. She frequently used her 'voices' as a reason for not answering. When asked in what form St Michael appeared to her, she countered: 'There is as yet no reply to that, for I have not had leave to answer.' She answered sharply when asked if the saint was naked when he came to her: 'Do you think God has not wherewithal to clothe him?' And when her questioner enquired if he had hair, she responded: 'Why should it be shorn off?'

The surviving tower of the castle at Rouen, where Joan of Arc was held prisoner during her trial.

Joan's appearance was a major issue in the trial. As far as she could, Joan had discarded her female identity. She cut her dark hair short, and dressed in men's clothes, with shirt, breeches, doublet and hose. It was argued that this was heretical, against divine law. Her opinion was clear: 'Since I do it by God's command and in His service I do not think I do wrong.' Her accusers' view was that, 'having cast aside all womanly decency, not only to the scorn of feminine modesty, but also of well-instructed men, she had worn the apparel and garments of most dissolute men'. There was, as result, 'nothing about her to display and announce her sex, save Nature's own distinctive marks'. What Joan wore became the evident and very public indication of whether or not she was prepared to admit to heresy. Eventually she did so, only to recant her confession four days later and put on men's garments once more. This, together with her admission that she was still listening to her 'voices', resulted in her condemnation. She was burned to death in Rouen in May 1431 at the age, she thought, of nineteen.

There have been many attempts to diagnose Joan in medical terms. She heard 'voices', which were accompanied by light, had delusions that God had sent her to save France, and ate very little. These symptoms could indicate anorexia, with its associated mental problems. The evidence, however, is insufficient to prove this. Nor does it explain Joan's determination, her powerful convictions and her self-belief.

Joan of Arc's brief military career transformed French morale, and marked a turning point in the Hundred Years War. However, her importance extends much further, for she has since become a vital element in the national identity of France.

Filippo Brunelleschi

ARCHITECT

1377–1446

How do you stand an egg upright on a slab of smooth marble? Filippo Brunelleschi knew the answer, and this is one of the reasons why he was chosen to construct the great dome on the cathedral in Florence.

Brunelleschi, Pippo to his friends, was born in 1377 in Florence. He began his career as a goldsmith and sculptor, and showed mechanical skill in making clocks. When, in 1401, a competition was held to design doors for the Baptistry in Florence, Brunelleschi was one of the entrants. He was, however, disappointed. Lorenzo Ghiberti claimed that he won fairly; Brunelleschi took a different view. After this, Brunelleschi went to Rome with his friend, the sculptor Donatello. He became obsessed with ancient buildings and intrigued by the technical details of their construction. The vast rotunda of the Pantheon in particular fascinated him, for in Florence there was much discussion about how to complete the city's cathedral with a great dome. This had been planned late in the thirteenth century, but there

The cathedral at Florence, dominated by Brunelleschi's great dome, remarkable for the ingenuity of its engineering.

had been much argument over how it could be built, with disputes over such issues as whether the octagon on which the dome would stand should have supporting buttresses, in the Gothic fashion. The powerful guild of wool merchants was in charge of the project, and held a competition in 1418 for proposals demonstrating how the dome could be built. Unlike everyone else, Brunelleschi claimed that he could construct it without using any temporary wooden formers or centring. At first, he was laughed out of court. It took two years, much canvassing and three further models before he was finally commissioned to build the dome. Doubtless to his despair, his rival Ghiberti was asked to undertake the task jointly with him. However, it was Brunelleschi's design that was used, and Ghiberti was removed from the project.

Brunelleschi's dome was to be a double structure: an inner lightweight shell, and a more solid outer one. He planned to build the outer dome by using the inner one as a scaffold. Ribs, and horizontal stone rings or chains, gave added strength. The clever use of a herringbone pattern for the brickwork helped direct weight on to the supporting structure. To aid construction, Brunelleschi devised a particularly ingenious great hoist to haul the building materials up to the workmen. This had a reverse gear, so that the oxen which supplied the motive power did not need to be constantly coupled and uncoupled. Construction, not surprisingly, did not go smoothly. Cracks were found in 1429. The budget was halved. The masons went on strike. Throughout the process, Brunelleschi's imagination was called upon to overcome a never-ending stream of obstacles – not least, how to feed his workmen without their having to come down to the ground. Sadly, he was not to see the final completion of the dome, for the great lantern at its apex was only finished in 1461, fifteen years after his death.

In building the dome, Brunelleschi was working to a largely predetermined design. It is more a demonstration of his engineering prowess than a display of his gifts as an architect. Other buildings provide a better illustration of his architectural style, which was strongly influenced by what he had seen in Rome. Round arches, and columns with Corinthian or Ionic capitals, characterized his work, as with the loggia of the Foundling Hospital in Florence. His contemporary biographer, in describing one of Brunelleschi's last buildings, the rotunda of Santa Maria degli Angeli, summed up his talents:

> Being completely in the antique manner inside and outside, it has rare and subtle innovations in what one can see as it stands now, because he attempted new and beautiful things. Problems which normally entail great inconvenience were remedied. He introduced new methods and saved a great deal of money.

Brunelleschi's expertise, like that of many of the great figures in late-medieval Florence, was not confined to a single field. Experience in surveying led him to work out, by 1413, the rules for linear perspective, which he demonstrated with a device that used mirrors to provide an accurate image. He constructed stage machinery, which enabled heavenly beings to descend from on high, and allowed Christ to rise to a cloud featuring revolving angels. However, he was not uniformly successful in his endeavours. The ship he built to transport

Brunelleschi is on the right in this fresco by Masaccio. From left to right, the others are Masolino, Masaccio himself, and Alberti.

marble up the river Arno to Florence for use in the cathedral sank in 1427, costing him an estimated ten years' wages. His plan to build a dam so as to flood an invading enemy's position ended in disaster when the Florentine camp was destroyed, along with Brunelleschi's own bed.

Unfortunately, Brunelleschi was secretive about much of what he did. His architectural models often lacked detail, so that others could not copy his designs. He scrupulously followed the advice he gave his friend Taccola (see pp. 254–56): 'Do not tell everyone about your ideas but speak only to the few who understand and appreciate science, because putting yourself about too much, and explaining your own inventions and actions is just squandering your own talent.' Consequently, too much of Brunelleschi's achievement, particularly in engineering, remains obscure. In architecture, he may have lacked the depth of theoretical knowledge that the great Renaissance architect and polymath Leon Battista Alberti, some thirty years his junior, would display. Yet his developed, Classical style marked a new beginning, a startling transformation in how churches and other public buildings might look. Although perspective was not new to painters, it was not consistently or accurately used until Brunelleschi. The first notable artist to apply his rules was his friend, Masaccio, whose work as a result marks a clear turning point in the evolution of European art.

As for the egg test, lateral thinking is all that's needed. Brunelleschi simply struck the egg on the marble slab, so that the end was crushed. It could then be stood upright.

Taccola
(Mariano di Jacopo)
SIENA'S ARCHIMEDES
1382–1453

Mariano di Jacopo, known as Taccola, or 'Little blackbird', was a Sienese official. Relatively little is known of his career; the major civic office to which he was appointed in 1441 was that of *viaio*, or superintendent of streets. Taccola had good contacts. He knew Brunelleschi (see pp. 251–53), and left a record of a conversation he had with him. His daughter's godfather was the celebrated sculptor Jacopo della Quercia. He established a short-lived, but particularly important connection, in 1432, when the emperor-elect Sigismund resided in Siena for nine months. Taccola was given a position in Sigismund's household, held discussions with him and drew his portrait.

Taccola's great interest lay in military and civil engineering. Through Sigismund, he came across the work of Conrad Kyeser, a German engineer whose book, *Bellifortis*, contained many drawings of siege engines and other devices. Taccola produced his own book on siege weapons and other military equipment, which he probably presented to Sigismund in 1433. In 1449, he finished another illustrated treatise, on machines. Many of his drawings were the product of his imagination rather than of his practical experience. Some derive from Kyeser, while others anticipate work by Leonardo da Vinci.

Some of Taccola's siege engines, such as trebuchets and rams, had been in use for centuries. He also had new ideas to offer. He designed movable platforms for various purposes, such as supporting scaling ladders. Crossing rivers was often a problem for armies. Taccola's solution was a six-wheeled cart carrying a hinged bridge. This was to be held in a vertical position until it reached the waterway, when it would be dropped into position. He also drew a sectional bridge, which could be expanded as was needed. Some of his ideas for warfare appear less practical. He drew a mounted knight, conventionally equipped with a lance, but whose horse was fitted with a pole carrying incendiary material in a brazier hung on the end. Another mounted warrior wielded a handgun, so heavy that it needed an elaborate arrangement of straps to hold it.

Taccola's civil engineering work is even more intriguing. He was fascinated by the problems presented by water. He depicted coffer dams and caissons, to demonstrate how bridges and other structures could be built in water. His books contain a number of pumping devices, notably a piston pump. A water tower and conduit showed how a supply system could work. Taccola also drew a number of waterwheels; one of them had a camshaft which operated two bellows that fed a blast furnace. An elaborate system of pumps with a reservoir might be used for a watermill in regions where water was scarce. In contrast, by the sea, the tide could be harnessed to power mills.

Taccola was interested in solving the load-moving problems that faced builders. It was perhaps his association with Brunelleschi that led him to show how a reversible gearing system could work, for the Florentine employed one in his hoist for building the dome of the cathedral in Florence. Large monolithic columns were hard both to quarry and to transport, and Taccola proposed possible solutions. He advocated the use of mobile cranes for placing heavy loads in the right places.

Not all of these inventions made sense. An amphibious wagon had a sail to power it on land. In water, however, it was pulled by oxen, for as Taccola explained, 'many oxen can stand being under water without breathing'. He suggested that a diver might ride a large fish underwater. Other ingenious, if impractical, ideas included a dog tied by a long rope to a lever fixed to the bell on a tower. When the hungry dog moved towards its dinner, it would pull the rope, and the bell would be sounded.

 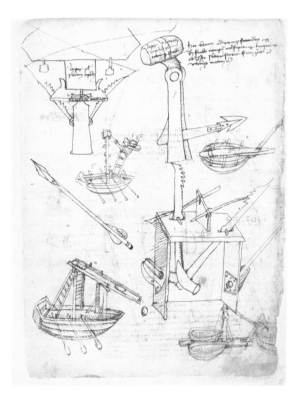

Two pages from Taccola's book De Ingeniis. *On the left, a mounted warrior equipped with a gun. On the right, ships equipped to deliver weapons, and various military machines.*

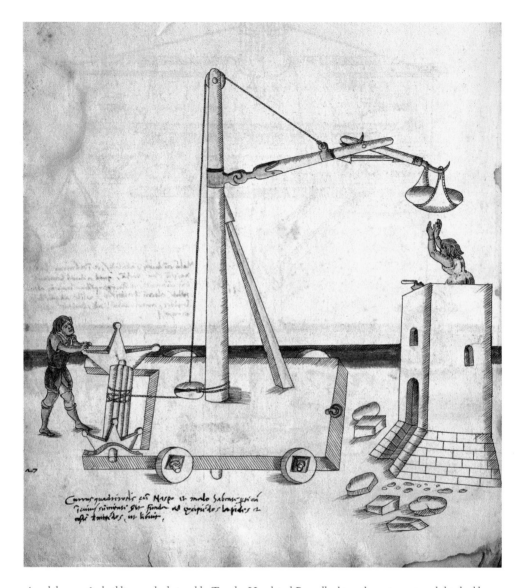

A mobile crane for building work, designed by Taccola. He advised Brunelleschi on the equipment needed to build the dome of the cathedral at Florence.

Taccola's work shows that medieval engineers did not lack imagination, or a desire to find new solutions. Nor, in Taccola's case, was there a lack of confidence, for he compared himself with Archimedes. Much of his work, though, is derivative, and hardly compares with that of the great Greek. It was, however, used and copied by Francesco di Giorgio, the Sienese military architect and engineer, who developed the concept of star-shaped defences in the fortifications he built for the duke of Urbino. It forms part of a tradition whose greatest exponent was to be Leonardo da Vinci.

Clara Sanuto

DISSOLUTE VENETIAN ABBESS

EARLY 1400S

Many medieval nuns possessed a genuine sense of religious calling. In the twelfth century, Christina of Markyate rejected her parents' plan for her to marry, and had no truck with the wicked designs of Ranulf Flambard, bishop of Durham, on her chastity. Like many holy women, she had visions which reinforced her faith. After years of solitude, she became the prioress of a small community of nuns. In other cases, where convents might meet the social need of providing for families with too many daughters, there might be less sense of vocation. This was very clear in fifteenth-century Venice.

Of noble birth, Clara Sanuto entered the Venetian convent of Sant'Angelo di Contorta, along with her sister, Filipa, early in the fifteenth century, and rose to be its abbess. Sant'Angelo was situated on a small island in the lagoon, not far from the Giudecca. A government scribe, Marco Bono, was a frequent visitor to the convent. On one enjoyable occasion, he and a friend, Benedetto Malipiero, took Clara and Filipa, along with some other nuns, to another island in the lagoon, where they 'committed numerous dissolute deeds'. Filipa was Marco's special favourite; however, he became suspicious about her other visitors, and one night, following Carnival celebrations, he came to the nunnery armed and ready for trouble. Filipa was entertaining a noble, Andrea Valier, at the time. Marco entered her cell, and drove the couple out. In the hubbub, several other nuns emerged with their visitors. Chaos ensued.

The matter came to the attention of the civic authorities in 1415, and the affairs

A nun joyfully disporting herself, from a fourteenth-century Flemish manuscript. A friar makes music for her, using a bellows as his instrument.

of the convent were investigated. It became clear that the good work done by the nuns in taking in abandoned foundlings was a convenient way of disguising the fact that the nuns were in fact the mothers of some of the babies. One, Constanza Balastro, had given birth recently. A number of young men, including the father of Constanza's baby, fled from Venice to avoid prosecution for fornication.

Sant'Angelo was investigated again, in 1439, when Clara had become abbess. One nun, Valeria Valier, already the mother of a girl, had a baby boy. The father could have been one of three men: a former servant of the nunnery, a seller of old clothes or a third individual, of unknown occupation. Valeria was of noble birth, and had disgraced her class as well as dishonouring her vows. As for Clara herself, it turned out that she had been having affairs, both with another of the convent servants for many years, and also with an official of a more suitable social background. Another of the nuns had been visited on a regular basis by a government scribe; he, in turn, had also been sleeping with a young novice.

The problems continued at Sant'Angelo. In 1447, Liseta de Buora, one of the nuns, assisted in the seduction of an underage girl by her relative, Marco de Buora, and had affairs with at least six men, including Marco, before she left to take up a full-time career as a courtesan. Marco did not limit himself to Sant'Angelo; in 1455, he was convicted along with four other men of fornication with Camilla Morosini, a nun from a notable Venetian family in the convent of San Biasio. Sant'Angelo, however, was the most notorious of the Venetian convents, and was eventually closed on papal orders in 1474.

Virtuous nuns, shown in at their devotions in King Henry VI's psalter.

There is no indication that the nuns of Sant'Angelo were forced to do what they did in order to make money; they were not running a commercial brothel. Rather, they appear to have enjoyed providing a service of which the young men of Venice were only too eager to take advantage. Nor was Sant'Angelo unique: in 1428, at San Nicolai di Torcello, one nun, Filipa Barbarigo (the abbess's sister), was found to have had ten lovers. There is, however, little in medieval history to parallel the scale of the activities of the Venetian nuns. In England, for example, the nearest equivalent is probably the recurrent problems at the convent at Godstow, just outside Oxford, where the nuns presented an obvious temptation to the university students. In 1284,

The marginal illustration at the foot of the page of this fourteenth-century manuscript shows nuns enjoying themselves playing piggyback.

there were rumours about the activities of the sub-prioress, and orders were issued that the nuns were not to speak to any students, unless they were related to them. There were further scandals in the late fourteenth century; as a result of one, the chaplain of Wolvercote was forbidden to enter the convent. In 1432, discipline was tightened again, for 'the scholars of Oxford say that they can have all kinds of good cheer with the nuns to their heart's desire'. Only a single nun, however, was discovered to have been unchaste.

Margaret of Anjou

CONTROVERSIAL QUEEN OF ENGLAND

1430–82

There was much celebration in London when the king of France's fifteen-year-old niece, Margaret of Anjou, entered the city in 1445 in order to marry King Henry VI. Pageants greeted her whenever the procession stopped. One of the fanciful constructions was a Noah's Ark. When she reached this, Margaret was compared to a dove of peace, for the marriage had been brokered in the expectation that it would provide the cornerstone for peace between England and France:

> Through your grace and high benignity,
> Between the two realms, England and France,
> Peace shall approach, rest and unity,
> Mars be set aside, with all his cruelty.

Though Margaret and Henry were close in the years following their marriage, it was some considerable time before she performed her queenly duty of producing an heir; it may be that the pious king lacked enthusiasm for his role in the process. Nevertheless, in 1453, a son, Edward, was born. Shortly before the birth, however, the king collapsed both physically and mentally, and was reduced to a catatonic state.

As mother to the infant prince of Wales, from the mid-1450s Margaret's position was transformed, and she began to take a leading political role. One commentator wrote that 'the queen is a great and strong laboured woman, for she spareth no pain to sue her things to an intent and conclusion'. The country was riven by faction, government finances were in an appalling state and the prospect either of rule by a timid and incapable king, or of a regency headed by a foreign queen, was dire. The challenge came from the duke of York. Civil conflict, the Wars of the Roses, was the outcome. In 1460, York was killed at the battle of Wakefield; the victory of his son, Edward, at the brutal battle of Towton the following year led to the latter's coronation as king. Margaret took refuge, first in Scotland, and then France. Her frantic diplomatic efforts to win support and oust Edward IV finally came to fruition in 1470, when, with the support of the earl of Warwick, the 'Kingmaker', Henry VI was restored to the English throne. Success was brief. When Margaret returned to England in 1471, it was to hear of the defeat of Lancastrian forces at Barnet and the death of Warwick. At Tewkesbury, three weeks later, her son, Edward, prince of Wales, was slain and she was taken prisoner. The death of Henry VI at Yorkist hands shortly afterwards marked the end of her dreams. She was held in custody by Edward IV until 1475, when she was ransomed by the French. She lived out the last seven years of her life in the land of her birth, Anjou.

Margaret's many enemies and hostile chroniclers have painted a damning picture of the queen. She brought an inadequate dowry with her, and there were suspicions that she was acting in French interests. It was rumoured that Henry VI was not the father of her son. A newsletter of 1454 reported that 'she desires to have the whole rule of this land', and that she wanted to appoint all royal officials, and even bishops. She was seen as an ambitious and unscrupulous power-seeker, responsible for the political breakdown of the mid-1450s, when she and her associates ruled as they wished.

In fact, the evidence for such a portrayal is scant. Margaret played no discernible political role until after her son was born, and even then the records do not suggest that she interfered much in government business. None of the royal warrants of the late 1450s specify that they were issued on the queen's instructions, whereas many were initialled by the king. She did, however, act on behalf of her son, and exercised control over the lands that he held, particularly in the Midlands and Cheshire.

Margaret spent much of her time in her castle of Tutbury in Staffordshire, for she disliked London intensely. She appreciated the importance of exercising good lordship, and her surviving letters show the care she took to look after her associates, servants and tenants. When her tenants at the Hertfordshire village of Hertingfordbury complained of the actions of a local knight, John Forester, in driving some of them off the land and imprisoning others, Margaret wrote to him in fierce terms, complaining that he had acted 'not only in great hindering and undoing of our said tenants, but also unto great derogation of us and of our said lordship, whereof we marvel greatly'.

Margaret's cultural interests were limited. The celebrated lawyer and propagandist, Sir John Fortescue, went into exile with her in the 1460s; she valued his political views. The earl of Shrewsbury presented her with a magnificently illustrated manuscript of romances, but it seems unlikely that she read it. She did not share her husband's piety, or his enthusiasm for education, for although she founded Queens' College in Cambridge in 1448, she did not attend the laying of the foundation

Margaret of Anjou, from the Guild Book of the London Skinners' Fraternity. She joined the fraternity in the 1470s.

stone or provide it with a substantial endowment, nor did she take much interest in its development. Her tastes were more conventional. She was, above all, a keen huntswoman. In one
of many letters on the subject, she wrote to the keeper of Lady Say's Falborne Park:

> We will and charge you, that the game there be favoured, cherished and kept, without
> suffering any person of whatsoever degree, estate or condition he be of, to hunt there,
> or have course, shot or other sport so reducing the aforesaid game, without a special
> command from us or Lady Say.

The building records for Margaret's manor of Plesaunce at Greenwich give some idea of
the state in which she liked to live. There were two courtyards, one for the king, and one for
the queen, each with their respective households. In hers, Margaret had a great chamber, a
parlour and a gallery. Heraldic stained-glass enhanced the windows. The garden, hedged all
round, had an arbour for her use.

The challenges Margaret faced in her life were immense. Her match with Henry did not
bring an end to the Hundred Years War. When peace came in 1453, it was not through any
influence she might have, but resulted from the defeat of English forces. A Frenchwoman
among a people who had learned to hate the French, queen to a feeble king prone to mental
collapse, Margaret did all she could to preserve her son's royal inheritance. She was, however,
no military commander, and her diplomatic efforts were ineffective. Although she failed, the
task was an impossible one, and she deserves admiration for her efforts. Her reputation has
been ill-served both by many of her contemporaries and, much later, above all by William
Shakespeare. The literary and dramatic merits of his plays about the English monarchy in
the fifteenth century are, unfortunately, outbalanced by their historical inaccuracy.

*John Talbot, earl of Salisbury, presenting Margaret of Anjou with a book of romances. She is seated, holding
hands with her husband, King Henry VI. This fine manuscript was produced in Normandy, and presented
to Margaret in 1445.*

Johannes Gutenberg

INVENTOR AND FAILED BUSINESSMAN

c. 1400–68

In 1438, a small consortium of artisans and businessmen in Strasbourg came up with a scheme to get rich quick. The emperor Charlemagne (see pp. 16–19) had presented a number of valuable relics to the cathedral at Aachen. These relics, which included the Virgin Mary's cloak and Christ's loincloth, were brought out only every seven years. There was money to be made from the pilgrims who flocked to see them. The scheme was to make mirrors which would capture images of the relics, trapping their power.

Unfortunately, floods caused the pilgrimage to be cancelled, and the project was abandoned. Instead, the partners turned to another venture, one so secret that its instigator, Johannes Gutenberg, was unwilling to reveal any details. This was almost certainly printing.

The scion of a wealthy family, Gutenberg left his home city of Mainz, probably as a result of a political upheaval directed against the better-off. He then settled in Strasbourg, but little is known of his activities there. Records show that, in 1434, in pursuit of a debt he claimed was owed to him, he had a visiting dignitary from Mainz arrested. A couple of years later, a young woman called Ennelin sued him for breach of promise. It seems unlikely that he ever married. He stayed in Strasbourg until 1444, and by 1448 had returned to Mainz. There he continued to develop printing.

In Mainz, Gutenberg obtained finance from a wealthy burgher, Johann

A seventeenth-century woodcut of Johannes Gutenberg. There are no contemporary images of him.

The opening of the Book of Proverbs in the Gutenberg Bible. While the text is printed, the illustrations are done by hand.

Fust. The first items Gutenberg printed may have been indulgences, produced as early as 1452. When the general chapter of Benedictine abbots in the Mainz diocese was held in 1451, Cardinal Nicholas of Cusa stressed the need for their libraries to hold good copies of the bible. Gutenberg saw his opportunity, and despite the scale and difficulty of the project, began to print them. In 1455, Aeneas Silvius Piccolomini, later to become Pope Pius II, and author among other things of an erotic novel, wrote to a friend that he had met a wonderful man in Frankfurt selling bibles so neatly written that his friend would be able to read the text without his glasses.

In the autumn of 1455, Gutenberg's partnership with Fust broke down catastrophically. Fust took Gutenberg to court. He claimed interest at 6 per cent on loans he had made to Gutenberg, but the latter claimed, implausibly, that although interest had been specified in the deeds, Fust had promised not to levy it. Fust took over the business, and ran it along with one of Gutenberg's workmen, Peter Schöffer. It was Fust and Schöffer who put their names to the magnificent Mainz Psalter, published in 1457, though Gutenberg must have done much of the initial work on it. Gutenberg did receive some recognition, however, when in 1465 he was granted a pension by the archbishop of Mainz, sufficient to keep him in some comfort for the last years of his life. He died in 1468.

The key to Gutenberg's method of printing was the use of movable metal type. His genius lay in the careful development of an entire system, from making the moulds for the type and the frame in which it was then set, to the press itself. He also made the oil-based ink that was required. Gutenberg's methods are still not fully understood in all their details; computer analysis has suggested that his letters may have been cast in sand, rather than made by using steel punches to create the matrices in which the type was moulded. Years of obsessive experimentation must have been needed to get the whole process right. To have produced something as magnificent as Gutenberg's bible was quite astonishing; it was an amazing technical achievement.

There have, inevitably, been claims that Gutenberg was not the originator of printing. There is evidence for the use of movable type in China from as early as the eleventh century, and in Korea from the thirteenth. However, there is no evidence for transmission of the technology from east to west. Suggestions that printing was invented in the Low Countries, and subsequently taken up by Gutenberg, have little credibility.

The new method of book production spread with astonishing speed. Gutenberg failed to make a commercial success of his invention, but others were remarkably quick to see its potential, and realize the demand for books. Venice was the most important centre, with the first press established in 1469. Thirty years later, some 400 printers were active in the city. In the 1470s printing began in England, Poland and the Low Countries. The revolution had begun. In the past, with books copied by hand, no one version was identical to another, and mistakes might well occur. Printing meant that copies were standardized. Above all, printing meant that multiple copies could be produced quickly and cheaply.

Johannes Gutenberg was a failure in business. A man of immense technical ability, he was incapable of taking forward the astonishing breakthrough that he made in book production. He lacked commercial acumen; when sued by Fust, he could not even provide accounts to demonstrate what he had spent on the printing project. Importantly, he failed to keep what he was doing secret. As a result, a revolution took place which transformed the world.

Charles the Bold

OVERAMBITIOUS DUKE OF BURGUNDY

1433–77

Charles the Bold was the last ruler of the great medieval state of Burgundy. It had come into being in 1363, when the French king John II granted the duchy to his youngest son, Philip. Through marriage to the daughter of the count of Flanders, Philip gained not only Flanders but also Brabant, Artois and the Franche-Comté. His successors, the Valois dukes of Burgundy, thus ruled an immense but patchwork state. The wealthy towns of the Low Countries provided resources for the dukes, but often challenged their authority. The ducal court, based at Brussels from the 1440s, was a notable

A scene at the Burgundian court, showing Charles the Bold being presented with a book.

artistic centre, as portraits of the dukes by Rogier van der Weyden and magnificent illustrated manuscripts commissioned by them show.

Charles the Bold came to power in 1465 when his father, Philip the Good, became too ill to govern, and inherited the title two years later, on Philip's death. As his sobriquet suggests, Charles was a warlike ruler, although his numerous campaigns were seldom decisive. He had initial success against France at the battle of Montlhéry in 1465, but it was not fully followed up. His invasion of France in 1471 took him as far as the Somme, but otherwise achieved little. In 1474, he began the siege of Neuss, in support of Rupprecht, archbishop of Cologne and brother of the count palatine of the Rhine. After almost a year, the siege had to be abandoned. In 1476, Charles suffered defeat at the hands of the Swiss at the battle of Grandson, and shortly afterwards was routed by them again at Murten. In the next year, he died attempting to recapture the city of Nancy.

Charles worked day and night. He supervised everything he could in person, writing a great many letters and instructions himself, in appalling handwriting. Yet he received little praise from contemporaries. The care he took on financial matters led to accusations of avarice. He was thought to be 'pompous and lofty' in speech; he did not believe in cutting what he had to say short. According to the Burgundian courtier and writer Philippe de Commynes, meetings between Charles and other rulers were usually disastrous; the duke was a difficult man. He spent little time with his duchess, Margaret, and did not have close companions. There was no one to prick his vanity.

The Burgundian dukes believed in government by display, and Charles took this to extremes. His court was splendid, and highly formal. If Charles wished to address his nobles, he would sit, magnificently dressed, on a throne to do so. In Brussels, he heard lawsuits three times a week, with his household officers and courtiers around him and the nobles seated on benches in order of precedence. His court chronicler, Georges Chastellain, observed: 'From the outside, it seemed a grand and magnificent thing, whatever fruit it might bear. But I have never heard nor seen a prince or king, or anyone else, do this.' With its complex pageantry the Burgundian court in many ways surpassed those of royalty. Etiquette was elaborate; everyone had to know their place. Meals were served in rigorous order, taking due account of seniority. There was something of a culture clash when the count palatine of the Rhine came to Brussels, for the Germans were irritated by the pomp and arrogance of the duke's servants, while the Burgundians were appalled by the way the Germans left dirty clothes and boots on the fine bedclothes.

Grand occasions were an opportunity for gargantuan displays of wealth. When Charles married Margaret of York – sister of Edward IV and Richard III – in 1468, there were ten days of feasting and jousting. The feasts featured elaborate reconstructions of the labours of Hercules. Men dressed as various animals, such as a unicorn, a lion and a dromedary

A sumptuous example of goldsmith's work from 1467. Charles the Bold kneels with a reliquary of St Lambert in his hands. St George stands behind him, the dragon at his feet.

paraded into the hall. When a griffin opened its beak, birds flew out. On the last day, the tables all featured gardens, with golden trees bearing artificial fruit being picked by little people. The high point was the entry of a whale, fully sixty feet long, which wiggled its fins and tail, and spat out two sirens and a troupe of dancers.

Charles's defeats by the Swiss at the end of his life suggest that he was thoroughly incompetent. This was far from the case. Charles made every effort to ensure that his armies were fully up to date and properly trained. He was an innovator, and created a standing army in 1471, which was some 5,000 strong, and was soon increased to 8,400, at least in theory. In an ordinance he wrote in 1473 he structured his forces into companies, which were divided into four squadrons and then into four units of five men. He ensured that the artillery was of the highest standard; new types of guns such as the harquebus and the serpentine were introduced. The men were to practice manoeuvring in the field, charging and retreating in good order. Charles used mercenaries, recruiting the best in Europe, and English archers in particular. He led his forces himself where he could: one eyewitness commented that, in battle, 'I saw the duke applying himself in person here and there admirably in organizing and commanding.'

Effective organization of his troops paid off for Charles at the battle of Brustem, in 1467, against the men of Liège. However, at Grandson, nine years later, his outnumbered army failed to stand up to the advance of the Swiss pikemen, and his artillery could not be brought into effective use. At Murten, Charles selected the ground for the battle with care, but the Swiss delayed their attack so long that his troops were quite unprepared when it came, and withdrawal soon turned into rout. At Nancy, Charles again drew up his troops carefully, with artillery in support. However, his troops were once again outnumbered, and their formations were broken by a flank assault they failed to anticipate. Charles fought courageously, suffering horrific wounds and dying on the battlefield. As Commynes wrote: 'The duke of Burgundy never wanted courage, but his conduct often failed him.'

In many ways, Charles showed the way forward for rulers; but, as his contemporaries noted, his judgment was fatally flawed, and he was badly shaken by his defeats. His ambition, however, was overweening:

> He had so many and so great enterprises in his head, as could not be compassed
> in one man's life. Besides, to speak the truth, they were but little better than impossible,
> for one half of Europe was not sufficient to content his insatiable desire of extending
> his dominions.

Charles's demise meant the end of Valois Burgundy. His daughter and heir, Mary, married the emperor Maximilian, a Habsburg, in 1477. The great, late-medieval Burgundian state could not be held together. Its lands were divided, with most of those in the Netherlands going to the Habsburgs, and the others to France. The death of Charles the Bold was one of the events that marked the beginning of a new age.

Piero della Francesca

PAINTER AND MATHEMATICIAN

c. 1412–92

As a boy, Piero della Francesca wanted to be a mathematician. It was not, however, until late in life that he was able to devote himself singlemindedly to this study. He wrote a practical guide to the abacus, with exercises about partnerships and profits, which illuminates medieval commercial preoccupations. A far more abstruse work on the geometry of solids examined five basic shapes – pyramid, square, circle, decahedron and icosahedron – and their derivatives. He was concerned with such problems as how to fit an icosahedron into a cube, and the various ways of fitting a cube into an octahedron, in order to establish the mathematical principles that underlay the representation of objects in painting. The geometrical problems he worked on were difficult, particularly given the limitation of the algebraic methods available, but he succeeded in proving new theorems in

Piero della Francesca's portraits of Federigo da Montefeltro, duke of Urbino, and his duchess.

The Baptism of Christ, *carefully composed by Piero della Francesca according to mathematical principles.*

original ways. A third treatise was on perspective, which he explained in mathematical terms.

Piero's work was extensively copied without acknowledgment by his student Luca Pacioli. Leonardo da Vinci, for example, thought he was using Pacioli, when in fact the concepts he was studying had been worked out by Piero. Giorgio Vasari, writing in the mid-sixteenth century, was aware of Pacioli's plagiarism, and described Piero as the best geometrician of his time, but it was only with the rediscovery in the twentieth century of Piero's manuscripts that his importance in the development of mathematics has become clear. He appears to have been largely self-taught; what he learned as a boy was no more than the straightforward arithmetic needed by merchants. University study passed him by, but princely patronage gave him access to the libraries that he needed.

Piero had been born in around 1412 in the small town of Borgo San Sepulcro in Tuscany, and it was there that he began his career as a painter. Florence, however, was the cultural hub for the most notable artists, and by 1439, Piero was working there with Domenico Veneziano. Success was not immediately forthcoming, and by 1442 he was back in his home town, where he was elected to the council. In the 1450s, he was employed by the wealthy merchant, Luigi Bacci, to paint one of his finest works, the frescoes in the church of San Francesco in Arezzo. It was, however, at the courts of the rulers of the Italian cities that Piero found the lavish patronage he desired. He was attracted to Ferrara by its marquis, Lionello d'Este. There, he met Rogier van der Weyden, from whom he learned a mastery of painting in oils. Sigismondo Malatesta, at Rimini, was another of the city despots to employ Piero, but it was Federigo da Montefeltro, at Urbino, who was the most notable of his patrons.

Federigo da Montefeltro was one of the greatest of the *condottiere*, the mercenary soldiers who dominated fifteenth-century Italy. In 1444, when in his early twenties, he seized the city of Urbino; and, while ruling there as a prince, continued to fight for a number of different masters until the 1470s. This tough soldier, one-eyed following a tournament injury, was also notable for his encouragement of literature and the arts. He built up a magnificent library, which was no doubt much used by Piero for his mathematical studies. Most of the work that Piero did at Urbino has not survived, but fortunately the remarkable portraits of Federigo and his wife have done. Both are shown in profile, Federigo from the left so as not to show his injury. The faces are not idealized; this is the couple as they were, skin blemishes, narrow lips and all. The gentle landscape backgrounds show the strong Flemish influence on Piero's work.

Unlike most earlier medieval artists, Piero arranged his paintings according to strict geometrical principles. In his *Baptism of Christ*, the right-hand edge of the tree trunk in the foreground is one third of the way across the picture. The dove is centrally positioned, two thirds of the way up, and is the centre point of a circle defined by the top of the picture, the Baptist's left arm and Christ's loincloth. In his book on perspective, Piero showed how to plot the shape of the human head, so as to depict it from any angle. The architectural backdrops in many of his paintings demonstrate very clearly how he used mathematical theory to guide his brush. The relevance of Piero's advanced study of polygonal solids to his painting is not so evident; in the end, art cannot be reduced to a set of mathematical formulae. However, his use of regular shapes and of blocks of colour perhaps helps to explain the often monumental, still quality of his figures, their draperies almost frozen in position.

From 1471, Piero was back in his home town, where he was commissioned to oversee building work on the city walls. In about 1480, he stopped painting. According to Vasari, this was because he became blind with cataracts, but it seems more likely that he suffered a deterioration of his eyesight, rather than a complete loss (he could still see to write in 1487). In 1482, he rented a house in Rimini, with a garden. It may have been there that he ended his days in 1492 – the year that heralded the start of a very different era, with the discovery of the New World.

Piero della Francesca's fresco of the battle of Nineveh, painted in 1452 at Arezzo.

Further Reading

The medieval period is long, and a great many outstanding books have been written on it. This list offers a limited selection, intended to provide no more than an initial guide which can lead to wider reading.

General Reading

This section is confined to books published since 1990. There are many other excellent works written before and after that date.

Abulafia, David (ed.), *Italy in the Central Middle Ages* (Oxford: Oxford University Press, 2004)

Abulafia, David, Christopher Allmand, Paul Fouracre, Michael Jones, Rosamond McKitterick, Timothy Reuter, David Luscombe and Jonathan Riley-Smith (eds), *The New Cambridge Medieval History*, 7 vols (Cambridge: Cambridge University Press, 1995–2005)

Barber, Malcolm, *The Two Cities: Medieval Europe 1050–1320* (London: Routledge, 1992)

Bartlett, Robert, *The Making of Europe: Conquest, Colonization and Cultural Change 950–1350* (London: Penguin, 1994)

Bartlett, Robert (ed.), *Medieval Panorama* (London: Thames & Hudson, 2001), republished as *The Medieval World Complete* (London: Thames & Hudson, 2010)

Bisson, Thomas N., *The Crisis of the Twelfth Century: Power, Lordship and the Origins of European Government* (Princeton, NJ: Princeton University Press, 2009)

Bull, Marcus (ed.), *France in the Central Middle Ages 900–1200* (Oxford: Oxford University Press, 2002)

Carpenter, David, *The Struggle for Mastery: Britain 1066–1284* (London: Penguin, 2003)

Coldstream, Nicola, *Medieval Architecture* (Oxford: Oxford University Press, 2002)

Moore, Robert I., *The War on Heresy: Faith and Power in Medieval Europe* (London: Profile, 2012)

Potter, David (ed.), *France in the Later Middle Ages 1200–1500* (Oxford: Oxford University Press, 2002)

Scales, Len, *The Shaping of German Identity: Authority and Crisis 1245–1414* (Cambridge: Cambridge University Press, 2012)

Tyerman, Christopher, *God's War: A New History of the Crusades* (London: Penguin, 2007)

Witt, Ronald G., *The Two Latin Cultures and the Foundations of Renaissance Humanism in Italy* (Cambridge: Cambridge University Press, 2012)

1. An Age of Empires

Charlemagne

Bullough, Donald, *The Age of Charlemagne*, 2nd edn (London: Elek, 1973)

McKitterick, Rosamond, *Charlemagne: The Formation of a European Identity* (Cambridge: Cambridge University Press, 2008)

Story, Joanna (ed.), *Charlemagne: Empire and Society* (Manchester: Manchester University Press, 2005)

Two Lives of Charlemagne: Einhard and Notker the Stammerer, ed. and trans. David Ganz (London: Penguin, 2008)

Hrotsvit of Gandersheim

Hrotsvit of Gandersheim, *The Plays of Hrotsvit of Gandersheim*, ed. and trans. Katharina M. Wilson (New York: Garland, 1989)

Wilson, Katharina M., *Hrotsvit of Gandersheim: The Ethics of Authorial Stance* (Leiden: E. J. Brill, 1988)

Wilson, Katharina M., 'The Saxon Canoness: Hrotsvit of Gandersheim', in Katharina M. Wilson (ed.), *Medieval Women Writers* (Manchester: Manchester University Press, 1984), pp. 30–63

King Olav I of Norway

Bagge, Sverre, *From Viking Stronghold to Christian Kingdom: State Formation in Norway c. 900–1350* (Copenhagen: Museum Tusculanum Press, 2010)

Helle, Knut (ed.), *The Cambridge History of Scandinavia, Volume I: Prehistory to 1520* (Cambridge: Cambridge University Press, 2003)

Jones, Gwyn, *A History of the Vikings* (Oxford: Oxford University Press, 1968)

Sturlason, Snorre, *The Heimskringla: A History of the Norse Kings*, trans. Samuel Laing, notes by Rasmus B. Anderson, vol. I (London: Norrœna Society, 1906)

Fulk Nerra

Bachrach, Bernard S., 'The Angevin Strategy of Castle Building in the Reign of Fulk Nerra 987–1040', *The American Historical Review*, vol. 88 (1963), pp. 533–60

Bachrach, Bernard S., *Fulk Nerra, the Neo-Roman Consul, 987–1040: A Political Biography of the Angevin Count* (Berkeley, CA: University of California Press, 1993)

Ibn Sīnā (Avicenna)

Afnan, Soheil A., *Avicenna: His Life and Works* (London: Allen & Unwin, 1958)

Goodman, Lenn E., *Avicenna* (London: Routledge, 1992)

Emma of Normandy

Keynes, Simon, 'Emma [Ælfgifu] (d. 1052), queen of England', in H[enry] Colin G[ray] Matthew and Brian H. Harrison (eds), *The Oxford Dictionary of National Biography: From the Earliest Times to the Year 2000*, 61 vols (Oxford: Oxford University Press, 2004) (http://www.oxforddnb.com/public/index.html)

Searle, Eleanor, 'Emma the Conqueror', in Christopher Harper-Bill, Christopher Holdsworth and Janet L. Nelson (eds), *Studies in Medieval History Presented to R. Allen Brown* (Woodbridge: Boydell, 1989), pp. 281–88

Stafford, Pauline, *Queen Emma and Queen Edith: Queenship and Women's Power in Eleventh-Century England* (Oxford: Blackwell, 1997)

Odo of Bayeux

Bates, David, 'Odo, earl of Kent (d. 1097)', *Oxford Dictionary of National Biography*

Gameson, Richard (ed.), *The Study of the Bayeux Tapestry* (Woodbridge: Boydell, 1997)

Ordericus Vitalis, *The Ecclesiastical History of Orderic Vitalis*, 6 vols, ed. Marjorie Chibnall (Oxford: Clarendon Press, 1969–80)

Wilson, David M., *The Bayeux Tapestry: The Complete Tapestry in Colour* (London: Thames & Hudson, 1985)

Rodrigo Díaz (El Cid)

Fletcher, Richard, *The Quest for El Cid* (Oxford: Oxford University Press, 1989)

Menéndez Pidal, Ramón, *The Cid and His Spain*, trans. Harold Sunderland (London: Frank Cass, 1929)

The Poem of the Cid, trans. Rita Hamilton and Janet Perry, introduction by Ian Michael (Harmondsworth: Penguin, 1984)

Matilda of Tuscany

Hay, David J., *The Military Leadership of Matilda of Canossa 1046–1115* (Manchester: Manchester University Press, 2008)

Spike, Michèle K., *Tuscan Countess: The Life and Extraordinary Times of Matilda of Canossa* (New York: Vendome Press, 2005)

Verzar, Christine B., 'Picturing Matilda of Canossa: Medieval Strategies of Representation', in Robert A. Maxwell (ed.), *Representing History 900–1300: Art, Music, History* (University Park, PA: Pennsylvania State University Press, 2010), pp. 73–90

Pope Urban II

Becker, Alfons, *Papst Urban II (1088–1099)*, 3 vols, Schriften der Monumenta Germaniae Historica 19 (Stuttgart and Hanover: Hiersemann and Hahnsche Buchhandlung, 1964–2012)

Tyerman, Christopher, *God's War: A New History of the Crusades*

Guibert de Nogent

Guibert, Abbot of Nogent-sous-Coucy, *Self and Society in Medieval France: The Memoirs of Abbot Guibert of Nogent (1064?–c. 1125)*, ed. John F. Benton (Toronto: University of Toronto Press, 1984)

Rubenstein, Jay, *Guibert of Nogent: Portrait of a Medieval Mind* (London: Routledge, 2002)

Anna Komnene

Buckler, Georgina, *Anna Comnena: A Study* (London: Oxford University Press, 1929)

Comnena, Anna, *The Alexiad of Anna Comnena*, trans. Edgar R. A. Sewter (Harmondsworth: Penguin, 1969)

Gouma-Peterson, Thalia (ed.), *Anna Komnene and Her Times* (New York: Garland, 2000)

2. An Age of Confidence

Abbot Suger

Crosby, Sumner McKnight, Jane Hayward, Charles T. Little and William D. Wixom, *The Royal Abbey of Saint-Denis in the Time of Abbot Suger (1122–1151)* (New York: The Metropolitan Museum of Art, 1981)

Gerson, Paula L. (ed.), *Abbot Suger and Saint-Denis: A Symposium* (New York: The Metropolitan Museum of Art, 1986)

Grant, Lindy, *Abbot Suger of St-Denis: Church and State in Early Twelfth-Century France* (Harlow: Longman, 1998)

Geoffrey of Monmouth

Crick, Julia C., 'Monmouth, Geoffrey of [Galfridus Arturus] (d. 1154/5)', *Oxford Dictionary of National Biography*

Geoffrey of Monmouth, *The History of Britain*, ed. and trans. Lewis Thorpe (Harmondsworth: Penguin, 1966)

Jankulak, Karen, *Geoffrey of Monmouth* (Cardiff: University of Wales Press, 2010)

Godric of Finchale

Ridyard, Susan, 'Functions of a Twelfth-Century Recluse Revisited: The Case of Godric of Finchale', in Richard Gameson and Henrietta Leyser (eds), *Belief and Culture in the Middle Ages* (Oxford: Oxford University Press, 2001), pp. 236–50

Tudor, Victoria, 'Durham Priory and Its Hermits in the Twelfth Century', in David Rollason, Margaret Harvey and Michael Prestwich (eds), *Anglo-Norman Durham 1093–1193* (Woodbridge: Boydell, 1994), pp. 67–78

Tudor, Victoria, 'Godric of Finchale [St Godric of Finchale] (c. 1070–1170)', *Oxford Dictionary of National Biography*

Héloïse

Clanchy, Michael T., *Abelard: A Medieval Life* (Oxford: Blackwell, 1997)

The Letters of Abelard and Heloise, ed. and trans. Betty Radice, revised by Michael T. Clanchy (Harmondsworth: Penguin, 2003)

McLeod, Enid, *Heloise: A Biography* (London: Chatto & Windus, 1938)

Mews, Constant J., *The Lost Love Letters of Heloise and Abelard* (New York, 1999)

Al-Idrisi

Brotton, Jerry, *A History of the World in Twelve Maps* (London: Allen Lane, 2012)

Harley, John B., and David Woodward (eds), *Cartography in the Traditional Islamic and South Asian Societies (The History of Cartography, vol. 11, bk 1)* (Chicago, IL: University of Chicago Press, 1992)

Johns, Jeremy, and Emilie Savage-Smith, 'The Book of Curiosities: A Newly Discovered Series of Islamic Maps', *Imago Mundi*, vol. 55 (2003), pp. 7–24

Hildegard of Bingen

Flanagan, Sabina, *Hildegard of Bingen 1098–1179: A Visionary Life* (London: Routledge, 1989)

Hildegard of Bingen, *The Personal Correspondence of Hildegard of Bingen*, ed. Joseph L. Baird (Oxford: Oxford University Press, 2006)

King-Lenzmaier, Anne H., *Hildegard of Bingen: An Integrated Vision* (Collegeville, MN: Michael Glazier, 2001)

Kotzur, Hans-Jürgen, Winfried Wilhelm and Ines Koring, *Hildegard von Bingen 1098–1179* (Mainz: P. von Zabern, 1998)

Thomas Becket

Barlow, Frank, 'Becket, Thomas [St Thomas of Canterbury, Thomas of London] (1120?–1170)', *Oxford Dictionary of National Biography*

Barlow, Frank, *Thomas Becket* (London: Weidenfeld & Nicolson, 1986)

Guy, John A., *Thomas Becket: Warrior, Priest, Rebel, Victim: A 900-Year-Old Story* (London: Viking, 2012)

Knowles, David M., *Thomas Becket* (London: Black, 1970)

The Lives of Thomas Becket: Selected Sources, ed. and trans. Michael Staunton (Manchester: Manchester University Press, 2001)

Usāma ibn Munqidh

Cobb, Paul M., 'Infidel Dogs: Hunting Crusaders with Usamah ibn Munqidh', *Crusades*, vol. 6 (2007), pp. 57–68

Cobb, Paul M., *Usama ibn Munqidh: Warrior-Poet of the Age of Crusades* (Oxford: Oneworld, 2006)

Usāma-Ibn-Munquid, *Memoirs of An Arab-Syrian Gentleman and Warrior*, ed. and trans. Philip K. Hitti (New York: Columbia University Press, 1929)

Frederick Barbarossa

The Deeds of Frederick Barbarossa by Otto of Freising and His Continuator, Rahewin, ed. and trans. Charles C. Mierow (New York: Norton, 1953)

Hampe, Karl, *Germany under the Salian and Hohenstaufen Emperors*, trans. Ralph F. Bennett (Oxford: Blackwell, 1973)

Haussherr, Reiner (ed.), *Die Zeit der Staufer: Geschichte, Kunst, Kultur*, 5 vols (Stuttgart: Württembergisches Landesmuseum, 1977)

Munz, Peter, *Frederick Barbarossa: A Study in Medieval Politics* (London: Eyre & Spottiswoode, 1969)

Eleanor of Aquitaine

Martindale, Jane, 'Eleanor [Eleanor of Aquitaine], suo jure duchess of Aquitaine (c. 1122–1204)', *Oxford Dictionary of National Biography*

Martindale, Jane, 'Eleanor of Aquitaine', in Janet L. Nelson (ed.), *Richard Coeur de Lion in History and Myth* (London: King's College London, 1992), pp. 17–50

Turner, Ralph V., *Eleanor of Aquitaine* (New Haven, CT, and London: Yale University Press, 2009)

Saladin (Ṣalāḥ ad-Dīn Yūsuf ibn Ayyūb)

Gibb, Hamilton A. R., *The Life of Saladin* (Oxford: Clarendon Press, 1973)

Lyons, Malcolm Cameron, and David E. P. Jackson, *Saladin: The Politics of the Holy War* (Cambridge: Cambridge University Press, 1982)

Möhring, Hannes, *Saladin: The Sultan and His Times 1138–1193*, trans. David S. Bachrach (Baltimore, MD: Johns Hopkins University Press, 2008)

William Marshal

Crouch, David, 'Marshal, William (I) [called the Marshal], fourth earl of Pembroke (c. 1146–1219)', *Oxford Dictionary of National Biography*

Crouch, David, *William Marshal: Court, Career and Chivalry in the Angevin Empire 1147–1219* (Harlow: Longman, 1990)

Painter, Sidney, *William Marshal: Knight Errant, Baron and Regent of England* (Baltimore, MD: Johns Hopkins University Press, 1933)

Pope Innocent III

Moore, John C. (ed.), *Pope Innocent III and His World* (Aldershot: Ashgate, 1999)

Moore, John C., *Pope Innocent III (1160/1–1216): To Root up and to Plant* (Leiden: Brill, 2003)

Sayers, Jane, *Innocent III: Leader of Europe 1198–1216* (Harlow: Longman, 1994)

3. An Age of Maturity

Chinggis Khan (Genghis Khan)

Jackson, Peter, *The Mongols and the West* (Harlow: Longman, 2005)

Juvaynī, 'Alā' al-Dīn 'Aṭā Malik, *The History of the World Conqueror by 'Ala-ad-Din 'Ata-Malik Juvaini*, ed. and trans. John A. Boyle, 2 vols (Manchester, Manchester University Press, 1958)

Marshall, Robert, *Storm from the East* (London, 1993)

Morgan, David, *The Mongols* (Oxford: Blackwell, 1986)

The Secret History of the Mongols, ed. and trans. Urgunge Onon (London: RoutledgeCurzon, 2001)

Simon de Montfort

Pegg, Mark Gregory, *A Most Holy War: The Albigensian Crusade and the Battle for Christendom* (Oxford: Oxford University Press, 2008)

Sumption, Jonathan, *The Albigensian Crusade* (London: Faber, 1978)

Dominic de Guzmán

Jarrett, Bede, *Life of St. Dominic (1170–1221)* (London: Burns Oates & Washbourne, 1924)

Tugwell, Simon, *Early Dominicans: Selected Writings* (London: SPCK, 1982)

Vicaire, Marie-Humbert, *Saint Dominic and His Times*, trans. Kathleen Pond (London: Darton, Longman and Todd, 1964)

Robert of Wetherby

Crook, David, 'The Sheriff of Nottingham and Robin Hood: The Genesis of the Legend?', in Peter R. Coss and Simon D. Lloyd (eds), *Thirteenth Century England: Proceedings of the Newcastle upon Tyne Conference 2* (Woodbridge: Boydell, 1988), pp. 59–68

Holt, James C., *Robin Hood* (London: Thames & Hudson, 1982)

Frederick II

Abulafia, David, *Frederick II: A Medieval Emperor* (London: Allen Lane, 1988)

Van Cleve, Thomas C., *The Emperor Frederick II of Hohenstaufen, Immutator Mundi* (Oxford: Oxford University Press, 1972)

Matthew Paris

Lewis, Suzanne, *The Art of Matthew Paris in the Chronica Majora* (Aldershot: Scolar Press, 1987)

Paris, Matthew, *Chronicles of Matthew Paris: Monastic Life in the Thirteenth Century*, ed. and trans. Richard Vaughan (Stroud: Alan Sutton, 1984)

Vaughan, Richard, *Matthew Paris* (Cambridge: Cambridge University Press, 1958)

King Håkon IV of Norway

Bagge, Sverre, *From Viking Stronghold to Christian Kingdom: State Formation in Norway c. 900–1350*

Helle, Knut (ed.), *The Cambridge History of Scandinavia, Volume I: Prehistory to 1520*

The King's Mirror, ed. and trans. Laurence M. Larson (London: Oxford University Press, 1917)

King Louis IX of France

Jordan, William Chester, *Louis IX and the Challenge of the Crusade* (Princeton, NJ: Princeton University Press, 1979)

Le Goff, Jacques, *Saint Louis*, trans. Gareth Evan Gollrad (Notre Dame, IN: University of Notre Dame Press, 2008)

Richard, Jean, *Saint Louis: Crusader King of France*, ed. and abridged by Simon D. Lloyd (Cambridge: Cambridge University Press, 1992)

Joinville, Jean de, 'The Life of Saint Louis', in Margaret R. B. Shaw (ed. and trans.), *Joinville & Villehardouin: Chronicles of the Crusades* (Harmondsworth: Penguin, 1963)

Alexander Nevsky

Dmytryshyn, Basil (ed.), *Medieval Russia: A Source Book 850–1700*, 3rd edn (Fort Worth, TX: Harcourt Brace Jovanovich College Publishers, 1991)

Fennell, John, *The Crisis of Medieval Russia 1200–1304* (London: Longman, 1983)

Nicolle, David, *Lake Peipus 1242: The Battle of the Ice* (Oxford: Osprey, 1996)

Thomas Aquinas

Aquinas, Thomas, *Thomas Aquinas: Selected Writings*, ed. and trans. Ralph McInerny (London: Penguin, 1998)

Kerr, Fergus, *Aquinas: A Very Short Introduction* (Oxford: Oxford University Press, 2009)

Torrell, Jean-Pierre, *Saint Thomas Aquinas*, 2 vols (Washington, DC: Catholic University of America Press, 1996)

Villard de Honnecourt

Barnes, Carl F., Jr, 'The Portfolio of Villard de Honnecourt', http://www.villardman.net/

Barnes, Carl F., Jr, *The Portfolio of Villard de Honnecourt (Paris, Bibliothèque Nationale de France, MS Fr 19093): A New Critical Edition and Color Facsimile* (Aldershot: Ashgate, 2009)

Honnecourt, Villard de, *Album de Villard de Honnecourt, architecte du XIIIe siècle*, ed. Henri Auguste Omont (Paris: Berthaud Frères, 1906)

Benedetto Zaccaria

Lopez, Roberto S., *Genova marinara nel Duecento: Benedetto Zaccaria ammiraglio e mercante*, (Messina and Milan: Giuseppe Principato, 1933)

Miller, William, 'The Zaccaria of Phocaea and Chios (1275–1329)', *Journal of Hellenic Studies*, vol. 31 (1911), pp. 42–55

Renouard, Yves, *Les hommes d'affaires Italiens du moyen age* (Paris: Armand Colin, 1949)

James of St George

Brown, R. Allen, Howard M. Colvin and Arnold J. Taylor (eds), *The History of the King's Works, Volume I: The Middle Ages* (London: H.M.S.O., 1963)

Taylor, Arnold J., 'Master James of St George', *English Historical Review*, vol. 65 (1950), pp. 433–57

Jacques de Molay

Barber, Malcolm, *The Trial of the Templars* (Cambridge: Cambridge University Press, 1978)

Frale, Barbara, 'The Chinon Chart: Papal Absolution to the Last Templar, Master Jacques de Molay', *Journal of Medieval History*, vol. 30 (2004), pp. 109–34

Nicholson, Helen, *The Knights Templar: A New History* (Stroud: Sutton, 2001)

Marco Polo

Larner, John, *Marco Polo and the Discovery of the World* (New Haven, CT, and London: Yale University Press, 1999)

Phillips, J. R. Seymour, *The Medieval Expansion of Europe* (Oxford: Oxford University Press, 1988)

The Travels of Marco Polo, ed. and trans. Ronald E. Latham (Harmondsworth: Penguin, 1958)

Wood, Frances, *Did Marco Polo Go to China?* (London: Secker & Warburg, 1995)

4. An Age of Plague

Dante Alighieri

Alighieri, Dante, *The Divine Comedy*, ed. and trans. Mark Musa, 3 vols (Harmondsworth: Penguin, 1984–86)

Jacoff, Rachel (ed.), *The Cambridge Companion to Dante* (Cambridge: Cambridge University Press, 1993)

Reynolds, Barbara, *Dante: The Poet, the Political Thinker, the Man* (London: I. B. Tauris, 2006)

William Lene

The Court Rolls of Walsham le Willows, ed. Ray Lock (Woodbridge: Boydell, 1998)

Dyer, Christopher, *Everyday Life in Medieval England* (London: Hambledon, 1994)

Lock, Ray, 'The Black Death in Walsham le Willows', *Proceedings of the Suffolk Institute of Archaeology*, vol. 37 (1992), pp. 316–37

Schofield, Philipp R., *Peasant and Community in Medieval England* (Basingstoke: Palgrave, 2003)

James Douglas

Barbour, John, *The Bruce*, ed. and trans. Archibald A. M. Duncan (Edinburgh: Canongate, 1997)

Brown, Michael, *The Black Douglases* (East Linton: Tuckwell Press, 1998)

Duncan, Archibald A. M., 'Douglas, Sir James [*called* the Black Douglas] (*d.* 1330)', *Oxford Dictionary of National Biography*

Giotto di Bondone

Cole, Bruce, *Giotto and Florentine Painting 1280–1375* (New York: Harper & Row, 1976)

Derbes, Ann, and Mark Sandona (eds), *The Cambridge Companion to Giotto* (Cambridge: Cambridge University Press, 2004

Eimerl, Sarel, *The World of Giotto c. 1267–1337* (New York: Time, inc., 1967)

Martindale, Andrew, and Edi Baccheschi, *The Complete Paintings of Giotto* (London: Weidenfeld & Nicolson, 1969)

Richard of Wallingford

Dohrn-van Rossum, Gerhard, *History of the Hour: Clocks and Modern Temporal Orders*, trans. Thomas Dunlap (Chicago, IL: University of Chicago Press, 1996)

North, John, *God's Clockmaker: Richard of Wallingford and the Invention of Time* (London: Hambledon, 2005)

Jean de Lamouilly

Hall, Bert S., *Weapons and Warfare in Renaissance Europe: Gunpowder, Technology, and Tactics* (Baltimore, MD: Johns Hopkins University Press, 1997)

Phillips, J. R. Seymour, *Aymer de Valence, Earl of Pembroke 1307–1324* (Oxford: Oxford University Press, 1972)

Smith, Robert Douglas, and Kelly DeVries, *The Artillery of the Dukes of Burgundy 1363–1477* (Woodbridge: Boydell 2005)

Petrarch (Francesco Petrarca)

Petrarcha, Francesco, *Petrarch in English*, ed. Thomas P. Roche (London: Penguin, 2005)

Robinson, John H., *Petrarch: The First Modern Scholar and Man of Letters* (London: G. P. Putnam's Sons, 1909)

Wilkins, Ernest Hatch, *Life of Petrarch* (Chicago, IL: University of Chicago Press, 1961)

John Crabbe

Lucas, Henry S., 'John Crabbe, Flemish pirate, merchant and adventurer', *Speculum*, vol. 20 (1945), pp. 334–50

Guillaume Cale

Luce, Siméon, *Histoire de la Jacquerie*, 2nd edn (Paris: Honoré Champion, 1894)

Sumption, Jonathan, *Trial by Fire: The Hundred Years War II* (London: Faber, 1999)

Guy de Chauliac

Benedictow, Ole J., *The Black Death 1346–1353: The Complete History* (Woodbridge: Boydell, 2004)

Chauliac, Guy de, *La Grande Chirurgie de Guy de Chauliac*, ed. Edouard Nicaise (Paris: Alcan, 1890)

Horrox, Rosemary (ed. and trans.), *The Black Death* (Manchester: Manchester University Press, 1994)

Thevenet, André, 'Guy de Chauliac, pere de la chirurgie', *Bulletin de l'Académie des sciences et lettres de Montpellier*, vol. 28 (1998), pp. 207–22 (http://www.ac-sciences-lettres-montpellier.fr/academie_edition/fichiers_conf/Thevenet1997.pdf)

Charles IV of Bohemia

Boehm, Barbara Drake, and Ji í Fajt (eds), *Prague: The Crown of Bohemia 1347–1437* (New Haven, CT, and London: Yale University Press, 2005)

Charles IV, *Autobiography of Emperor Charles IV and His Legend of St Wenceslas*, ed. and trans. Balász Nagy and Frank Schaer, introduction by Ferdinand Seibt (Budapest: Central European University Press, 2001)

Crossley, Paul, 'The Politics of Presentation: The Architecture of Charles IV in Bohemia', in Sarah Rees Jones, Richard Marks and Alastair J. Minnis (eds), *Courts and Regions in Medieval Europe* (Woodbridge: Boydell, 2000), pp. 99–172

Rosario, Iva, *Art and Propaganda: Charles IV of Bohemia 1346–1378* (Woodbridge: Boydell, 2000)

King Pedro IV of Aragon

Bisson, Thomas N., *The Medieval Crown of Aragon* (Oxford: Oxford University Press, 1986)

Cawsey, Suzanne F., *Kingship and Propaganda: Royal Eloquence and the Crown of Aragon c. 1200–1450* (Oxford: Oxford University Press, 2002)

Hillgarth, Jocelyn N., *The Spanish Kingdoms 1250–1516, Volume I: 1250–1410: Precarious Balance* (Oxford: Clarendon Press, 1976)

Pedro, king of Aragon, *Chronicle*, ed. and trans. Mary Hillgarth and Jocelyn N. Hillgarth (Toronto: Pontifical Institute of Medieval Studies, 1980)

Ruiz, Teofilo F., *Spain's Centuries of Crisis 1300–1474* (Oxford: Blackwell, 2007)

Coluccio Salutati

Ullman, Berthold L., *The Humanism of Coluccio Salutati* (Padua: Antenori, 1963)

Witt, Ronald G., *Hercules at the Crossroads: The Life, Works, and Thought of Coluccio Salutati* (Durham, NC: Duke University Press, 1983)

Catherine of Siena (Catherine Benincasa)

Gardner, Edmund G., *Saint Catherine of Siena* (London: J. M. Dent, 1907)

Luongo, F. Thomas, *The Saintly Politics of Catherine of Siena* (Ithaca, NY: Cornell University Press, 2006)

Raymond of Capua, *The Life of Catherine of Siena by Raymond of Capua*, ed. and trans. Conleth Kearns (Wilmington, DE: Glazier, 1980)

Tylus, Jane, *Reclaiming Catherine of Siena* (Chicago, IL: University of Chicago Press, 2009)

John Hawkwood

Cafero, William, *John Hawkwood: An English Mercenary in Fourteenth-Century Italy* (Baltimore, MD: Johns Hopkins University Press, 2006)

Cooper, Stephen, *Sir John Hawkwood: Chivalry and the Art of War* (Barnsley: Pen & Sword, 2008)

Fowler, Kenneth, 'Hawkwood, Sir John (d. 1394)', *Oxford Dictionary of National Biography*

Mallett, Michael, *Mercenaries and Their Masters: Warfare in Renaissance Italy* (London: Bodley Head, 1974)

John of Gaunt

Armitage-Smith, Sydney, *John of Gaunt: King of Castile and Leon, Duke of Aquitaine and Lancaster, Earl of Derby, Lincoln and Leicester, Seneschal of England* (London: Constable, 1904)

Goodman, Antony, *John of Gaunt: The Exercise of Princely Power in Fourteenth-Century Europe* (London: Longman, 1992)

Geoffrey Chaucer

Chaucer, Geoffrey, *The Canterbury Tales*, trans. Neville Coghill (Harmondsworth: Penguin, 1951)

Crow, Martin M., and Clair C. Olson (eds), *Chaucer Life-Records* (Oxford: Clarendon Press, 1966)

Pearsall, Derek, *The Life of Geoffrey Chaucer: A Critical Biography* (Oxford: Blackwell, 1992)

Jean Froissart

Ainsworth, Peter F., *Jean Froissart and the Fabric of History* (Oxford: Clarendon Press, 1990)

Froissart, Jean, *Chronicles*, ed. and trans. Geoffrey Brereton (Harmondsworth: Penguin, 1968)

Jones, Michael, 'Froissart, Jean (1337?–c. 1404)', *Oxford Dictionary of National Biography*

5. An Age of Transition

Temür (Tamerlane)

Manz, Beatrice Forbes, *The Rise and Rule of Tamerlane* (Cambridge: Cambridge University Press, 1989)

Marozzi, Justin, *Tamerlane: Sword of Islam, Conqueror of the World* (London: HarperCollins, 2004)

Boucicaut (Jean II le Maingre)

Lalande, Denis, *Jean II le Meingre, dit Boucicaut (1366–1421): Etude d'une biographie héroïque* (Geneva: Droz, 1988)

Le Livre des Faitz du Bon Messire Jehan le Maingre dit Boucicaut, Mareschal de France, ed. Denis Lalande (Geneva: Droz, 1985)

Jan Žižka

Fudge, Thomas A., *The Crusade against Heretics in Bohemia 1418–1437* (Aldershot: Ashgate, 2002)

Heymann, Frederick G., *John Žižka and the Hussite Revolution* (Princeton, NJ: Princeton University Press, 1955)

Turnbull, Stephen, *The Hussite Wars 1419–36* (Oxford: Osprey, 2004)

Joan of Arc

DeVries, Kelly, *Joan of Arc: A Military Leader* (Stroud: Sutton, 1999)

Taylor, Craig, *Joan of Arc, La Pucelle* (Manchester: Manchester University Press, 2006)

Taylor, Larissa J., *The Virgin Warrior: The Life and Death of Joan of Arc* (New Haven, CT, and London: Yale University Press, 2009)

Warner, Marina, *Joan of Arc: The Image of Female Heroism* (London: Weidenfeld & Nicolson, 1981)

Filippo Brunelleschi

Battisti, Eugenio, *Brunelleschi: The Complete Work* (London: Thames & Hudson, 1981)

King, Ross, *Brunelleschi's Dome: The Story of the Great Cathedral in Florence* (London: Chatto & Windus, 2000)

Prager Frank D., and Gustina Scaglia, *Brunelleschi: Studies of His Technology and Inventions* (Cambridge, MA: MIT Press, 1970)

Taccola (Mariano di Jacopo)

Gille, Bertrand, *The Renaissance Engineers* (London: Lund Humphries, 1966)

Prager, Frank D., *Mariano Taccola and His Book De Engeneis* (Cambridge, MA: MIT Press, 1972)

Clara Sanuto

Ruggiero, Guido, *The Boundaries of Eros: Sex Crime and Sexuality in Renaissance Venice* (New York: Oxford University Press, 1985)

Margaret of Anjou

Dunn, Diana E. S., 'Margaret [Margaret of Anjou] (1430–1482), queen of England', *Oxford Dictionary of National Biography*

Hilton, Lisa, *Queens Consort* (London: Weidenfeld & Nicolson, 2008)

Laynesmith, Joanna L., *The Last Medieval Queens: English Queenship 1445–1503* (Oxford: Oxford University Press, 2004)

Johannes Gutenberg

Füssel, Stephan, *Gutenberg and the Impact of Printing*, trans. Douglas Martin (Aldershot: Ashgate, 2003)

Kapr, Albert, *Johann Gutenberg: The Man and His Invention*, trans. Douglas Martin (Aldershot: Scolar Press, 1995)

Man, John, *The Gutenberg Revolution: The Story of a Technical Genius and an Invention That Changed the World* (London: Headline, 2002)

Charles the Bold

Smith, Robert Douglas, and Kelly DeVries, *The Artillery of the Dukes of Burgundy 1363–1477* (Woodbridge: Boydell, 2005)

Vaughan, Richard, *Charles the Bold: The Last Valois Duke of Burgundy* (London: Longman, 1973)

Piero della Francesca

Bertelli, Carlo, *Piero della Francesca*, trans. Edward Farrelly (New Haven, CT, and London: Yale University Press, 1992)

Clark, Kenneth, *Piero della Francesca*, 2nd edn (London: Phaidon, 1969)

Sources of Quotations

Introduction: The Medieval World. 'at any ... to taste': P. J. Corfield, *Time and the Shape of History* (New Haven and London: Yale UP, 2007), p. 146.

1. An Age of Empires. **Charlemagne.** 'the emperor ... into everyone': Henry R. Loyn and John Percival, *The Reign of Charlemagne: Documents on Carolingian Government and Administration* (London: Edward Arnold, 1973), p. 20. 'We have ... understood us.': cited by Rosamond McKitterick, *Charlemagne and the Written Word* (Cambridge: Cambridge UP, 1989), p. 29. 'Who is ... his wrongdoings.' (my trans.): *Monumenta Germaniae Historica, Capitularia Regum Francorum*, vol. I, ed. Alfred Boretius (Hannover: Impensis Bibliopolii Hahniani, 1883), p. 163. 'flour, wine ... them properly'; 'they shall ... to us'; 'so that ... Christian people'; 'concerning adultery ... among laymen': *The Reign of Charlemagne*, pp. 69, 76, 80. 'Often some ... incorrect books.': quoted by Rosamund McKitterick, *Charlemagne: The Formation of a European Identity* (Cambridge: Cambridge UP, 2008), p. 317. **Olav I.** 'The king ... into banishment.': Snorre Sturlason, *The Heimskringla: A History of the Norse Kings*, trans. Samuel Laing, notes by Rasmus B. Anderson, vol. I (London: Norrœna Soc., 1906), p. 185. **Fulk Nerra.** 'of his overwhelming ferocity'; 'ferocity was ... a time'; 'O Lord ... repentant soul.'; 'who has ... my bishopric': quoted by Bernard. S. Bachrach, *Fulk Nerra, the Neo-Roman Consul, 987–1040: A Political Biography of the Angevin Count* (Berkeley: California UP, 1993), pp. 88, 104, 243, 252. **Ibn Sīnā.** 'Medicine is ... in it.': quoted by R. D. Smith, 'Avicenna and the *Canon of Medicine*: A Millennial Tribute', *Western Journal of Medicine* 133 (October, 1980), p. 367. 'As the ... God's mysteries.': quoted by Lenn E. Goodman, *Avicenna* (London and New York: Routledge, 1992), p.167. 'He was ... and dominant.': quoted by Smith, 'Avicenna and the *Canon of Medicine*', p. 369. **Emma of Normandy.** 'It is ... them both.': *Encomium Emmae Reginae*, ed. and trans. Alistair Campbell (London: Royal Historical Society, Camden 3rd ser., lxxii, 1949), pp. 34–35. 'was driven ... raging winter': *English Historical Documents 500–1042* (London: Eyre & Spottiswoode, 1955), p. 233. 'because she ... as well': *English Historical Documents 1042–1189* (London: Eyre & Spottiswoode, 1953), pp. 111–12. **Odo of Bayeux.** 'was more ... spiritual contemplation'; 'a slave to worldly trivialties': Ordericus Vitalis, *The Ecclesiastical History of Orderic Vitalis*, ed. Marjorie Chibnall (Oxford: Clarendon, 1969–80), vol. II, p. 267; vol. IV, p. 117. **Rodrigo Díaz.** 'Rodrigo the ... with them.'; 'exalted and ... the kingdom'; 'Because of ... almost completely'; 'He took ... for himself.' (my trans.): *Gestas de Rodrigo el Campeador*, ed. Adolfo Bonila y San Martin (Madrid: Victoriano Suarez, 1911), pp. 74, 42, 75–76, 81. **Matilda of Tuscany.** 'most beloved and loving daughter'; 'the stench ... another's wife': quoted by David J. Hay, *The Military Leadership of Matilda of Canossa 1046–1115* (Manchester: Manchester UP, 2008), pp. 49, 63. **Urban II.** 'French by ... great courtesy'; 'corrected many ... amend practices' (my trans.): *The Ecclesiastical History of Orderic Vitalis*, vol. IV, p. 167; vol. V, p. 10. **Guibert de Nogent.** 'utterly unskilled ... verse composition'; 'left deserted ... and master': Guibert, Abbot of Nogent-sous-Coucy, *The Autobiography of Guibert, Abbot of Nogent-sous-Coucy*, trans. C. C. Swinton-Bland (London: George Routledge & Sons , 1925), pp. 19, 55. 'it raises ... castration complex': Guibert, Abbot of Nogent-sous-Coucy, *Self and Society in Medieval France*, ed. John F. Benton (Toronto:

Toronto UP, 1984), p. 26. 'the carnal ... fleshly longings'; 'swarms of ... holy habit'; 'No one ... and torture.'; 'a Judaizer and a heretic'; 'What a ... windy talk!'; 'no exception ... of women': *The Autobiography of Guibert*, pp. 62, 123, 128–29, 174, 204. **Anna Komnene.** 'I am ... of history'; 'a natural ... of slander'; 'absolute refusal ... of war'; 'the supreme mischief maker': Anna Comnena, *The Alexiad of Anna Comnena*, trans. Edgar R. A. Sewter (Harmondsworth: Penguin, 1969), pp. 104, 108, 329, 349.

2. An Age of Confidence. **Abbot Suger.** 'We had ... way round.': Suger, *The Book of Suger, Abbot of St.-Denis on What Was Done under His Administration*, ch. xxxiii (http://www.learn.columbia.edu/ma/htm/ms/ma_ms_gloss_abbot_sugar.htm). **Godric of Finchale.** 'athlete of Christ': Reginald of Durham, *Libellus de Vita et Miraculis S. Godrici, Heremitae de Finchale*, ed. Joseph Stevenson (London: J. B. Nichols & Son, etc. etc., for the Surtees Soc., 1847). **Héloïse.** 'Our desires ... welcomed it.': *The Letters of Abelard and Heloise*, ed. Betty Radice, rev. Michael T. Clanchy (Harmondsworth: Penguin, 2003), p. 11. 'You are ... my prayers.'; 'to one ... and taste' (my trans.): Constant J. Mews, *The Lost Love Letters of Heloise and Abelard: Perceptions of Dialogue in Twelfth-Century France* (Basingstoke: Palgrave, 2001), p. 278. 'During the ... my prayers.'; 'It frequently ... in public.' (my trans.): *Heloïsa und Abelard* (http://www.abaelard.de/mainl.htm). 'by composing ... words new': Mews, *The Lost Love Letters*, p. 130. **Al-Idrisi.** 'His knowledge ... extraordinary discoveries.' (my trans.): *Géographie d'Edrisi*, ed. and trans. Pierre Amédée Jaubert (Paris: Imprimerie Royale, 1836–40), vol. I, p. viii. 'From Southampton ... sixty miles.': Alfred F. L. Beeston, 'Idrisi's Account of the British Isles', *Bulletin of the School of Oriental and African Studies* 13 (1950), p. 279. **Hildegard of Bingen.** 'a light ... my brain' (my trans.): Sabina Flanagan, *Hildegard of Bingen (1098–1179)* (http://www.hildegard.org/documents/flanagan.html#scivias). 'Many turn ... true prophetess.' (my trans.): *Analecta Sanctae Hildegardis Opera Spicilegio Solesmensi parata*, ed. Jean Baptiste Pitra (Monte Cassino: typis sacri Montis Casinensis, 1882), pp. 484–85. 'Then I ... the light.' (my trans.): Flanagan, *Hildegard of Bingen*. 'When a ... man's seed.': quoted by Anne H. King-Lenzmaier, *Hildegard of Bingen. An Integrated Vision* (Collegeville, Minnesota: Michael Glazier, 2001), p. 139. 'When the ... a man.': quoted by Bruce Wood Holsinger, 'The Flesh of the Voice: Embodiment and the Homoerotics of Devotion in the Music of Hildegard of Bingen (1098–1179)', *Signs* 19 (1993), p. 117. **Thomas Becket.** 'What miserable ... low-born clerk!': quoted by Frank Barlow, *Thomas Becket* (London: Weidenfeld & Nicolson, 1986), p. 235. 'Humble at ... leopard without': Guernes de Pont-Saint-Maxence, *La vie de Saint Thomas le Martyr, par Guernes de Pont-Saint-Maxence*, ed. Emmanuel Walberg (Lund: Gleerup, 1922), p. 12. 'in an ... in him.': *The Lives of Thomas Becket*, ed. and trans. Michael Staunton (Manchester: Manchester UP, 2001), p. 138. **Usāma-Ibn-Munquidh.** 'as animals ... nothing else'; 'mighty and ... is he!'; 'an accursed ... own kin'; 'Eat, be ... their cooking.'; 'So, I ... at me.'; 'This case ... upon them.': Usāma-Ibn-Munquid, *Memoirs of An Arab-Syrian Gentleman and Warrior*, ed. and trans. Philip K. Hitti (New York: Columbia UP, 1929), pp. 161, 166, 168, 159, 169, 179–80. **Frederick Barbarossa.** 'meum est ... morientis ori.' (my trans.): Peter Dronke, *Sources of Inspiration: Studies in Literary Transformation: 400–1500* (Rome: Edizioni di storia e letteratura, 1997), p. 91. 'A glorious ... for Christ.' (my trans.): *Codex Strahoviensis*, ed. Hippolyt Tauschenski and Matthias Pangerl (*Fontes Rerum Austricarum* V, Vienna: Kaiserlich-Königlichen Hof- und Staatsdrückerei, 1863), p. 5. **Eleanor of Aquitaine.** 'If you ... be done.': *English Historical Documents 1042–1189*, p. 936. 'Eleanor, by ... of England': quoted by Ralph V. Turner, *Eleanor of Aquitaine* (New Haven and London: Yale UP, 2009), p. 271. 'a matchless ... and eloquent': *Chronicles of the Crusades*, trans. John A. Giles and others (London: Henry G. Bohn, 1848), p. 19. **Saladin.** 'he gave ... to work'; 'God, having ... them victory.'; 'God alone ... than he.'; 'displayed such ... sturdy resistance'; 'The Franks ... and lance.'; 'acknowledged that ... be done': Bahā' ad-Dīn Yūsuf Ibn Rāfi' Ibn Šaddād, *The Life of Saladin by Beha ad-Din*, ed. Charles W. Wilson (London: Palestine Pilgrim Texts Society, 1897), pp. 55, 112, 273, 280, 359, 375. 'He was ... beyond measure.': quoted by Hamilton A. R. Gibb, *The Life of Saladin* (Oxford: Clarendon, 1973), p. 16. **William Marshal.** 'Have I ... finer sons?' (my trans.): *Histoire de Guillaume le Maréchal, comte de Striguil et de Pembroke, régent d'Angleterre*, ed. Paul Meyer (Paris: Librairie Renouard, 1891–1901), vol. I, pp. 19–20. **Pope Innocent III.** 'power to ... to plant': quoted by John C. Moore, *Innocent III. To Plant and to Build* (Leiden: Brill, 2003), p. 127. 'We don't ... the matter.' (my trans.): *Chronicon Abbatiae de Evesham*, ed. William D. Macray (London: Longman etc., Rolls Series, 1863), p. 189.

3. An Age of Maturity. **Chinggis Khan.** 'struck the ... of annihilation'; 'If you ... upon you.': 'Alā' al-Dīn 'Aṭā' Malik Juvaynī, *The History of the World Conqueror by 'Ala-ad-Din 'Ata-Malik Juvaini*, ed. and trans. John A. Boyle (Manchester: Manchester UP, 1958), pp. 38, 98. 'While we ... no more.''': *The Secret History of the Mongols*, ed. and trans. Urgunge Onon (London: RoutledgeCurzon, 2001). 'the bowl ... rich soup': *The History of the World Conqueror*, p. 98. 'Spare your ... used up.'; 'he was ... carried off': *The Secret History*, pp. 183, 231. 'had much ... and concubines'; 'the children ... ten thousand': *The History of the World Conqueror*, pp. 40, 43. **Simon de Montfort.** 'Attack the ... more evil.'; 'Oh what ... the prince!': quoted by Mark Gregory Pegg, *A Most Holy War: The Albigensian Crusade and the Battle for Christendom* (Oxford: Oxford UP, 2008), pp. 7, 88. 'Kill them ... are His.': *Internet Medieval Sourcebook: Caeserius of Heisterbach, Medieval Heresies* (http://www.fordham.edu/halsall/source/caesarius-heresies.html). **Dominic de Guzmán.** 'he penetrated ... his heart' (my trans.): Jordan of Saxony, *Livret sur les origines de l'ordre des prêcheurs par Jourdain de Saxe*, ed. Marie-Humbert Vicaire (http://www.fordham.edu/Halsall/basis/jordan-french.txt), ch. 7. **Robert of Wetherby.** 'seek the ... hang him': quoted by David Crook, 'The Sheriff of Nottingham and Robin Hood: The Genesis of the Legend?' in Peter R. Coss and Simon D. Lloyd (eds) *Thirteenth century England: proceedings of the Newcastle upon Tyne conference 2* (Woodbridge: Boydell, 1988), p. 59. **Frederick II.** 'full of ... in devices'; 'crafty, wily ... malicious, wrathful': quoted by George G. Coulton, *From St Francis to Dante* (London: Duckworth, 1908), p. 240. 'It was ... to mention.': *Mathew Paris's English History*, trans. John A. Giles (London: Henry G. Bohn, 1853), vol II, p. 4. **Matthew Paris.** 'memory exhales ... infernal odour': Matthew Paris, *English History*, ed. and trans. J. A. Giles, vol. iii (London: Bohn, 1854), p. 133. **King Håkon IV of Norway.** 'God give ... lord king.'; 'Eh'; 'Hm'; 'What?'; 'to maintain ... before him'; 'stooping shield ... and flame': *The King's Mirror*, ed. and trans. Laurence M. Larson (London: Oxford UP, 1917), pp. 183, 209, 226, 298. 'The leader ... ruddy gold.': *The Norwegian Account of King Haco's Expedition*

against Scotland, trans. James Johnstone (Edinburgh: privately printed, 1885), p. 28. **King Louis IX of France.** 'would never ... with her': *The Memoirs of the Lord of Joinville*, ed. and trans. Ethel Kate Bowen-Wedgwood (London: John Murray, 1906), p. 311. 'Gracious Lord ... for me!': Joinville, Jean de, 'The Life of Saint Louis' in *Joinville & Villehardouin: Chronicles of the Crusades*, ed. and trans. Margaret R. B. Shaw (Harmondsworth and Baltimore: Penguin, 1963), p. 216. **Alexander Nevsky.** 'The clash ... with blood.': *Medieval Russia. A Source Book, 850–1700*, ed. Basil Dmytryshyn (Fort Worth: Harcourt Brace Jovanovich College, 3rd ed., 1991), p. 103. 'He cut ... to evil.': *The Chronicle of Novgorod, 1014–1471*, trans. Robert Mitchell and Nevill Forbes (London: Camden 3rd series, xxv, 1914), p. 96. **Thomas Aquinas.** 'If anyone ... of truth.': quoted by Jean-Pierre Torrell, *Saint Thomas Aquinas* (Washington DC: Catholic University of America, 2 vols, 1996), vol. I, p. 91. 'That settles the Manichees!': quoted by Brian Davies, *The Thought of Thomas Aquinas* (Oxford: Clarendon, 1992), p. 8. 'I cannot ... have seen.': quoted by Torrell, *Saint Thomas Aquinas*, vol. I, p. 289. **Master James of St. George.** 'The king ... Master James.' (my trans.): Arnold J. Taylor, 'Master James of St George', *English Historical Review* 65 (1950), p. 450. **Jacques de Molay.** 'Brother Jacques ... a river.': *Le procès des Templiers*, ed. Jules Michelet, vol. 2 (Paris: Imprimerie Nationale, 1851), p. 208. **Marco Polo.** 'I will ... good purpose'; 'they reckon ... be willing': *The Book of Ser Marco Polo*, trans. Sir Henry Yule (London: John Murray, 1902), vol. II, pp. 32, 40. 'in my ... the world': *The Travels of Marco Polo*, ed. and trans. Thomas Wright (London: Henry G. Bohn, 1854), p. 73.

4. An Age of Plague. **Dante Alighieri.** 'wandered, a ... of fortune': quoted by Guiseppe Mazzotta, 'Dante and the Virtues of Exile', *Poetics Today* 5 (1984), p. 655. 'somewhat haughty ... with laymen': *Selections from the First Nine Books of the Chroniche Fiorentine of Giovanni Villani*, trans. Rose E. Selfe, ed. Philip H. Wicksteed (Westminster: Archibald Constable, 1897), p. 450. **William Lene.** 'condemned to ... and villeins' (my trans.): Thomas Walsingham, *Historia Anglicana*, ed. Henry T. Riley (London: Longman etc., Rolls Series, 1863–64), vol II, p. 2. **James Douglas.** 'As long ... his life.': quoted by Archibald A. M. Duncan, *The Nation of Scots and the Declaration of Arbroath* (London: Historical Association, 1970), p. 36. **Giotto di Bondone.** 'introducing the ... hundred years': Giorgio Vasari, *Lives of the Most Excellent Painters, Sculptors, and Architects* (http://www.casasantapia.com/art/giorgiovasari/lives/giotto.htm). 'be welcomed ... said city': quoted by Bruce Cole, *Giotto and Florentine Painting 1280–1375* (New York: Harper & Row, 1976), p. 13. 'more than ... the life': quoted by Ann Derbes and Mark Sandona (eds), *The Cambridge Companion to Giotto* (Cambridge: Cambridge UP, 2004), p. 3. 'Giotto, if ... a little.'; 'And so ... were you.': Vasari, *Lives*. **Jean de Lamouilly.** 'for making ... said castle' (my trans.): British Library, Add. MS 8835, f. 44. **Petrarch.** ''Twas on ... any shield.': Francesco Petrarcha, *The Sonnets, Triumphs and Other Poems of Petrarch*, ed. Thomas Campbell (London: Henry G. Bohn, 1859), p. 3. 'I find ... not writing.'; 'Few indeed ... woman's person.': quoted by James H. Robinson, *Petrarch. The First Modern Scholar and Man of Letters* (New York: G. P. Putnam's Sons 1909), pp. 60, 95. 'a disgusting ... to me'; 'although I ... and liberty'; 'comely enough ... best days': *Petrarch: The First Modern Scholar and Man of Letters*, pp. 162, 403, 62. 'deep-seated and ... city life': quoted by Robinson, *Petrarch: The First Modern Scholar*, p. 69. 'the only ... the stream.'; 'Grapes, figs ... the river.'; 'to see

... to offer': quoted by Henry Calthrop Hollway-Calthrop, *Petrarch His Life and Times* (London: Methuen & Co., 1907), pp. 161–62; 308. **John Crabbe.** 'He wrought ... of another.': quoted by Henry S. Lucas, 'John Crabbe, Flemish pirate, merchant and adventurer', *Speculum* 20 (1945), p. 342. 'that worst ... many years' (my trans.): *Chronicles of Edward I and Edward II*, ed. William Stubbs (London: Longman etc., Rolls Series, 1882–83), vol. II, p. 109. **Guillaume Cale.** 'Death to the villeins!': Siméon Luce, *Histoire de la Jacquerie d'aprés des documents inédits* (Paris, Honoré Champion, 1895), p. 155. 'pillaged, set ... other evils' (my trans.): Siméon Luce, *Histoire de la Jacquerie* (Paris: H. Champion, 2nd ed., 1894), p. 260. **Guy de Chauliac.** 'They do ... their course.': Guy de Chauliac, *La Grande Chirugie de Guy de Chauliac*, ed. Edouard Nicaise (Paris: Alcan, 1890), p. 171. 'to drink ... opportunity offered': quoted in *The Black Death*, ed. and trans. Rosemary Horrox (Manchester: Manchester UP, 1994), p. 29. **Charles IV of Bohemia.** 'We had ... this day.' (my trans.): Charles IV, *Autobiography of Emperor Charles IV*, ed. Balász Nagy and Frank Schaer, introduction by Ferdinand Seibt (Budapest and New York, 2001), pp. 68, 70. **King Pedro IV of Aragon.** 'We spoke ... of retelling.' (my trans.): Pere III of Catalonia, *Crónica del rey de Arago En Pere IV lo Ceremonios ó del Punyalet*, ed. Joseph Coroleu (Barcelona: La Renaixensa, 1885), p. 226. 'I will ... for me.'; 'We entered ... and Roussillon.': Pere III of Catalonia (Pedro IV of Aragon), *Chronicle*, trans. Mary Hillgarth, intro. and notes by Jocelyn N. Hillgarth (Toronto: Pontifical Institute of Mediaeval Studies, 1980), vol. ii. pp. 310, 550. **Coluccio Salutati.** 'Imagine me ... the city.' (my trans.): *Epistolario di Coluccio Salutati*, ed. Francesco Novati (Rome: Forziani E.C. Tipografal del Senato, 1891–1911), vol. II, p. 193. **Catherine of Siena.** 'I have ... ears hear.': Catherine Benincasa, *Saint Catherine of Siena as Seen in Her Letters*, ed. and trans. Vida D. Scudder (London: J.M Dent, 1911), p. 111. 'her ecstasies ... heavenly favour'; 'to hear ... her ecstasies': Raymond of Capua, *The Life of St Catharine of Sienna*, ed. Etienne Cartier (Philadelphia: Peter F. Cunningham, 1860), pp. 74, 261. 'You who ... incarnate demons.'; 'I have ... against you.': *Saint Catherine of Siena as Seen in Her Letters*, pp. 122, 286. 'Take that ... to pieces.': *The Life of St Catharine of Siena*, p. 310. 'I wish ... and temporal.': *Saint Catherine of Siena as Seen in Her Letters*, p. 231. **John of Gaunt.** 'I saw ... a treasure.' (spelling modernized): Geoffrey Chaucer, *The Complete Works of Geoffrey Chaucer*, ed. Walter W. Skeat (Oxford: Clarendon, 1915), pp. 91–92. **Jean Froissart.** 'I eagerly ... my memory'; 'there was ... himself gallantly'; 'in such ... to come'; 'I well ... in it.': Jean Froissart, *Chronicles of England, France, Spain ... by Sir John Froissart*, ed. and trans. Thomas Johnes (London: William Smith, 1839), vol . ii, pp. 369, 465, 574, 688.

5. An Age of Transition. Temür. 'the butler ... bitter cup'; 'I am ... for learning.': 'Abdalwahhāb b Aḥmad Ibn 'Arābšāh, *Tamerlane or Timur the Great Amir*, trans. John H. Sanders (London: Luzac, 1936), pp. 127, 232. 'he is ... not know': *Islamic Central Asia: an Anthology of Historical Sources*, ed. Scott C. Levi and Ron Sela (Bloomington, Indiana: Indiana UP, 2010), p. 175. **Boucicaut.** 'grand, and ... and gentlemen' (my trans.): *Nouvelle collection des mémoires pour servir à l'histoire de France depuis le xiiie siècle jusqu'à la fin du xviii*, ed. Joseph F. Michaud and Jean-Joseph-François Poujoulat (Paris: Éditeur du Commentaire analytique du Code civil, 1836–54), vol. II, p. 233. 'Those who ... against evil-doers': Christine de Pisan, *Oeuvres poétiques de Christine de Pisan*, ed. Maurice Roy (Paris: Firmin Diderot et c^ie,

1886–96), vol. I, p. 220. 'to gain ... the soul'; 'set in ... all eternity': Geffroi de Charny, *The Book of Chivalry of Geffroi de Charny*, ed. and trans. Richard W. Kaeuper and Elspeth Kennedy (Philadelphia: Pennsylvania UP, 1996), p. 177. **Jan Žižka.** 'a vile ... serpent's egg': quoted by Norman Housley, *The Later Crusades* (Oxford: Oxford UP, 1992), p. 253. 'everyone capable ... a stone': quoted by Thomas A. Fudge, *The Crusade against Heretics in Bohemia, 1418–1437* (Aldershot: Ashgate, 2002), p. 123. 'that we ... holy glory'; 'Flogging, slaying ... burning, drowning' quoted by Count Franz von Lützow, *The Hussite Wars* (London, 1914) pp. 368, 370. 'Everyone must ... own battalion.': quoted by Fudge, *The Crusade against Heretics in Bohemia*, p. 67. 'seeking the ... the commonwealth': quoted by Lützow, *The Hussite Wars* p. 30. **Joan of Arc.** 'She was ... up artillery.' (my trans.): *Procès de rehabilitation de Jeanne d'Arc*, ed. J. Fabre (Paris, 1888), vol. I, p. 172. 'hard clouts and buffets': Wilfred P. Barrett, *The Trial of Jeanne d'Arc* (London, 1931), p. 63. 'from God ... of Orléans'; 'Have you ... of Lorraine?': *Joan of Arc. La Pucelle*, ed. and trans. Craig Taylor (Manchester, 2006), pp. 36, 63. 'In God's ... revictualling them.': *Procès de rehabilitation de Jeanne d'Arc*, vol. I, p. 226. 'perpetually changing ... times not'; 'The country ... was noticed.': Enguerrand de Monstrelet, *The Chronicles of Enguerrand de Monstrelet*, ed. and trans. Thomas Johnes (London: Henry G. Bohn, 1840), pp. 554, 560. 'There is ... to answer.'; 'Do you ... clothe him?'; 'Why should ... shorn off?'; 'Since I ... do wrong.'; 'having cast ... dissolute men'; 'nothing about ... distinctive marks': Barrett, *The Trial of Jeanne d'Arc*, pp. 59, 74, 117, 162, 235, 246. **Filippo Brunelleschi.** 'Being completely ... of money.' (trans. slightly modified): Antonio di Tuccio Manetti di Marabottino, *The Life of Brunelleschi by Antonio di Tuccio Manetti*, ed. Howard Saalman (Philadelphia: Pennsylvania State UP, 1970), pp. 102–3. 'Do not ... own talent.': Eugenio Battisti, *Brunelleschi: The Complete Work* (London: Thames & Hudson, 1981), p. 20. **Taccola.** 'many oxen ... without breathing': Frank D. Prager, *Mariano Taccola and his book De Engeneis* (Cambridge, Mass: MIT, 1972), p. 120. **Clara Sanuto.** 'committed numerous dissolute deeds.': quoted by Guido Ruggiero, *The Boundaries of Eros: Sex Crime and Sexuality in Renaissance Venice* (New York, Oxford UP, 1985), p. 79. 'the scholars ... heart's desire': quoted in *The Victoria History of the County of Oxford*, vol. II, ed. William Page (London: Archibald Constable, 1907), p. 74. **Margaret of Anjou.** 'Through your ... his cruelty.' (wording and spelling modernized): John Lydgate, *Mummings and Entertainments*, Appendix: *Margaret of Anjou's Entry into London, 1445*, ed. Claire Sponsler (Kalamazoo: Medieval Institute Publications, Western Michigan University, 2010, and at http://www.lib.rochester.edu/camelot/teams//scjl.htm). 'the queen ... and conclusion'; 'she desires ... this land' (spelling modernized): *The Paston Letters*, ed. James Gairdner (London: Archibald Constable, 1872–75), vol. I, pp. 265, 378. 'not only ... marvel greatly'; 'We will ... Lady Say.': *Letters of Queen Margaret of Anjou and Bishop Beckington*, ed. Cecil Monro (Westminster: Camden Society, 1863), pp. 106, 127. **Charles the Bold.** 'pompous and lofty': Philip de Commines, *The Memoirs of Philip de Commines, Lord of Argenton*, ed. Andrew R. Scoble (London: G. Bell & Sons, 1906), vol I, p. 124. 'From the ... do this.' (my trans.): Georges Chastellain, *Oeuvres de Georges Chastellain*, ed. le baron Kervyn de Lettenhove (Brussels: F. Heussner, 1863–66), vol. V, p. 370. 'I saw ... and commanding.': quoted by Richard Vaughan, *Charles the Bold* (2nd ed., Woodbridge, 2002), p. 204. 'The duke ... failed him.'; 'He had ... his dominions.': *Memoirs of Philip de Commines*, vol. I, pp. 151, 180.

Acknowledgments

My first debt is to Colin Ridler, who suggested that I write this book, and gave me every encouragement. I also owe thanks to others at Thames & Hudson. Alice Reid has chivvied me into meeting the timetable, and has provided much help. Maria Ranauro undertook the major task of sourcing the illustrations. Kit Shepherd did far more than could possibly be expected of a copy-editor, and saved me from many blunders.

As ever, my wife Maggie has provided constant help; her suggestions have been invaluable. I am grateful to Durham University, for continuing to allow me access to its library after my retirement. There are also many, whose identity is not known to me, who have done much to make this book possible by setting up and maintaining such internet sites as Gallica, the Internet Archive, the Internet Medieval Sourcebook, and *De Re Militari*.

Sources of Illustrations

2 Basilica di Santa Maria del Fiore, Florence; 8 British Library, Add. 28681, f. 9; 10 Bibliothèque nationale de France, Ms. Es. 30, Morel-Fatio 119, Pl. V; 11 Bibliothèque nationale de France, Ms. Fr. 5054, f. 13; 12 Cathedral Treasury, Aachen. Photo Ann Münchow; 15 Bibliothèque nationale de France, Ms. Lat. 1, f. 423; 17 Musée du Louvre, Paris. Photo Scala, Florence; 18 Photo akg-images/Hilbich; 19 Cathedral's Treasury, Rheims; 20 Metropolitan Museum of Art. The Cloisters Collection, 1988 (1988.15)/Art Resource/Scala, Florence; 21 Bayerische Staatsbibliothek, Munich, cod. Lat. 4453, f. 24v; 22 Photo © Martin M. Miles; 23 Private collection; 24 Photo Werner Karrasch. © The Viking Ship Museum, Denmark; 25 Arni Magnusson Institute, Reykjavik/Bridgeman Art Library; 27 Photo bilwissedition Ltd. & Co. KG/Alamy; 28 © Paul Shawcross/Alamy; 29 Biblioteca Universitaria, Bologna. Photo Scala, Florence; 30 Bibliothèque nationale de France, Ms. Fr. 9136, f. 1v; 31 Bibliothèque nationale de France/Bridgeman Art Library; 33 British Library, Add. 33241, ff.1v-2; 34 British Library, Stowe 944, f. 6; 37, 38 Bayeux Tapestry Museum, Normandy; 39 ITV Global/The Kobal Collection; 40 imagebroker.net/SuperStock; 43 Biblioteca Apostolica Vaticana, Vatican City/Flammarion/Bridgeman Art Library; 44 De Agostini/SuperStock; 47 De Agostini Picture Library/Bridgeman Art Library; 48 Bibliothèque nationale de France, Ms Fr 22495, f. 15/Giraudon/Bridgeman Art Library; 50 Bibliothèque nationale de France, Ms. Lat. 2502, f. 1; 51 Bibliothèque nationale de France, Ms. Fr. 2813, f. 200; 53 The Granger Collection/TopFoto; 54 Biblioteca Nacional, Madrid; 55 Biblioteca Nacional, Madrid; 56 British Library Board/Robana/TopFoto; 58 British Library, Royal 20 C VII, f. 24v; 61 Basilique Saint-Denis, France. Photo White Images/Scala, Florence; 62 Photo Stan Parry; 63 Photo Painton Cowen; 65 British Library, Harley 1808, f. 30v. British Library Board/Robana/TopFoto; 66 British Library, Add 10292, f. 164. British Library Board/Robana/TopFoto; 67 British Library, Royal 20 A II, f. 3v. British Library Board/Robana/TopFoto; 69 British Library, Royal 10 E IV, f. 113v; 70 © Jonathan Bailey/English Heritage/Arcaid/Corbis; 71 Bodleian Library, Oxford. MS Douce 6, f. 160v; 73 British Library, Royal 16 F II, f. 137. British Library Board/Robana/TopFoto; 75 Bodleian Libraries, University of Oxford, Ms Pococke 375; 76 Bodleian Libraries, University of Oxford, Ms Pococke 375, ff. 3v-4; 79, 81 Biblioteca Governativa, Lucca, Ms 1942; 83 British Library, Royal 2 B VII, f. 288v; 84 British Library, Royal 20 A II, f. 7v. British Library Board/Robana/TopFoto; 86 Bibliothèque nationale de France, Ms. Lat. 10483, f. 118; 87 British Library, Royal 16 G VI, f. 442; 88 British Library, Yates Thompson 12, f. 132; 91 Catholic Parish Church, Cappenberg, Germany; 92 Photo Ann Ronan/Heritage Images/Scala, Florence; 93 University Library, Leipzig; 95 Chapelle de Sainte Radegonde, Chinon, France. Photo DeAgostini Picture Library/Scala, Florence; 96 Photo Ann Ronan/Heritage Images/Scala, Florence; 97 Album/Oronoz/SuperStock; ; 99 Museum of Islamic Art, Cairo; 100 © Kevin Fleming/Corbis; 101 Bibliothèque nationale de France, Ms. Fr. 22495, f. 229; 103 © The Art Gallery Collection/Alamy; 104 © Pembrokeshire Pictures/Alamy; 107 Photo Scala, Florence, courtesy of the Ministero Beni e Att. Culturali; 108 British Library, Harley 2356, f. 8v. British Library Board/Robana/TopFoto; 109 British Library Board/Robana/Scala, Florence; 110 © Peter Barritt/Alamy; 112 Radius/SuperStock; 115 National Palace Museum, Taipei, Taiwan; 116 British Library Board/Robana/TopFoto; 119 Archives Nationales, Paris, cat. no. D708; ; 120 British Library/Bridgeman Art Library ; 123 Santa Maria Novella, Florence; 124 Bibliothèque nationale de France, Ms. 280, f. 31; 126 Lebrecht Music and Arts Photo Library/Alamy; 127 British Library, Add. 42130, f. 45. British Library Board/Robana/TopFoto; 129 Vatican Library, Vatican City/Photo De Agostini Picture Library/Scala, Florence; 130 Biblioteca Apostolica Vaticana, Ms. Pal. Lat. 1071; 132 Bibliothèque nationale de France, Ms. Fr. 12400, f. 54; 133 British Library, Royal 14 C VII, f. 6; 135 British Library, Cotton Nero D I, f. 169v; 137 Photo Regin Hjertholm/Bergen City Museum; 138 Werner Forman Archive/

Index

Page numbers in *italics* refer to illustrations.